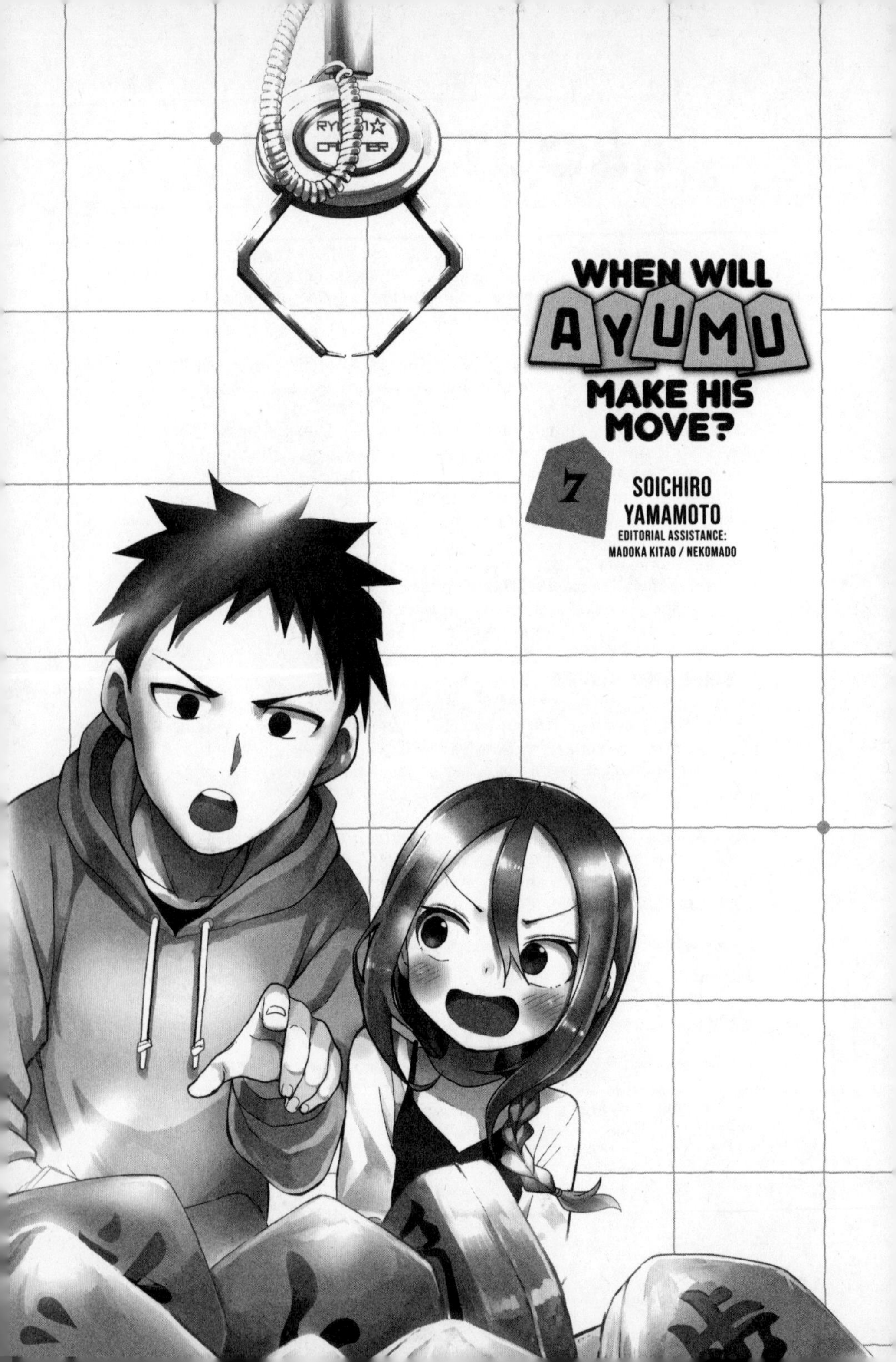
WHEN WILL AYUMU MAKE HIS MOVE?
7
SOICHIRO YAMAMOTO
EDITORIAL ASSISTANCE:
MADOKA KITAO / NEKOMADO

ABOUT SHOGI

This manga is a nearly-rom-com set in a high school shogi club. This game isn't well known outside Japan, but if you're familiar with chess, it's easy to grasp! Check out this explainer before reading, or jump right in and come back if you want to learn more!

Shogi is a two-player board game in the same family as chess. It's ancestor arrived in Japan over a thousand years ago and evolved into roughly its current form around the sixteenth century. Two players face off across a board with nine ranks (rows) and nine files (columns). Each player has a small army of pieces that start on their side of the board, and players can move one of these pieces per turn. The goal, like in chess, is to "checkmate" the other player's king piece by putting it into a situation where it cannot avoid being captured.

The two players are called *sente* and *gote* ("moves first" and "moves next"). These are sometimes called "black" and "white" in English; however, all pieces in shogi are the same color. They are differentiated by orientation, with the pointed end facing the opposing player.

PIECES AND MOVES
There are many different types of pieces, each with its own set of legal moves. Some of these will be familiar to chess players: For example, pawns move one square forward, while bishops move any number of squares diagonally. See the following pages for a detailed list of pieces and their moves.

When a piece legally moves into a square already occupied by an enemy piece, the enemy piece is "captured"—meaning that it is removed from the board and held "in hand" by the capturing player. (Pieces cannot move into squares occupied by friendly pieces.)

DROPPING
One big difference between shogi and chess is that, instead of moving a piece players can use their turn to place a piece they have in hand back on the board under their control. This is called "dropping" a piece.

A piece can be dropped almost anywhere on the board, although there are some restrictions. A player can never have two unpromoted pawns on the same file, and a piece cannot be dropped onto a square from which it has no legal move.

PROMOTION

If a piece reaches the three ranks at the far end of the board (the "enemy camp"), it can be "promoted." The piece is flipped over to reveal its other side, and gains a new set of moves. For example, a promoted pawn becomes a *tokin*, which moves like a gold general. (Note that kings and gold generals cannot be promoted.)

Promotion is not compulsory unless the piece would have no legal move otherwise. If a piece is left unpromoted, it can be promoted at the end of any subsequent move that begins within the enemy camp.

CHECK AND CHECKMATE

Moving a piece into a position that would let the enemy king be captured on the next move is called an *ote* ("king move"). This corresponds to "check" in chess. The "checked" player must protect their king, either by moving it, capturing the checking piece, or placing (or dropping) another piece in between the two. If the checked player has no way to save the king, they lose the game. This corresponds to "checkmate" in chess. As in chess, it is also against the rules for a player to make a move that puts their own king in check.

CASTLES

A key concept in shogi strategy is the castle (in Japanese, *kakoi*, "enclosure"). A castle is a formation of pieces that protects your king. Over the centuries, shogi players have come up with many types of castles, and also ways to undermine and attack them.

Note that building a castle involves arranging pieces using standard legal moves. This makes it different from the special move of "castling" in chess, although the objective (protect the king) is similar.

SHOGI PIECES

 FUHYO
English name: Pawn (P)
Move: One square directly forward
Comments: Unlike in chess, pawns do not capture diagonally

 TOKIN
English name: Tokin (+P)
Move: Replaced by gold general rules
Comments: Most English-speaking players use the Japanese name for this piece instead of "promoted pawn"

 KYOSHA
English name: Lance (L)
Move: Any number of squares directly forward

 NARIKYO
English name: Promoted lance (+L)
Move: Replaced by gold general rules

 KEIMA
English name: Knight (N)
Move: L-shaped "jump" two squares forward and one square to left or right
Comments: Knights can "jump" over pieces that are in their way. Unlike in chess, they cannot jump in any direction.

 NARIKEI
English name: Promoted knight (+N)
Move: Replaced by gold general rules

 GINSHO
English name: Promoted knight (S)
Move: One square in any direction except left, right, or directly back

NARIGIN

English name: Promoted silver (+S)
Move: Replaced by gold general rules

 KINSHO

English name: Gold general (or just "Gold") (G)
Move: One square in any direction except diagonally backward (left or right)
Comments: Gold generals cannot be promoted.

 KAKUGYO

English name: Bishop (B)
Move: Any number of squares diagonally

 RYUMA

English name: Promoted bishop (or "Dragon horse") (+B)
Move: Any number of squares diagonally OR one square in any direction

 HISHA

English name: Rook (R)
Move: Any number of squares forward, back, left, or right

 RYUO

English name: Promoted rook (or "Dragon king") (+R)
Move: Any number of squares forward, back, left, or right, OR one square in any direction

 OSHO

English name: King (K)
Move: One square in any direction
Comments: Kings cannot be promoted. This tile is used by the higher-ranking player, while the lower-ranking player traditionally uses the *gyokusho* tile (below) for their king.

 GYOKUSHO

English name: King (or "Jewel") (K)
Move: One square in any direction
Comments: This tile is used as the king of the lower-ranking player, but the rules are the same as for the *osho* tile.

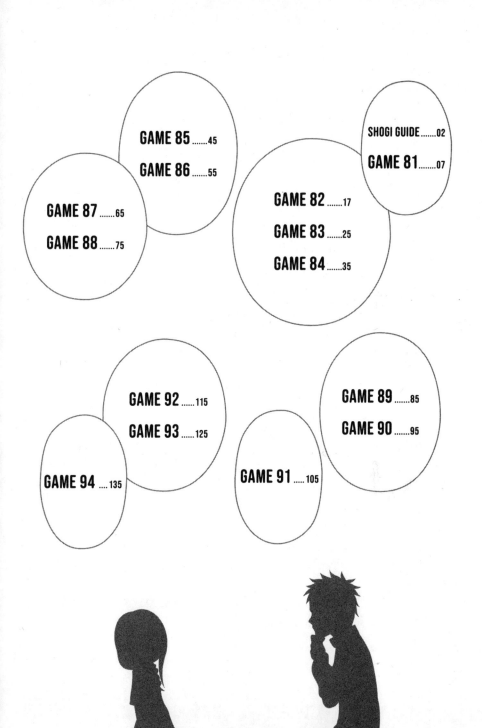

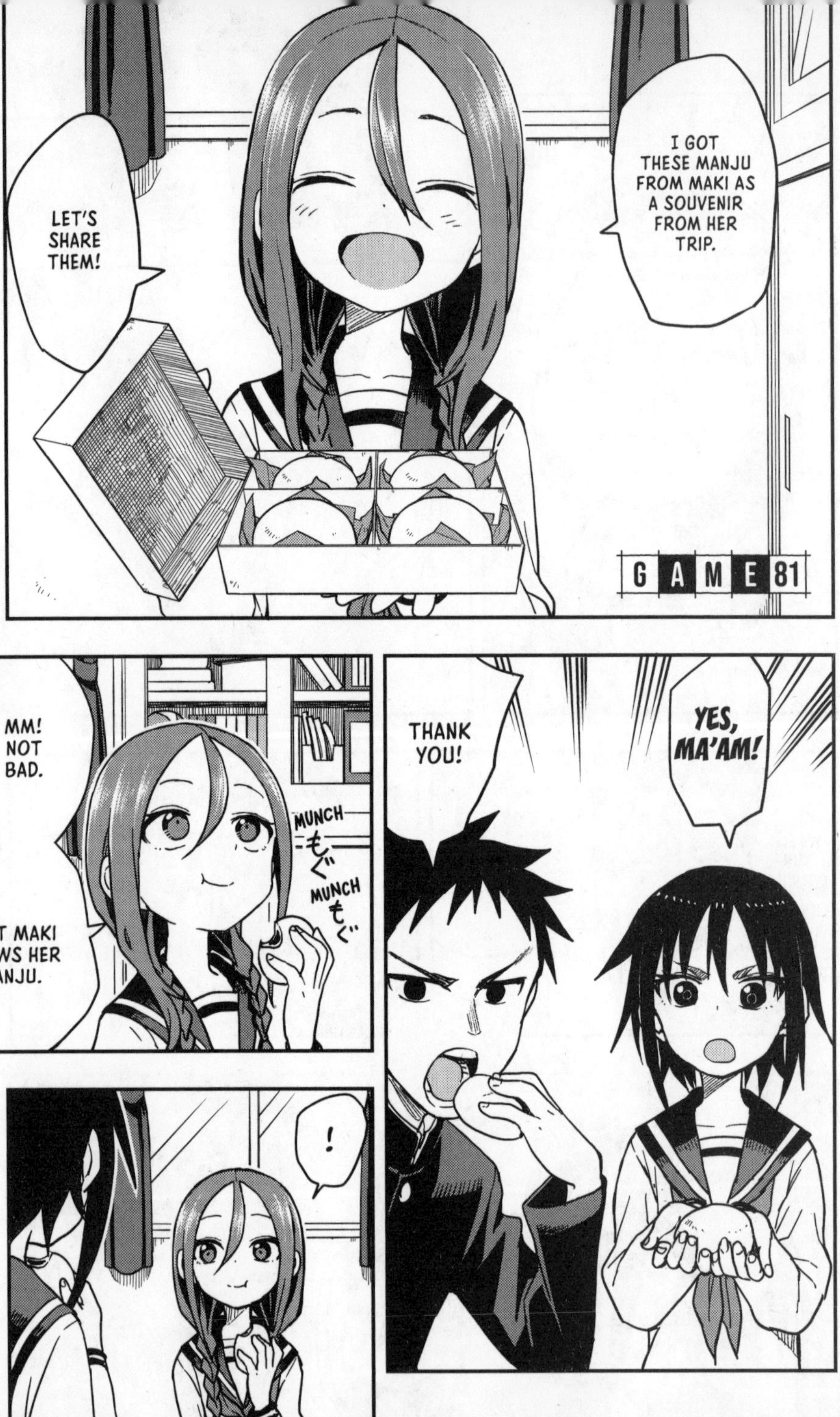
I GOT THESE MANJU FROM MAKI AS A SOUVENIR FROM HER TRIP.
LET'S SHARE THEM!
GAME 81
YES, MA'AM!
THANK YOU!
MM! NOT BAD.
MUNCH もぐ
MUNCH もぐ
THAT MAKI KNOWS HER MANJU.
!

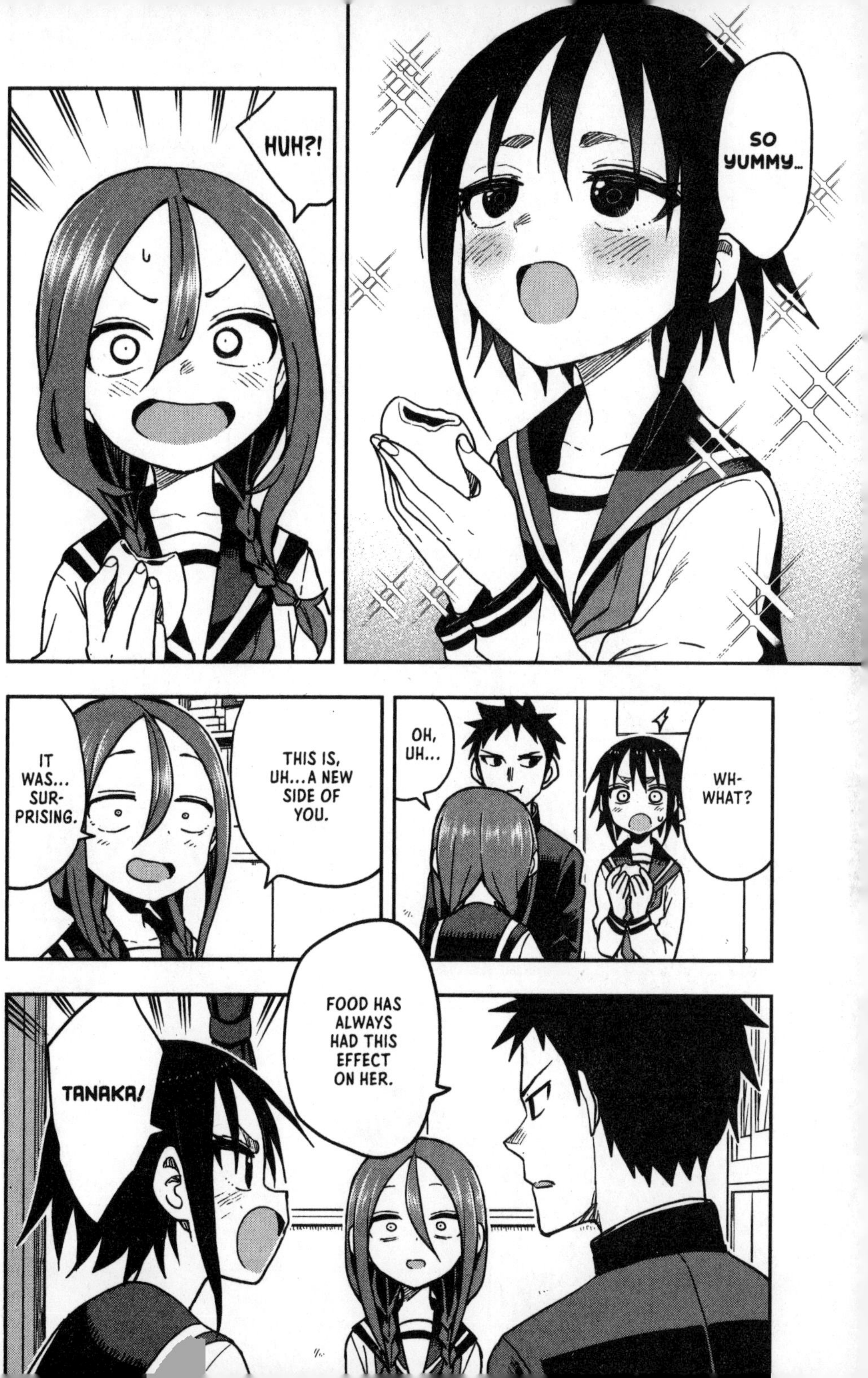
SO YUMMY...
HUH?!
WH-WHAT?
OH, UH...
THIS IS, UH...A NEW SIDE OF YOU.
IT WAS... SURPRISING.
FOOD HAS ALWAYS HAD THIS EFFECT ON HER.
TANAKA!

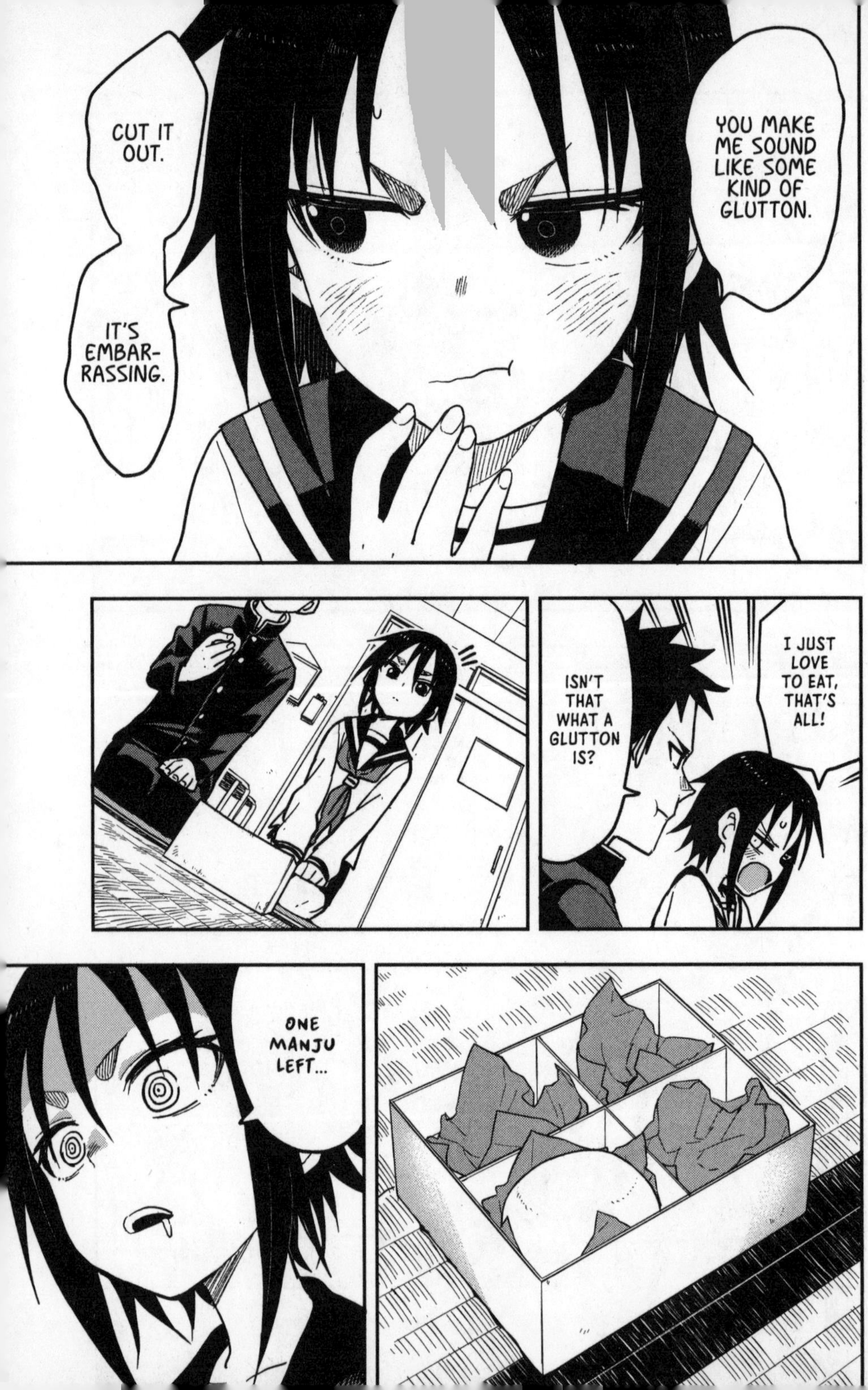
YOU MAKE ME SOUND LIKE SOME KIND OF GLUTTON.
CUT IT OUT.
IT'S EMBAR-RASSING.
I JUST LOVE TO EAT, THAT'S ALL!
ISN'T THAT WHAT A GLUTTON IS?
ONE MANJU LEFT...

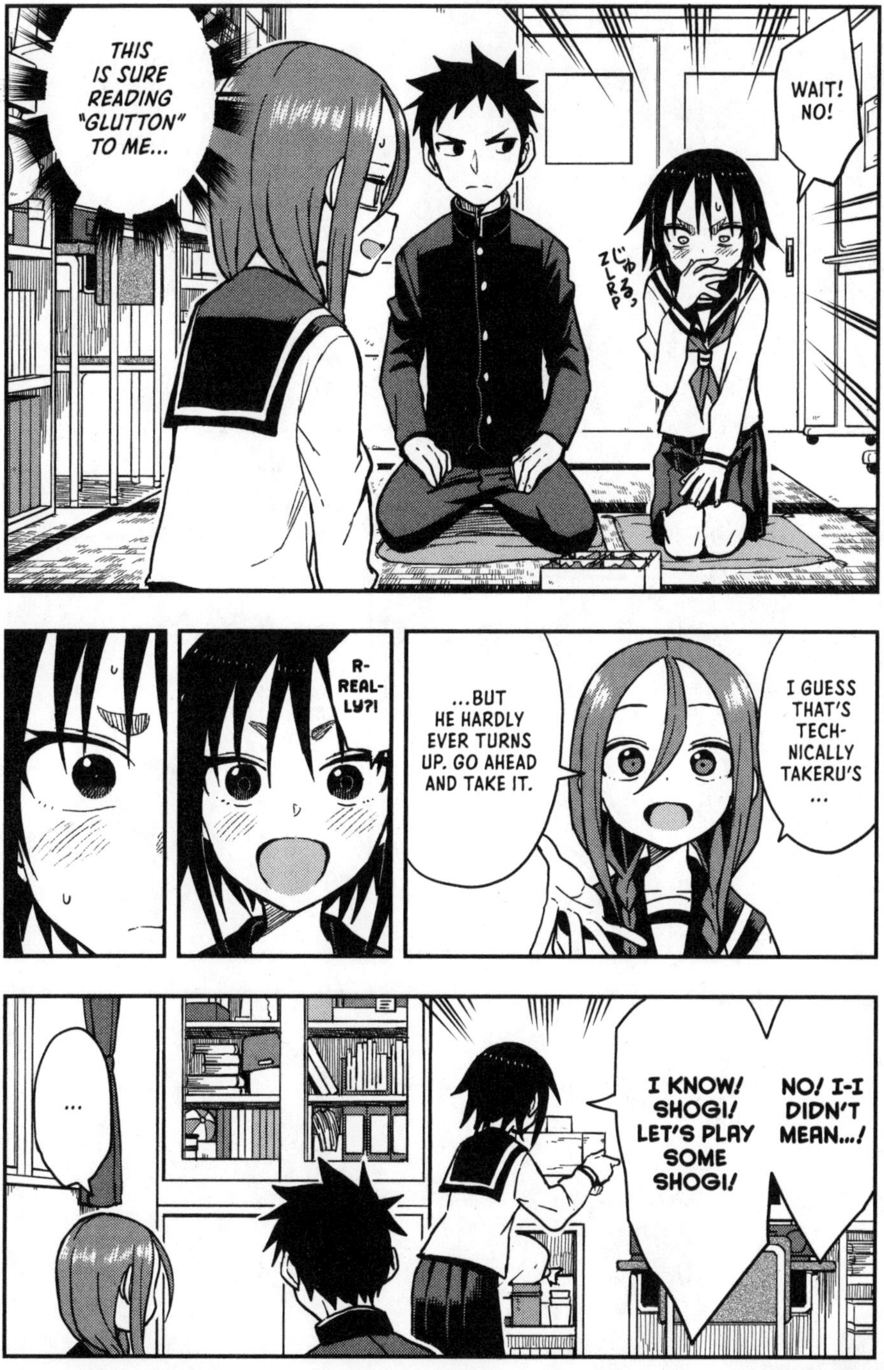
WAIT! NO!
じゅるっ
ZLRP
THIS IS SURE READING "GLUTTON" TO ME...
I GUESS THAT'S TECHNICALLY TAKERU'S ...
...BUT HE HARDLY EVER TURNS UP. GO AHEAD AND TAKE IT.
R-REALLY?!
NO! I-I DIDN'T MEAN...!
I KNOW! SHOGI! LET'S PLAY SOME SHOGI!
...

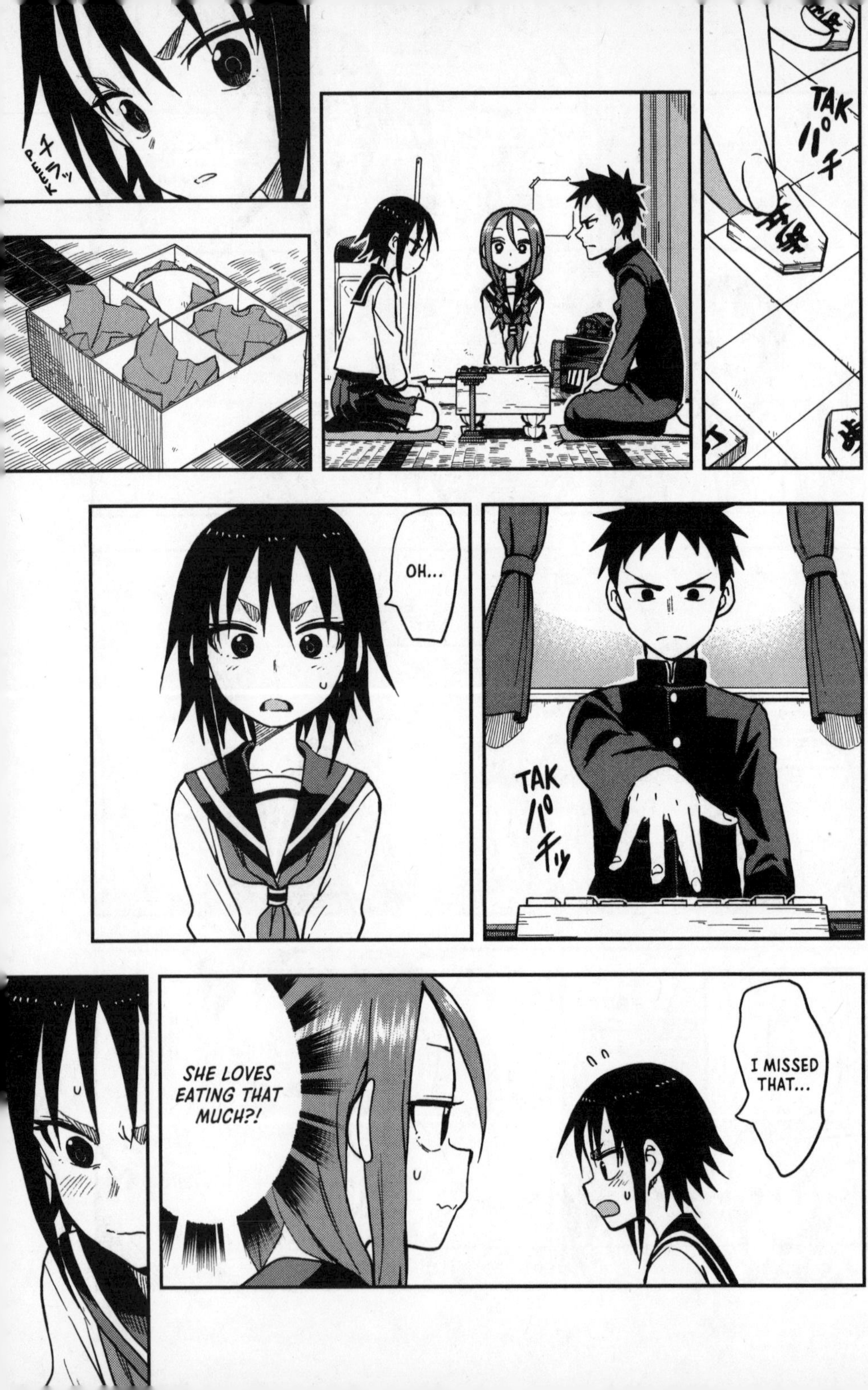
TAK
パチ
チラッ
PEEK
TAK
パチッ
OH...
I MISSED THAT...
SHE LOVES EATING THAT MUCH?!

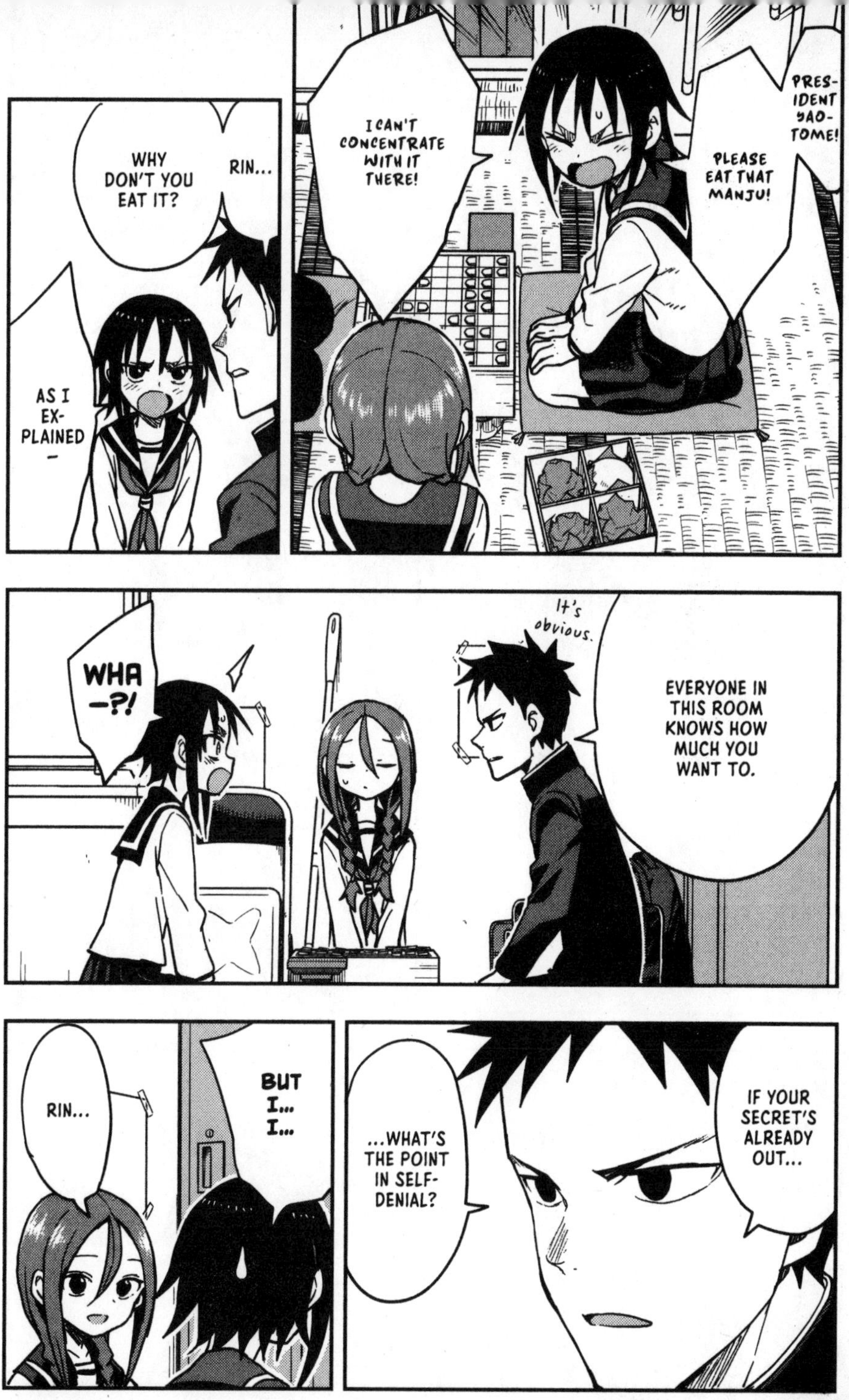
PRESIDENT YAOTOME!
PLEASE EAT THAT MANJU!
I CAN'T CONCENTRATE WITH IT THERE!
RIN...
WHY DON'T YOU EAT IT?
AS I EXPLAINED —
It's obvious.
EVERYONE IN THIS ROOM KNOWS HOW MUCH YOU WANT TO.
WHA—?!
IF YOUR SECRET'S ALREADY OUT...
...WHAT'S THE POINT IN SELF-DENIAL?
BUT I... I...
RIN...

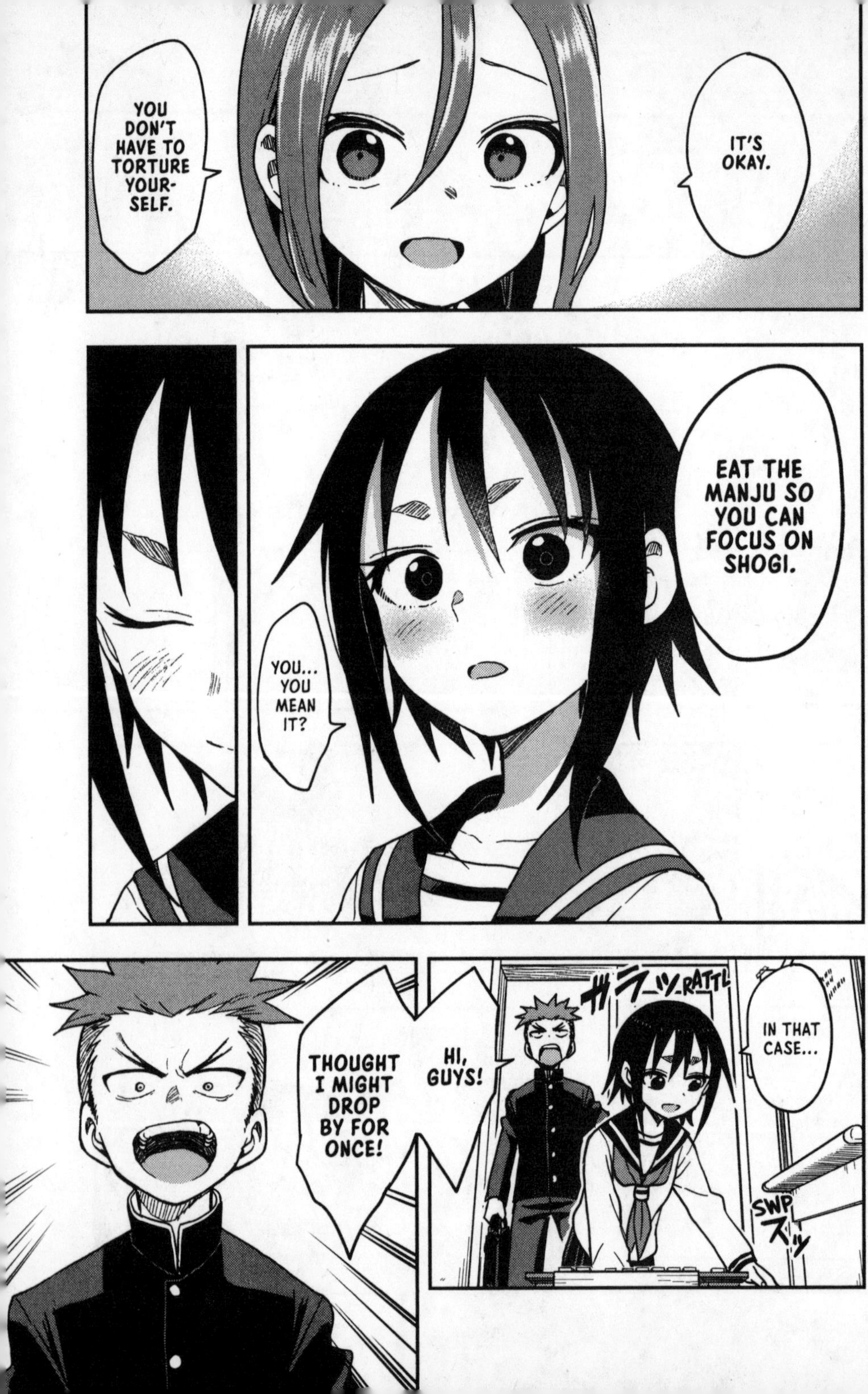
IT'S OKAY.
YOU DON'T HAVE TO TORTURE YOUR-SELF.
EAT THE MANJU SO YOU CAN FOCUS ON SHOGI.
YOU... YOU MEAN IT?
IN THAT CASE...
RATTL
HI, GUYS!
SWP
THOUGHT I MIGHT DROP BY FOR ONCE!

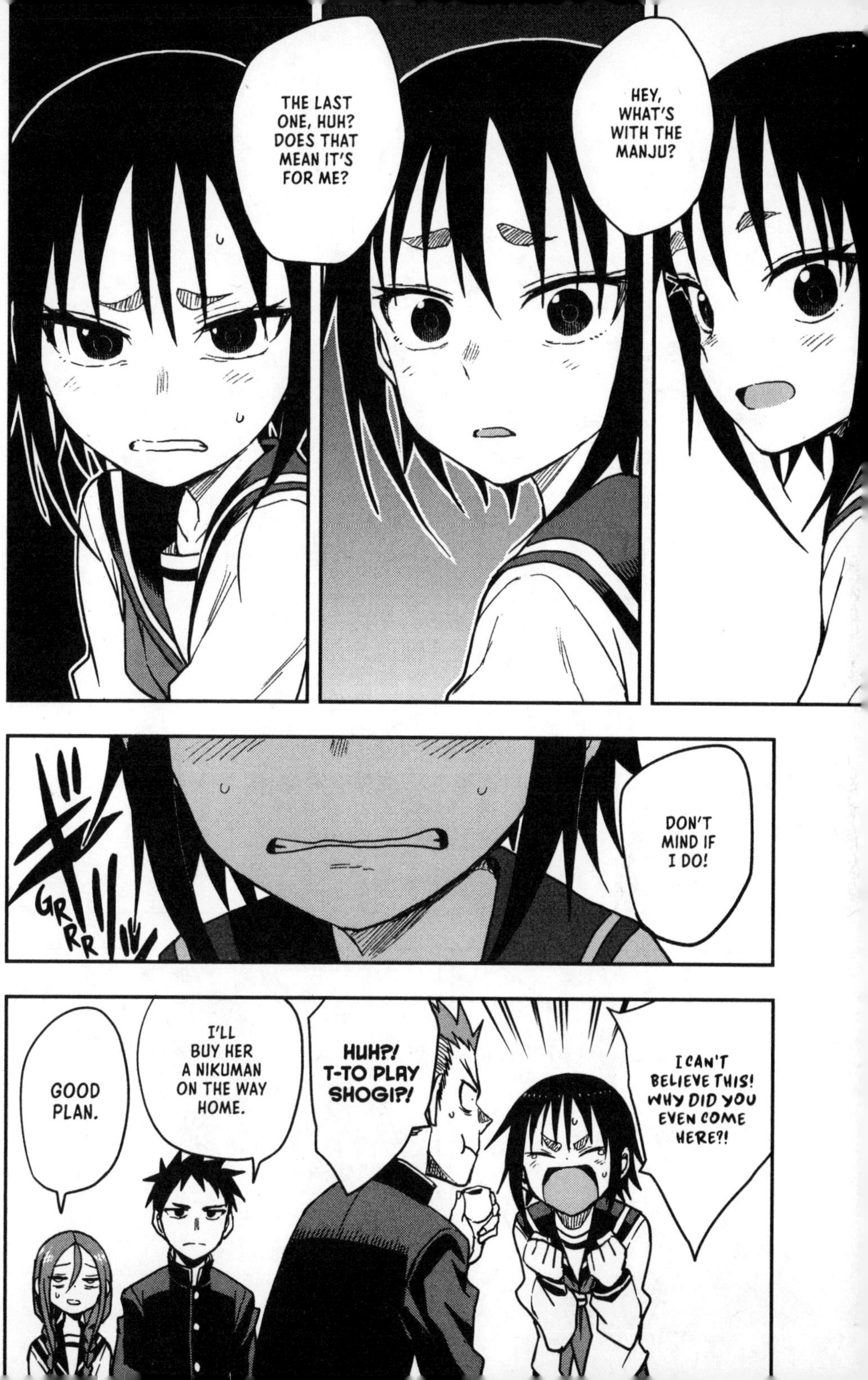
HEY, WHAT'S WITH THE MANJU?
THE LAST ONE, HUH? DOES THAT MEAN IT'S FOR ME?
DON'T MIND IF I DO!
GRRR
I CAN'T BELIEVE THIS! WHY DID YOU EVEN COME HERE?!
HUH?! T-TO PLAY SHOGI?!
I'LL BUY HER A NIKUMAN ON THE WAY HOME.
GOOD PLAN.

GAME 81 RECORD

▲ BLACK (SENTE): AYUMU TANAKA △ WHITE (GOTE): RIN KAGAWA

(DIAGRAM SHOWS BOARD AFTER MOVE 98, △ G×5H)

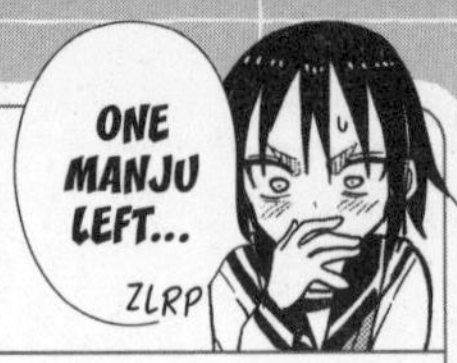

ONE MANJU LEFT...
ZLRP

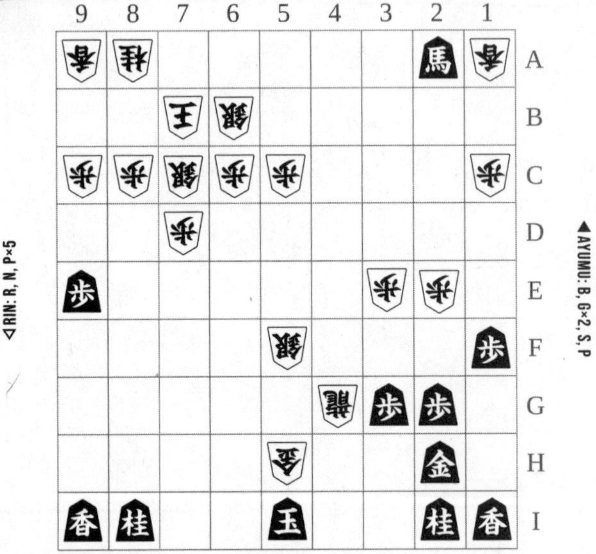

9 8 7 6 5 4 3 2 1
A B C D E F G H I
◁RIN: R, N, P×5
▲AYUMU: B, G×2, S, P

▲	△
▲ P-7F	△ P-3D
▲ P-6F	△ P-4D
▲ R-6H	△ R-3B
▲ K-4H	△ K-6B
▲ S-3H	△ K-7B
▲ K-3I	△ G4A-5B
▲ G6I-5H	△ S-4B
▲ S-7H	△ G6A-6B
▲ S-6G	△ B-3C
▲ S-5F	△ S-4C
▲ P-6E	△ S-8B
▲ P-6D	△ P-3E
▲ P×6C+	△ G6B×6C
▲ P×6D	△ G6C-6B
▲ S-6E	△ S-3D
▲ P-7E	△ P-2D
▲ P-7D	△ P×7D
▲ S×7D	△ P×7C
▲ P-6C+	△ G5B×6C
▲ S×6C+	△ G×6C
▲ P×6D	△ G×6D
▲ R×6D	△ P×6C
▲ R-6H	△ P-7D
▲ P-1F	△ S-7C
▲ P-9F	△ R-2B
▲ B-9G	△ S×6B
▲ P-4F	△ P-4E
▲ B-8H	△ B×8H+
▲ R×8H	△ B×3C
▲ R-9H	△ P×4F
▲ P-9E	△ P-2E
▲ R-9F	△ S-4E
▲ G×4C	△ B-8H+
▲ B×3A	△ R-2C
▲ B-4B+	△ +B×8G
▲ R-6F	△ +B×4C
▲ +B×4c	△ R×4C
▲ B×3B	△ R-4D
▲ B×2A+	△ G×4G
▲ G5H-5I	△ G×3H
▲ G×3H	△ S×4G
▲ G-2H	△ B×7E
▲ R-6G	△ S4E-5F
▲ R-7G	△ B×5G+
▲ N×4H	△ S×4H+
▲ G×4H	△ +B×4H
▲ K×4H	△ P-4G+
▲ R×4G	△ S×4G+
▲ K-5I	△ G×5H

(RIN WINS AT MOVE 98)

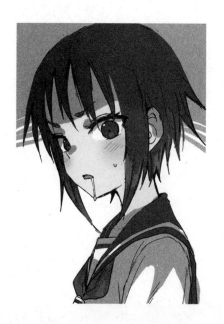

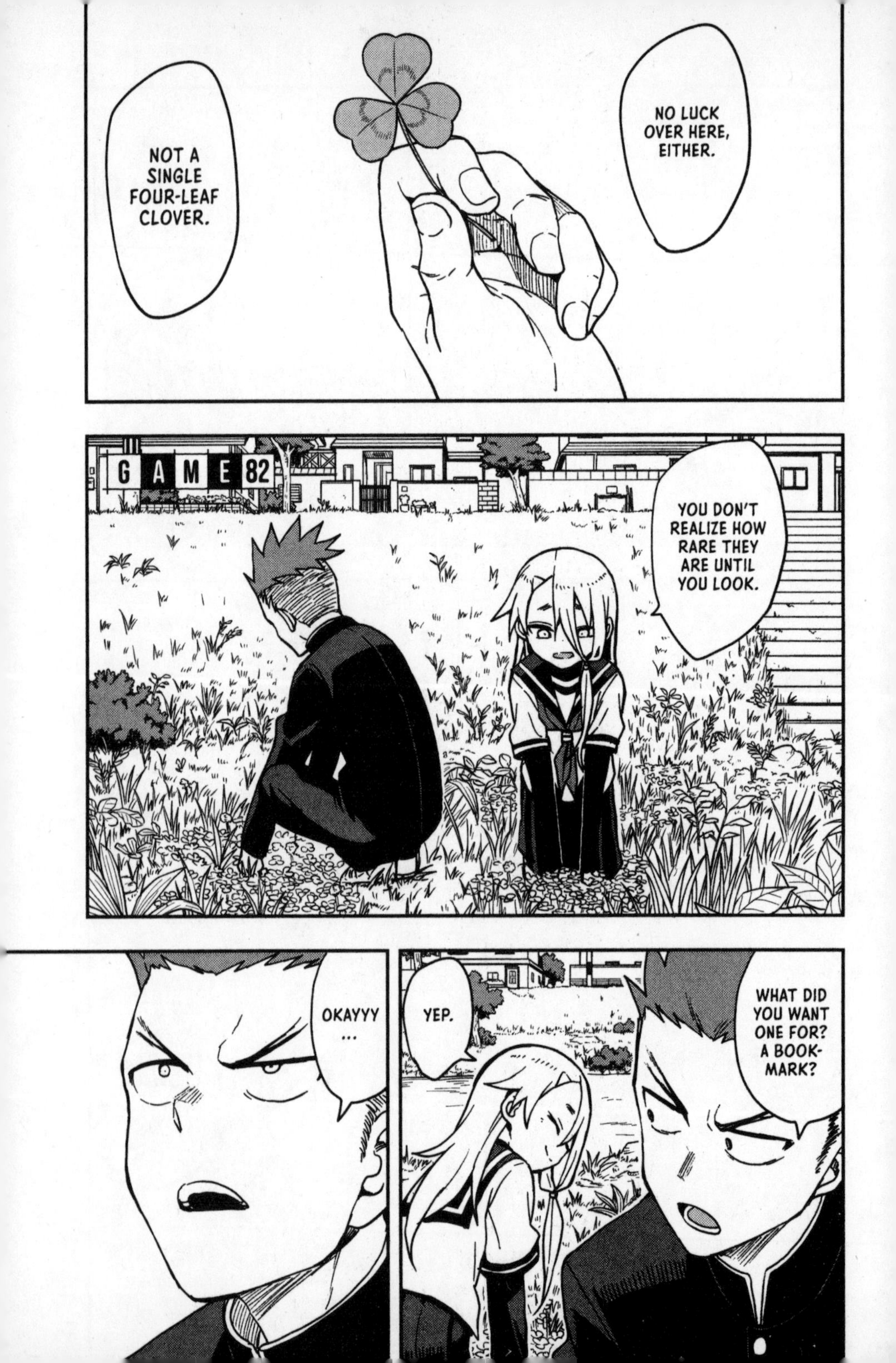
NO LUCK OVER HERE, EITHER.
NOT A SINGLE FOUR-LEAF CLOVER.
GAME 82
YOU DON'T REALIZE HOW RARE THEY ARE UNTIL YOU LOOK.
WHAT DID YOU WANT ONE FOR? A BOOK-MARK?
YEP.
OKAYYY ...

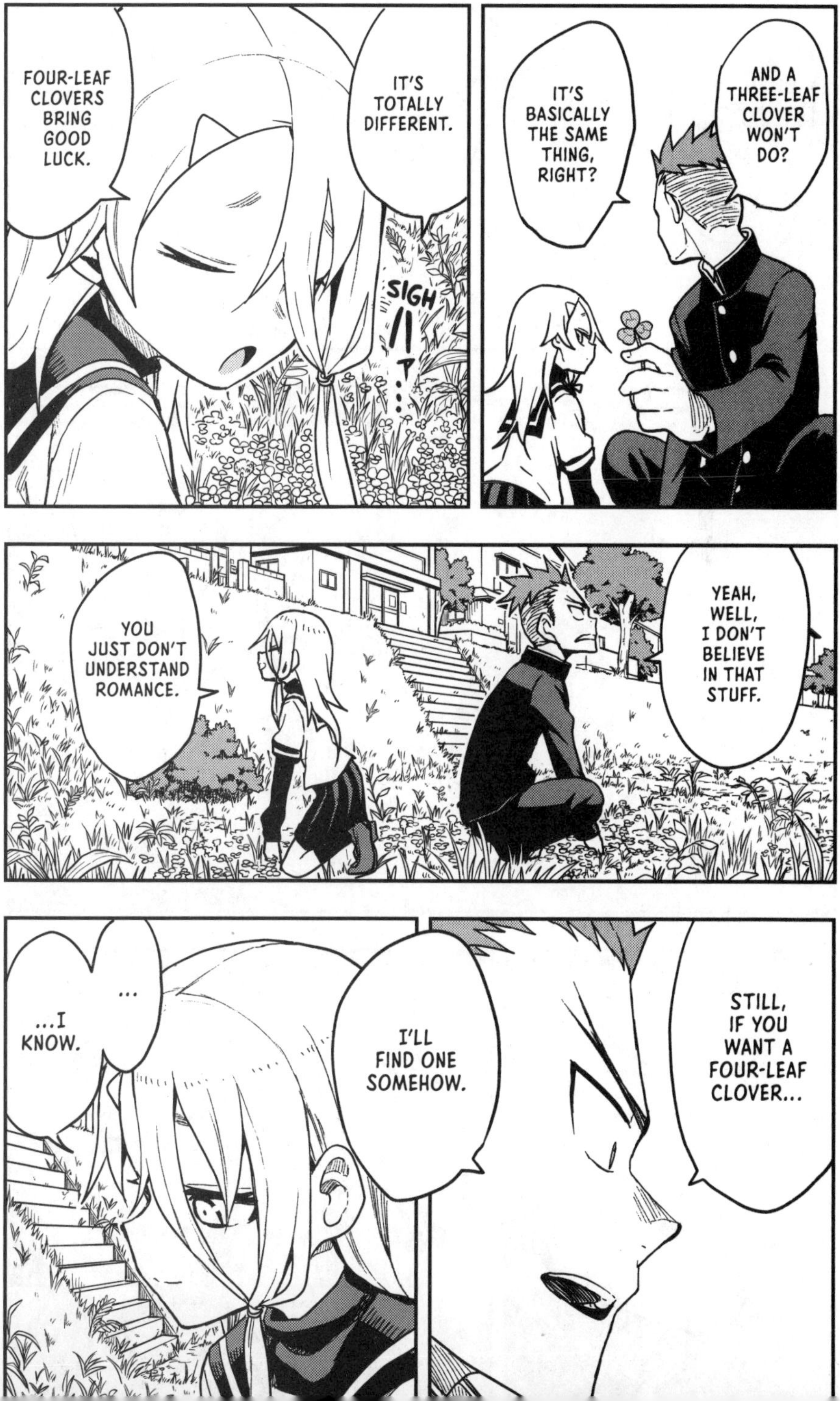
AND A THREE-LEAF CLOVER WON'T DO?
IT'S BASICALLY THE SAME THING, RIGHT?
IT'S TOTALLY DIFFERENT.
FOUR-LEAF CLOVERS BRING GOOD LUCK.
SIGH
YEAH, WELL, I DON'T BELIEVE IN THAT STUFF.
YOU JUST DON'T UNDERSTAND ROMANCE.
STILL, IF YOU WANT A FOUR-LEAF CLOVER...
I'LL FIND ONE SOMEHOW.
...
...I KNOW.

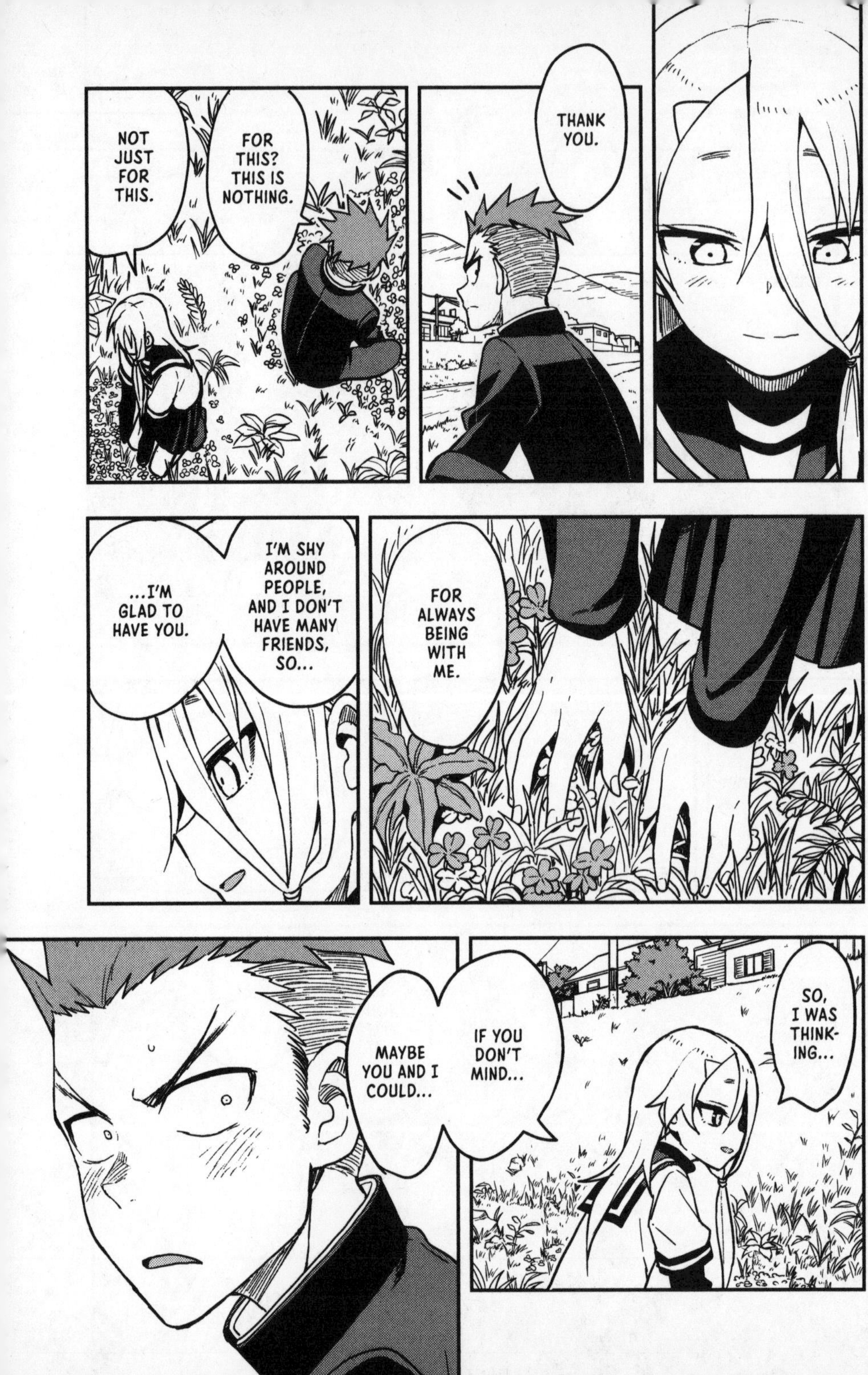
THANK YOU.
FOR THIS? THIS IS NOTHING.
NOT JUST FOR THIS.
FOR ALWAYS BEING WITH ME.
I'M SHY AROUND PEOPLE, AND I DON'T HAVE MANY FRIENDS, SO...
...I'M GLAD TO HAVE YOU.
SO, I WAS THINKING-ING...
IF YOU DON'T MIND...
MAYBE YOU AND I COULD...

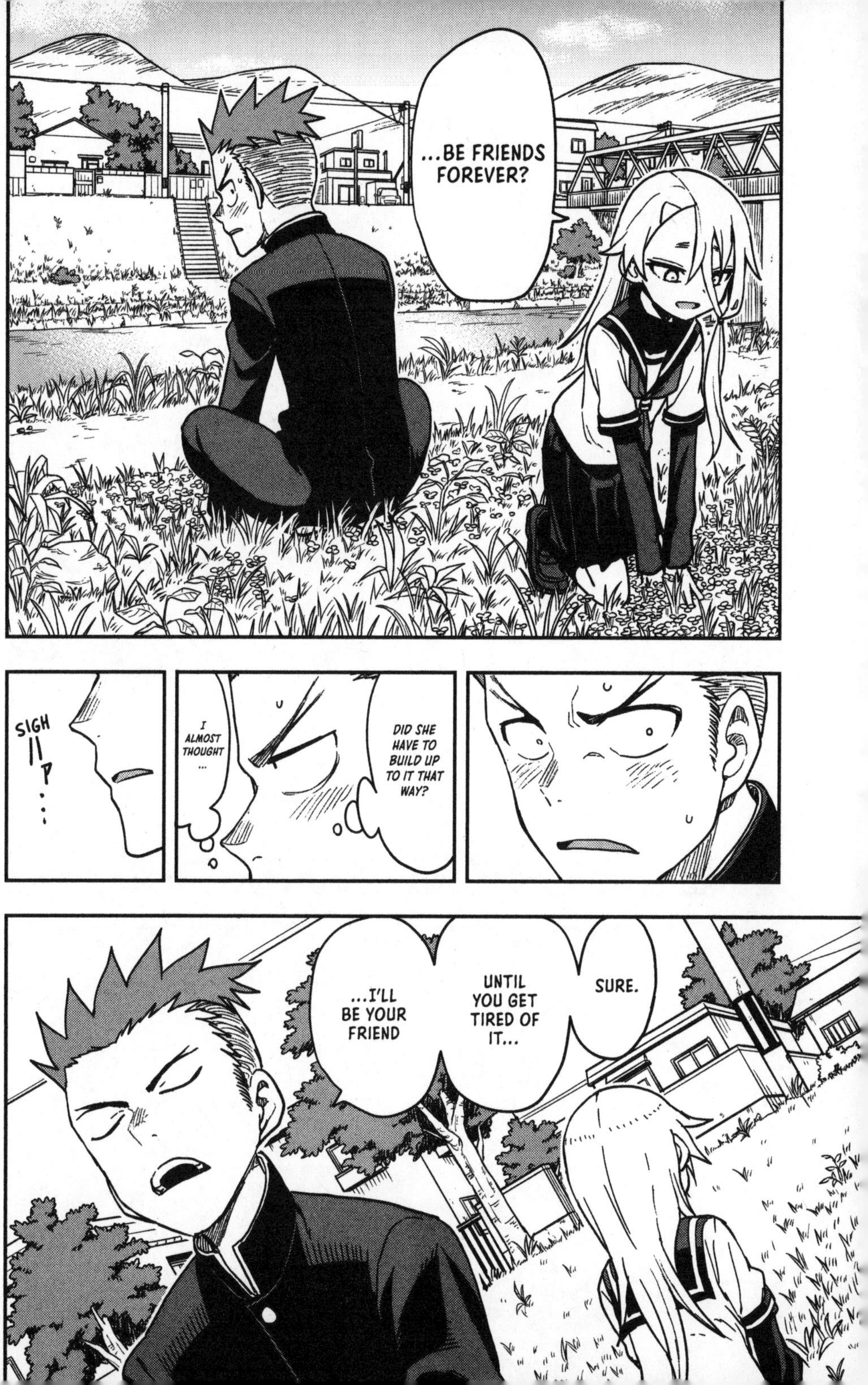
...BE FRIENDS FOREVER?
DID SHE HAVE TO BUILD UP TO IT THAT WAY?
I ALMOST THOUGHT ...
SIGH
SURE.
UNTIL YOU GET TIRED OF IT...
...I'LL BE YOUR FRIEND

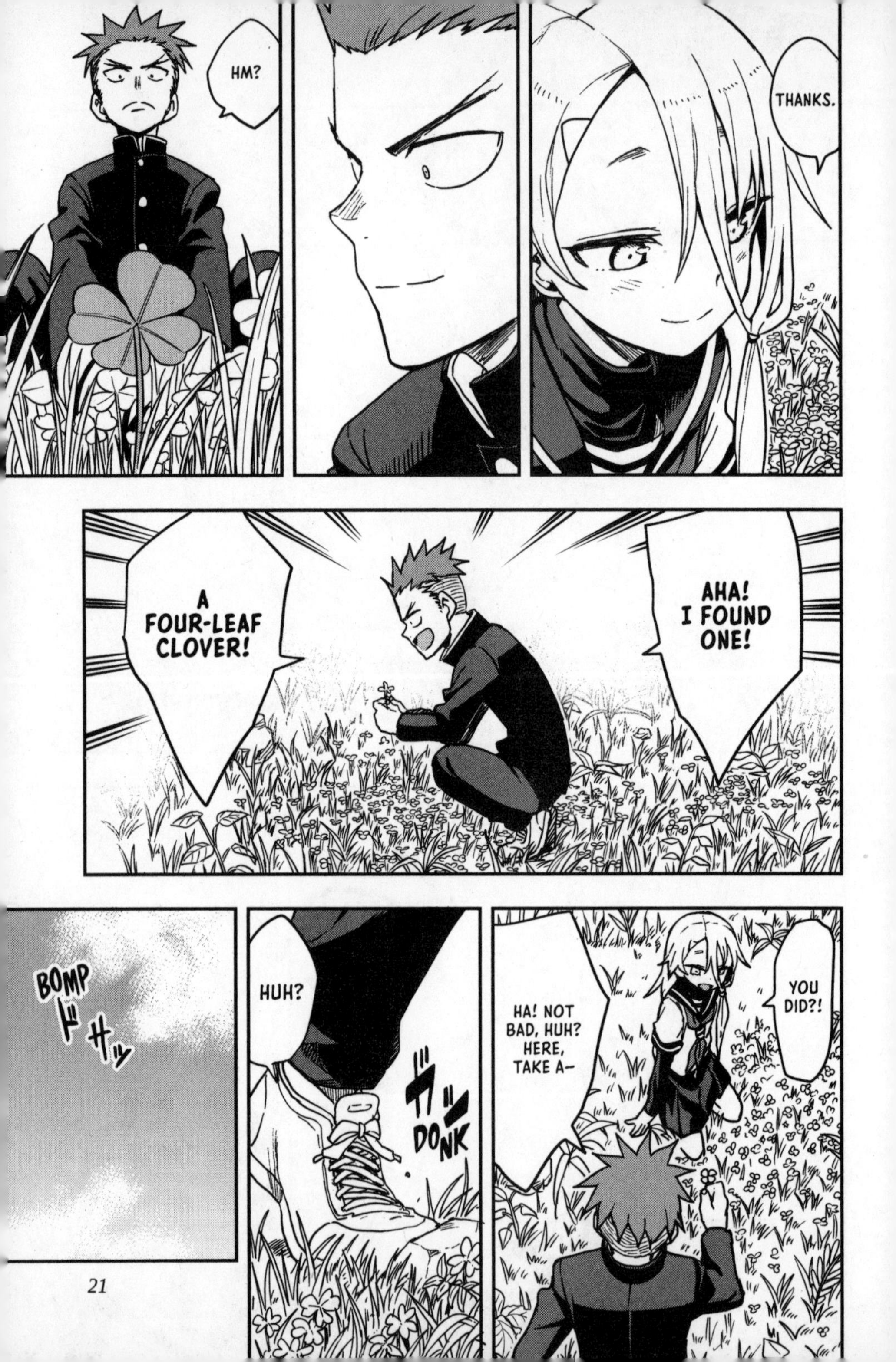
THANKS.
HM?
AHA! I FOUND ONE!
A FOUR-LEAF CLOVER!
YOU DID?!
HA! NOT BAD, HUH? HERE, TAKE A—
HUH?
DONK
BOMP
ドサッ

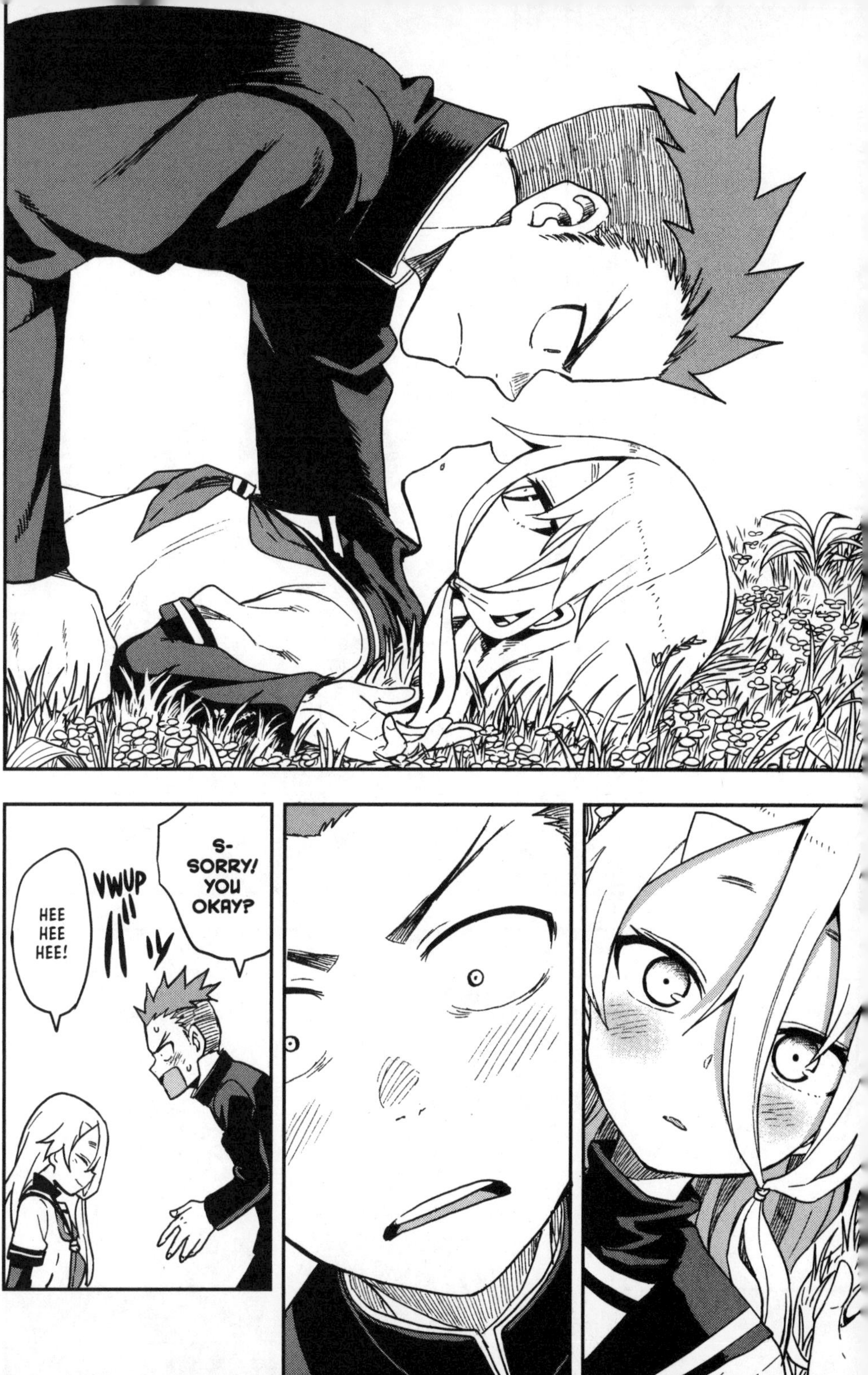
S-SORRY! YOU OKAY?
VWUP
HEE HEE HEE!

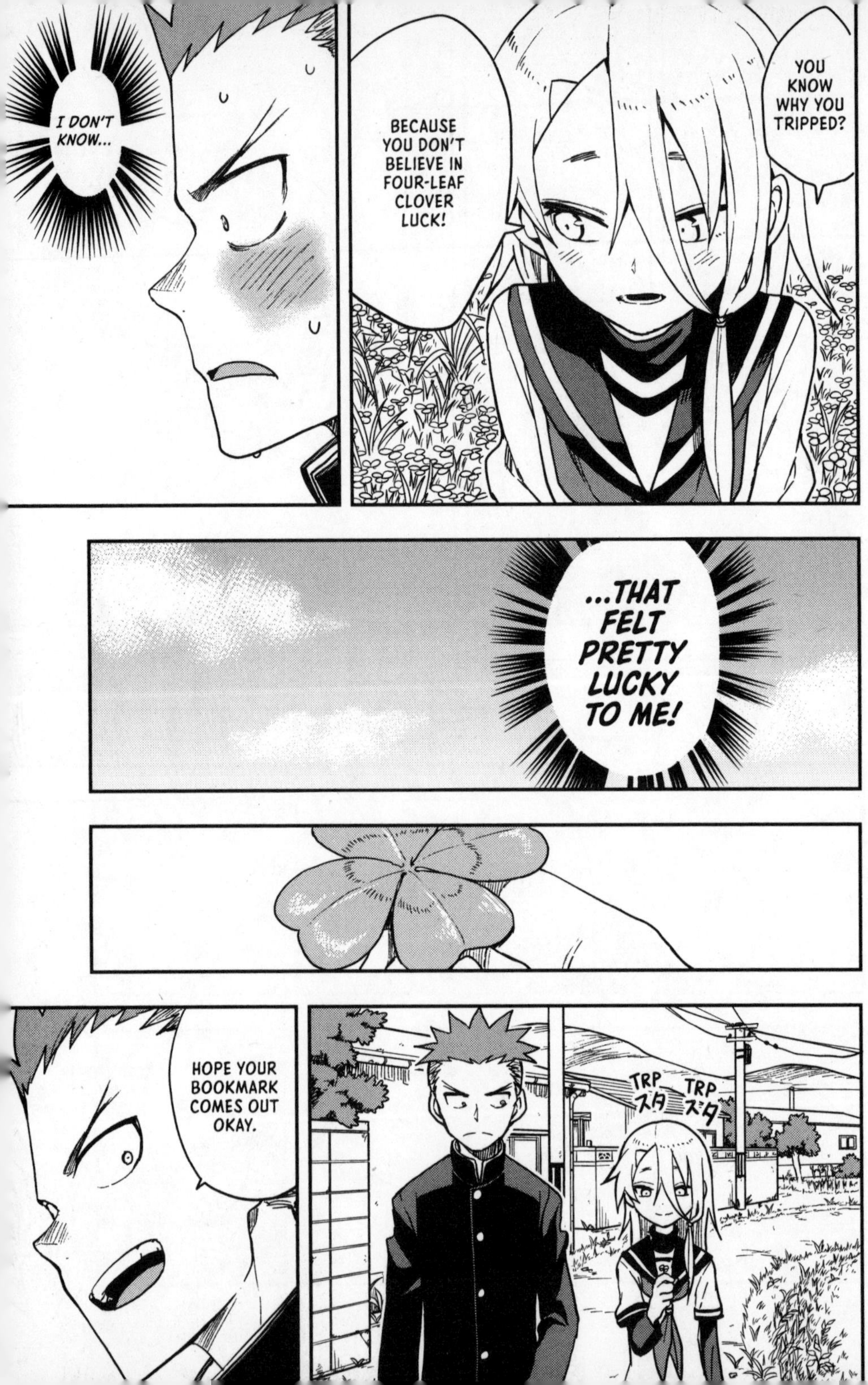
YOU KNOW WHY YOU TRIPPED?
BECAUSE YOU DON'T BELIEVE IN FOUR-LEAF CLOVER LUCK!
I DON'T KNOW...
...THAT FELT PRETTY LUCKY TO ME!
TRP スタ
TRP スタ
HOPE YOUR BOOKMARK COMES OUT OKAY.

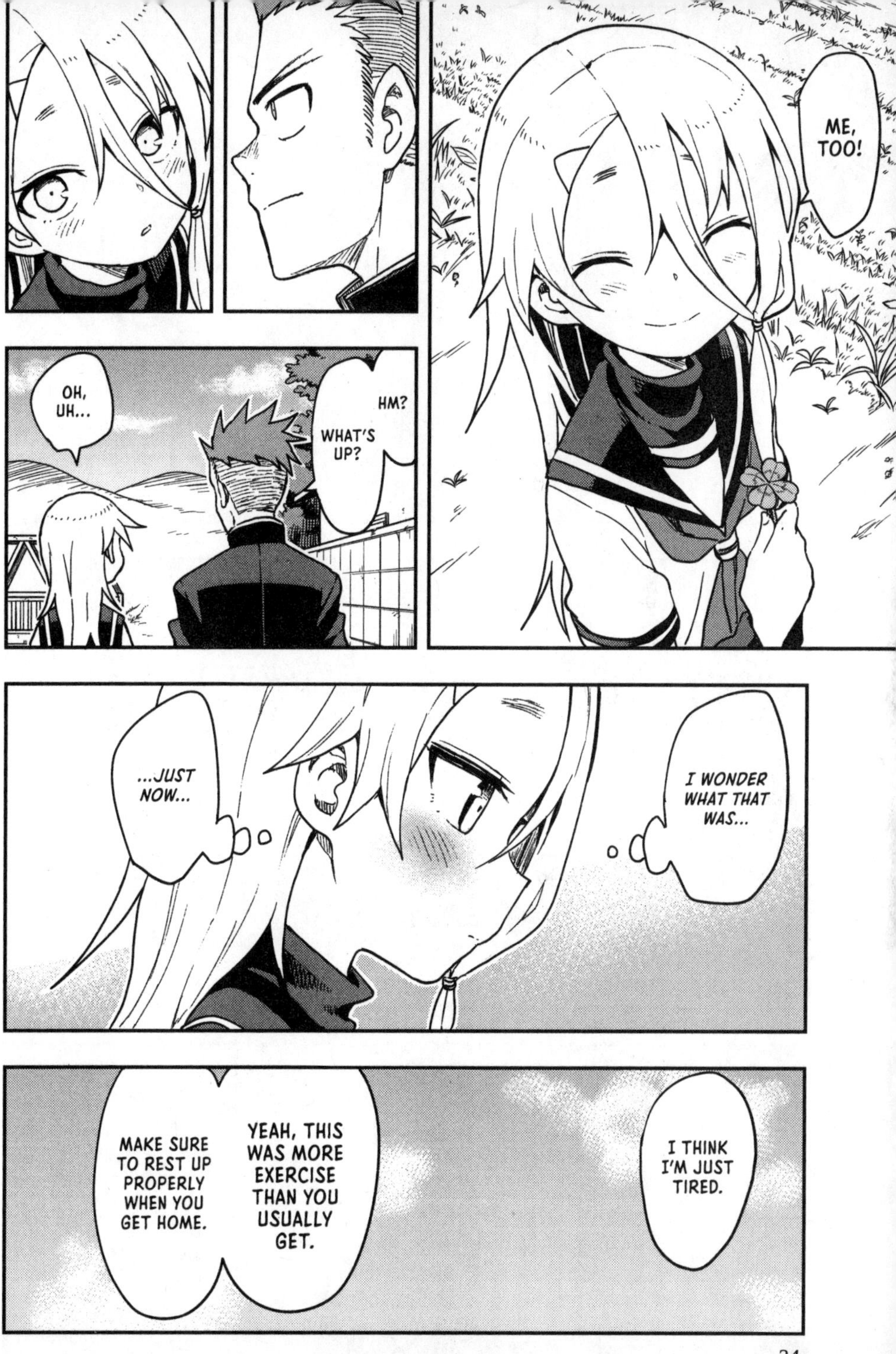
ME, TOO!
HM? WHAT'S UP?
OH, UH...
I WONDER WHAT THAT WAS...
...JUST NOW...
I THINK I'M JUST TIRED.
YEAH, THIS WAS MORE EXERCISE THAN YOU USUALLY GET.
MAKE SURE TO REST UP PROPERLY WHEN YOU GET HOME.

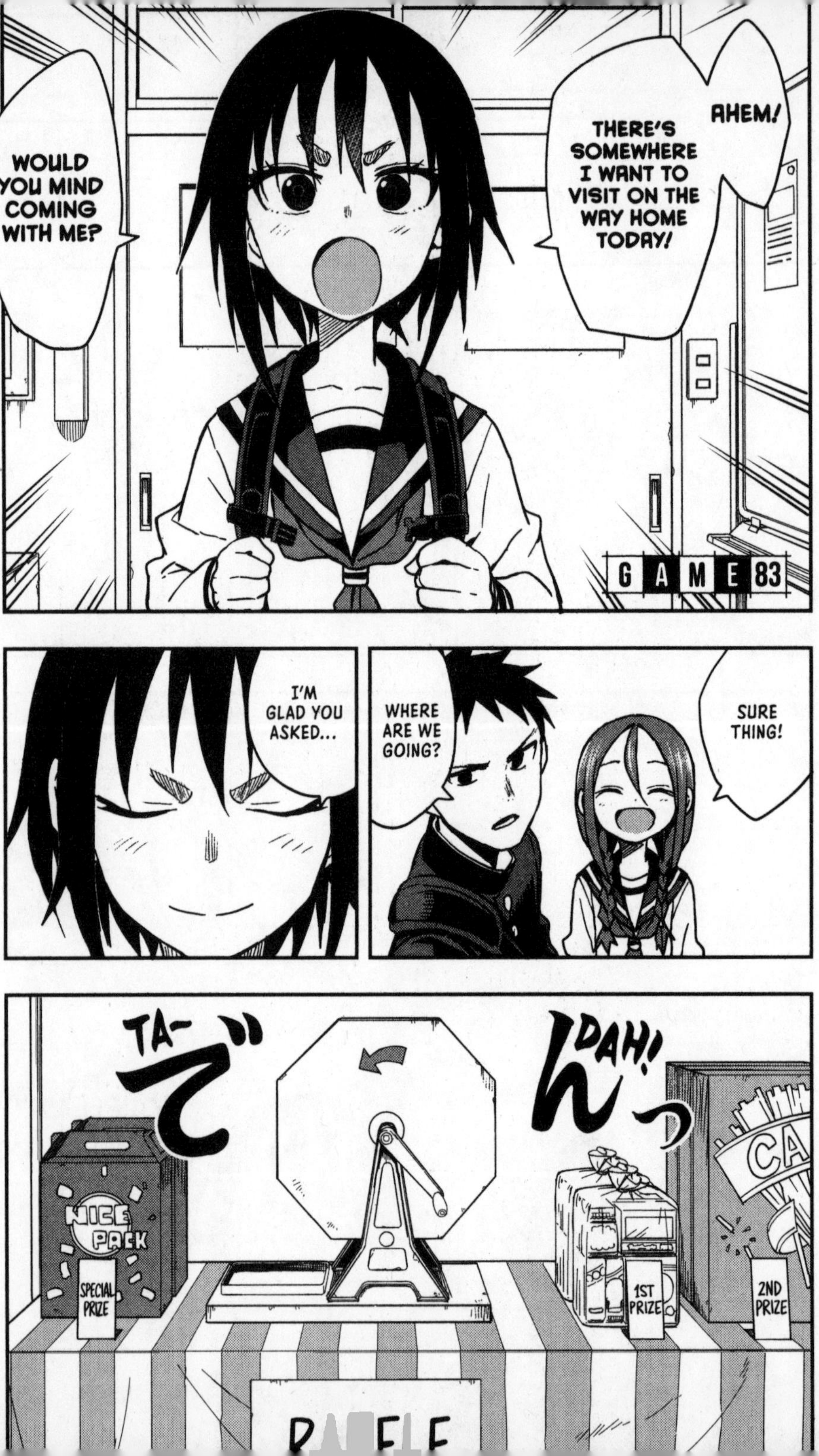

AHEM!
THERE'S SOMEWHERE I WANT TO VISIT ON THE WAY HOME TODAY!
WOULD YOU MIND COMING WITH ME?
GAME 83
SURE THING!
WHERE ARE WE GOING?
I'M GLAD YOU ASKED...
でんっ
TA- DAH!
2ND PRIZE
1ST PRIZE
NICE PACK
SPECIAL PRIZE

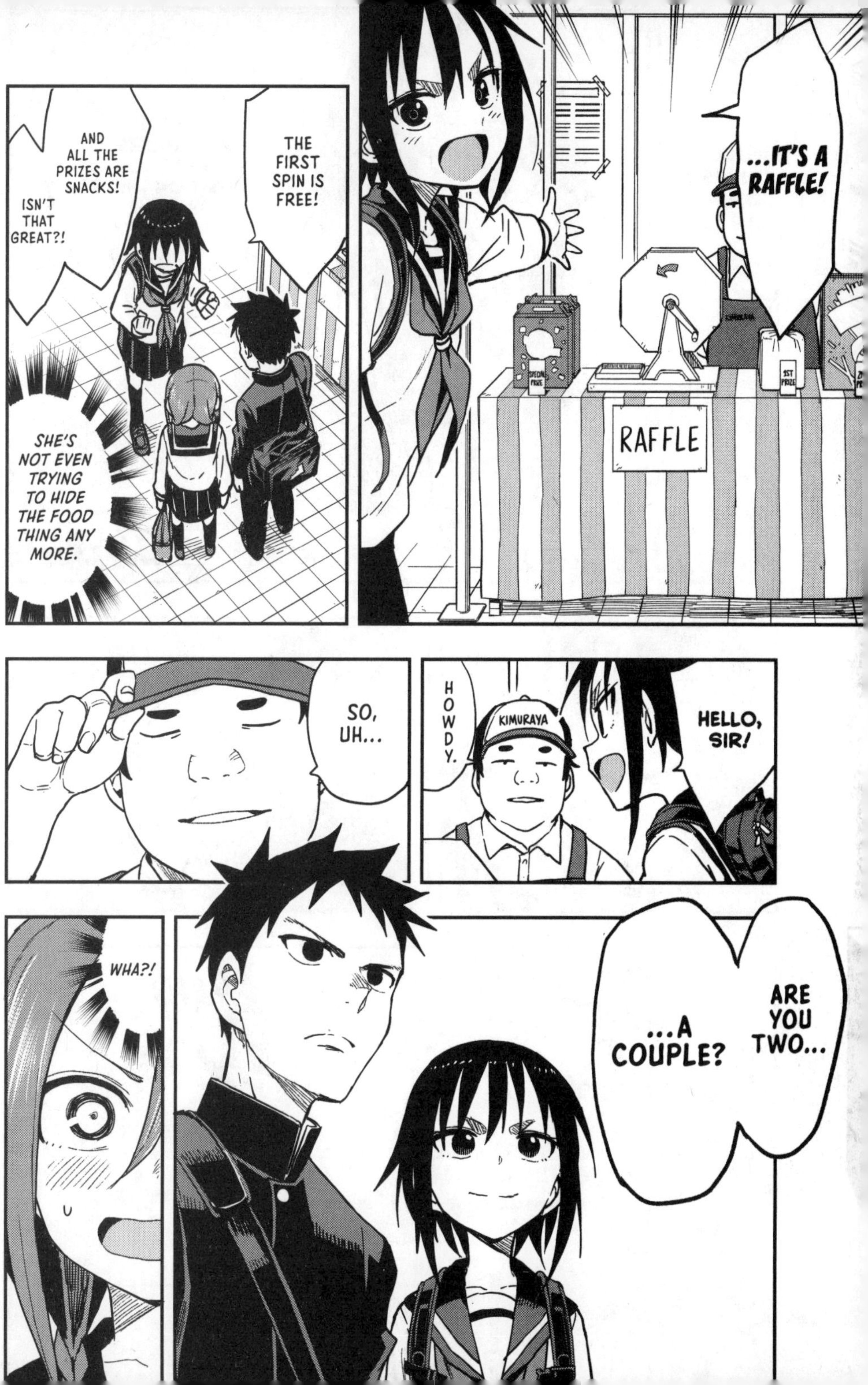
...IT'S A RAFFLE!
RAFFLE
THE FIRST SPIN IS FREE!
AND ALL THE PRIZES ARE SNACKS!
ISN'T THAT GREAT?!
SHE'S NOT EVEN TRYING TO HIDE THE FOOD THING ANY MORE.
HELLO, SIR!
KIMURAYA
HOWDY.
SO, UH...
ARE YOU TWO...
...A COUPLE?
WHA?!

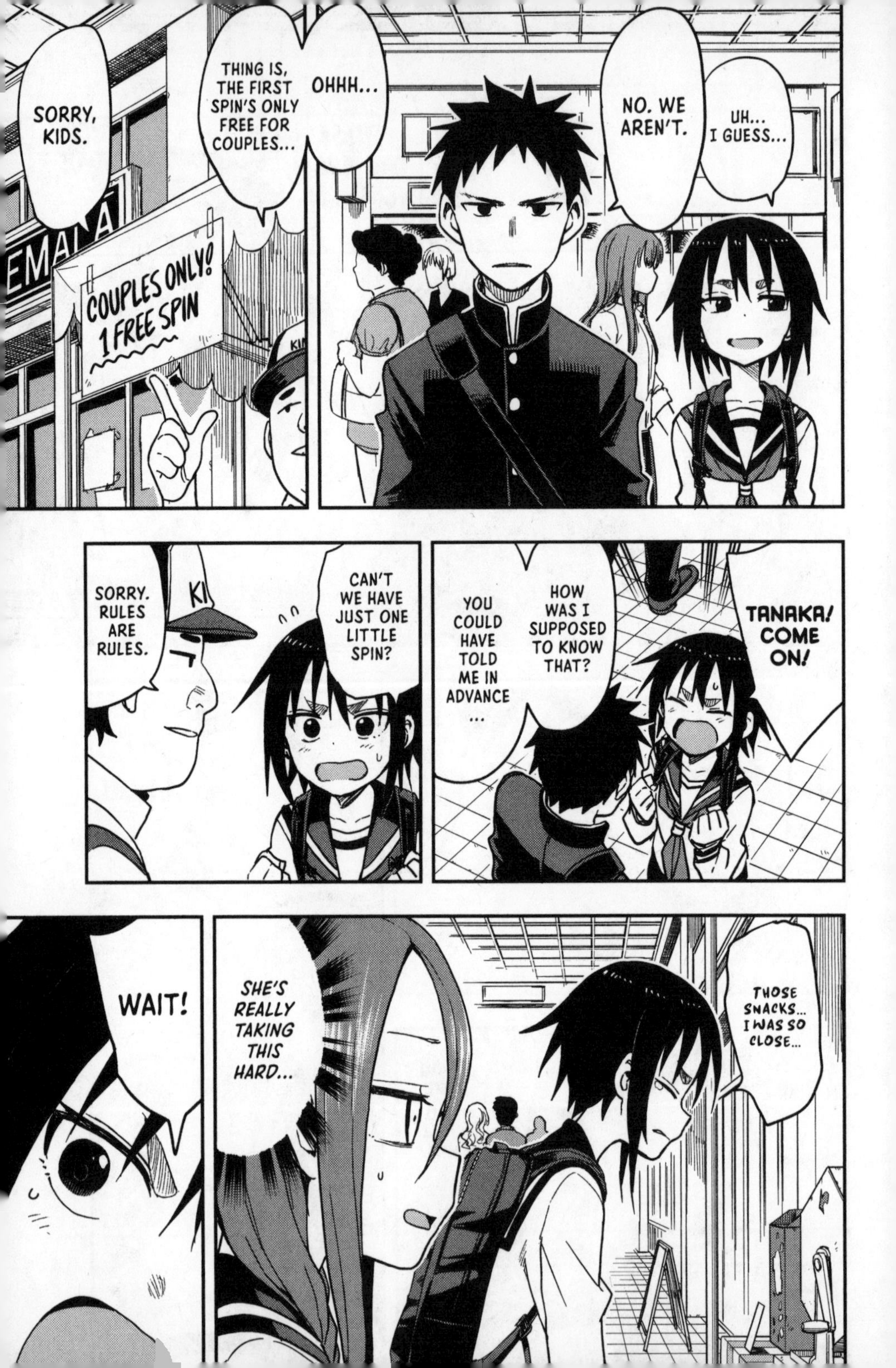
UH... I GUESS...
NO. WE AREN'T.
OHHH...
THING IS, THE FIRST SPIN'S ONLY FREE FOR COUPLES...
SORRY, KIDS.
COUPLES ONLY! 1 FREE SPIN
TANAKA! COME ON!
HOW WAS I SUPPOSED TO KNOW THAT?
YOU COULD HAVE TOLD ME IN ADVANCE ...
CAN'T WE HAVE JUST ONE LITTLE SPIN?
SORRY. RULES ARE RULES.
THOSE SNACKS... I WAS SO CLOSE...
SHE'S REALLY TAKING THIS HARD...
WAIT!

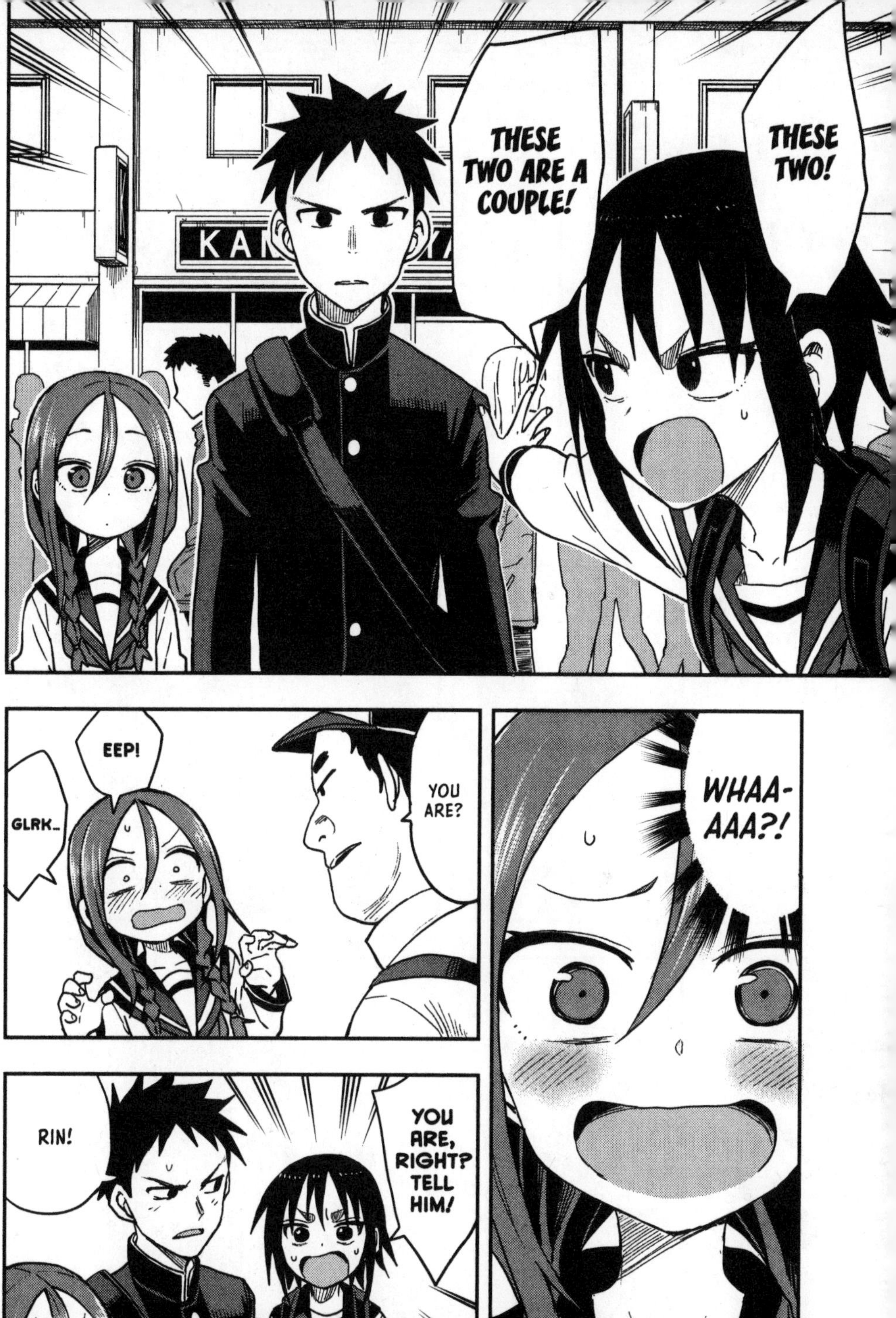

THESE TWO!
THESE TWO ARE A COUPLE!
KA
WHAAA-AAA?!
YOU ARE?
EEP!
GLRK...
YOU ARE, RIGHT? TELL HIM!
RIN!

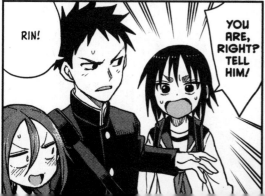

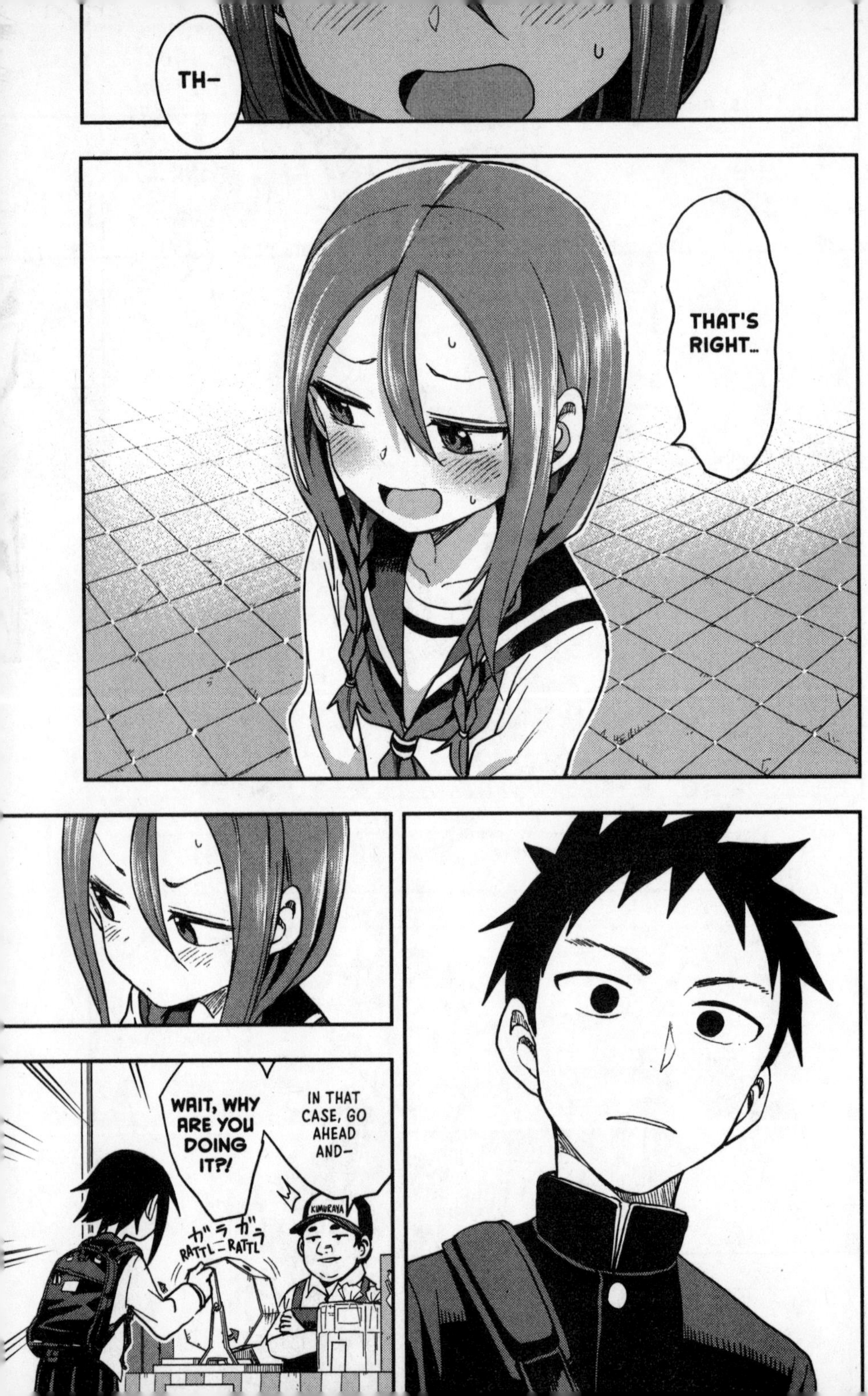
TH-
THAT'S RIGHT...
IN THAT CASE, GO AHEAD AND-
WAIT, WHY ARE YOU DOING IT?!
KIMURAYA
ガラガラ
RATTL RATTL

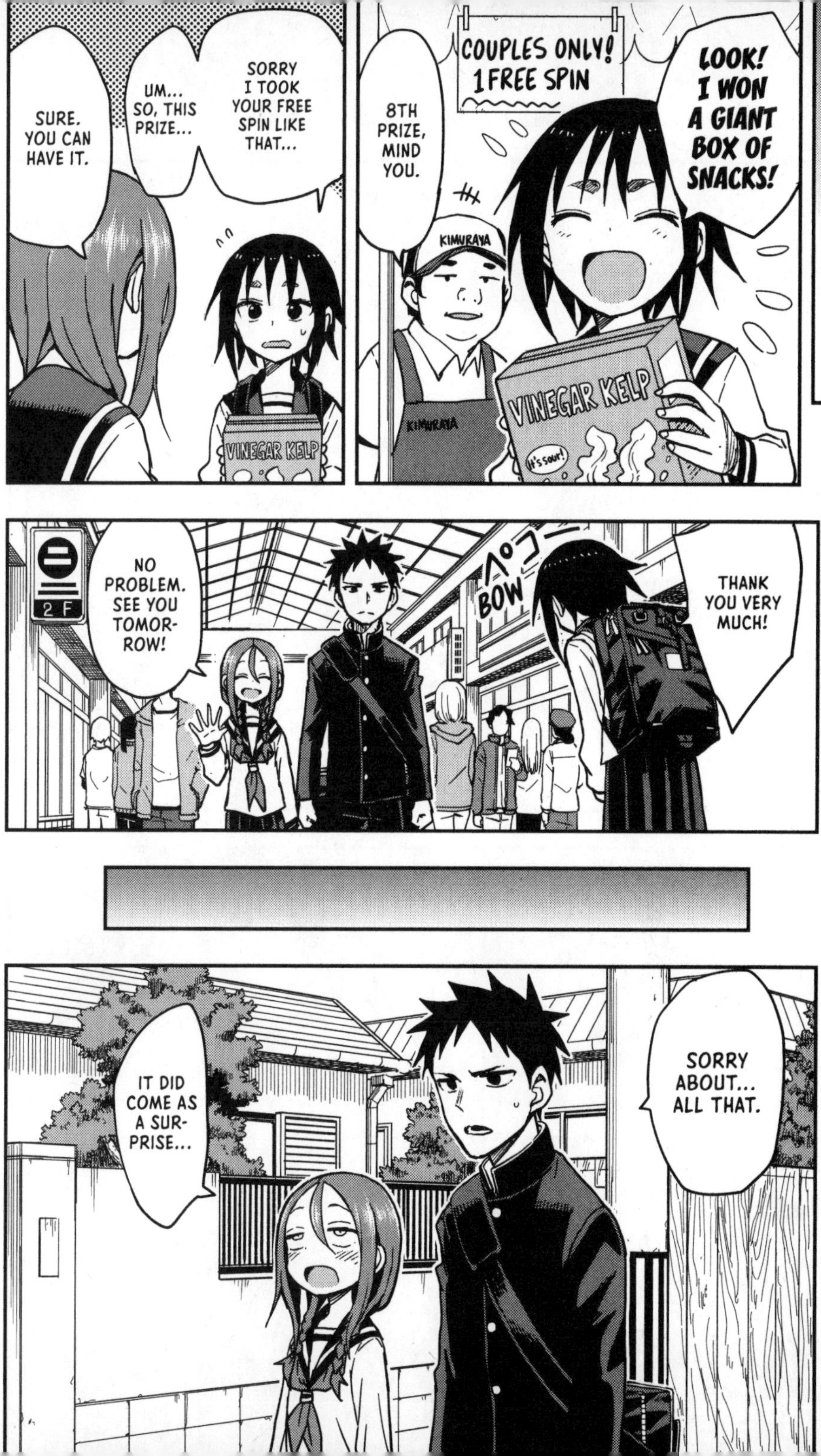
COUPLES ONLY! 1 FREE SPIN
LOOK! I WON A GIANT BOX OF SNACKS!
8TH PRIZE, MIND YOU.
KIMURAYA
KIMURAYA
VINEGAR KELP
It's sour!
SORRY I TOOK YOUR FREE SPIN LIKE THAT...
UM... SO, THIS PRIZE...
SURE. YOU CAN HAVE IT.
VINEGAR KELP
THANK YOU VERY MUCH!
ペコー BOW
NO PROBLEM. SEE YOU TOMORROW!
2 F
SORRY ABOUT... ALL THAT.
IT DID COME AS A SURPRISE...

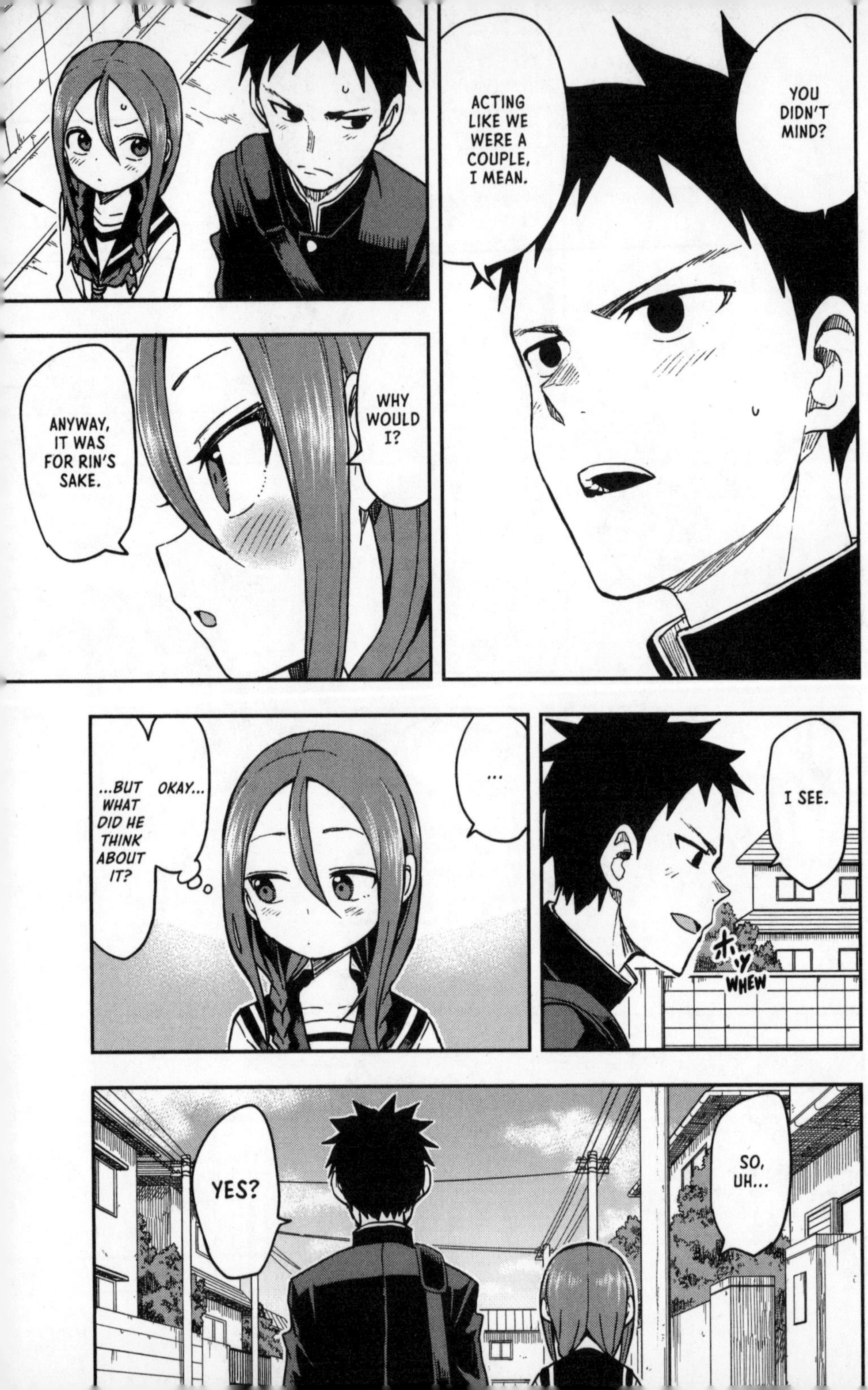
YOU DIDN'T MIND?
ACTING LIKE WE WERE A COUPLE, I MEAN.
WHY WOULD I?
ANYWAY, IT WAS FOR RIN'S SAKE.
I SEE.
ホッ
WHEW
...
OKAY...
...BUT WHAT DID HE THINK ABOUT IT?
SO, UH...
YES?

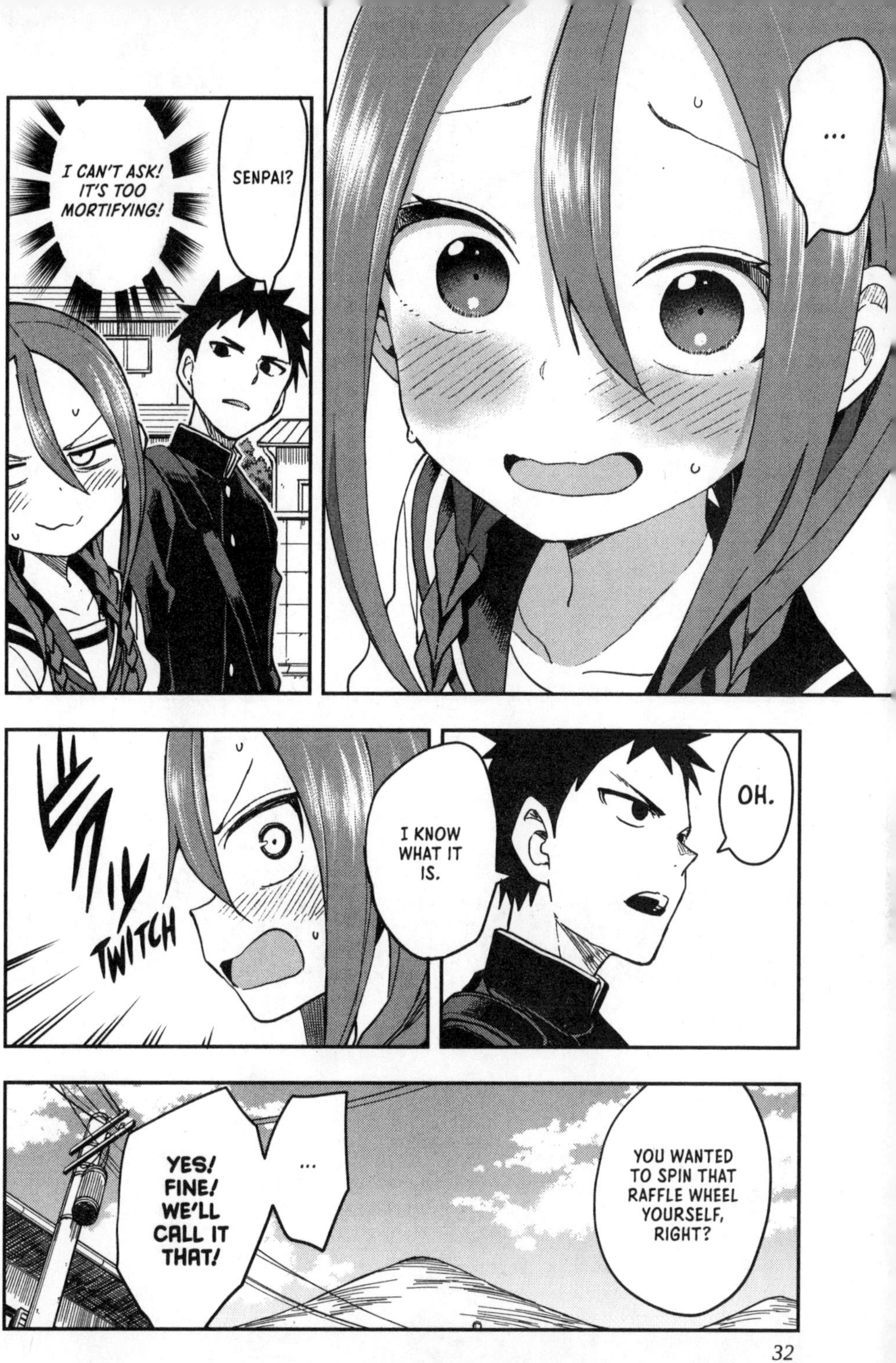
...
SENPAI?
I CAN'T ASK! IT'S TOO MORTIFYING!
OH.
I KNOW WHAT IT IS.
TWITCH
YOU WANTED TO SPIN THAT RAFFLE WHEEL YOURSELF, RIGHT?
...
YES! FINE! WE'LL CALL IT THAT!

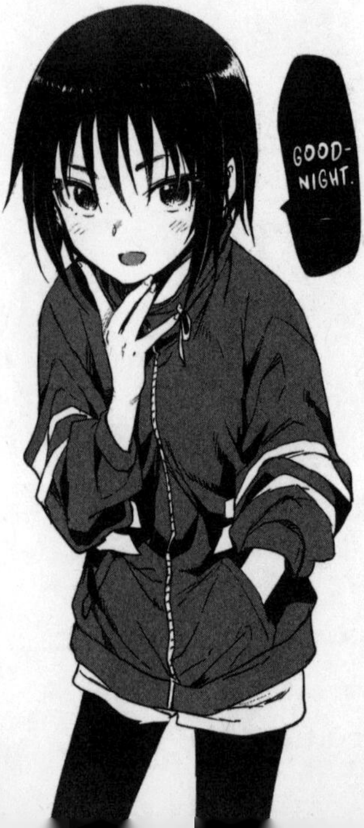
GOOD-NIGHT.

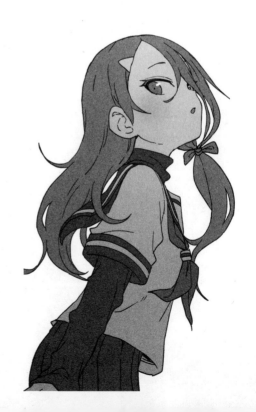

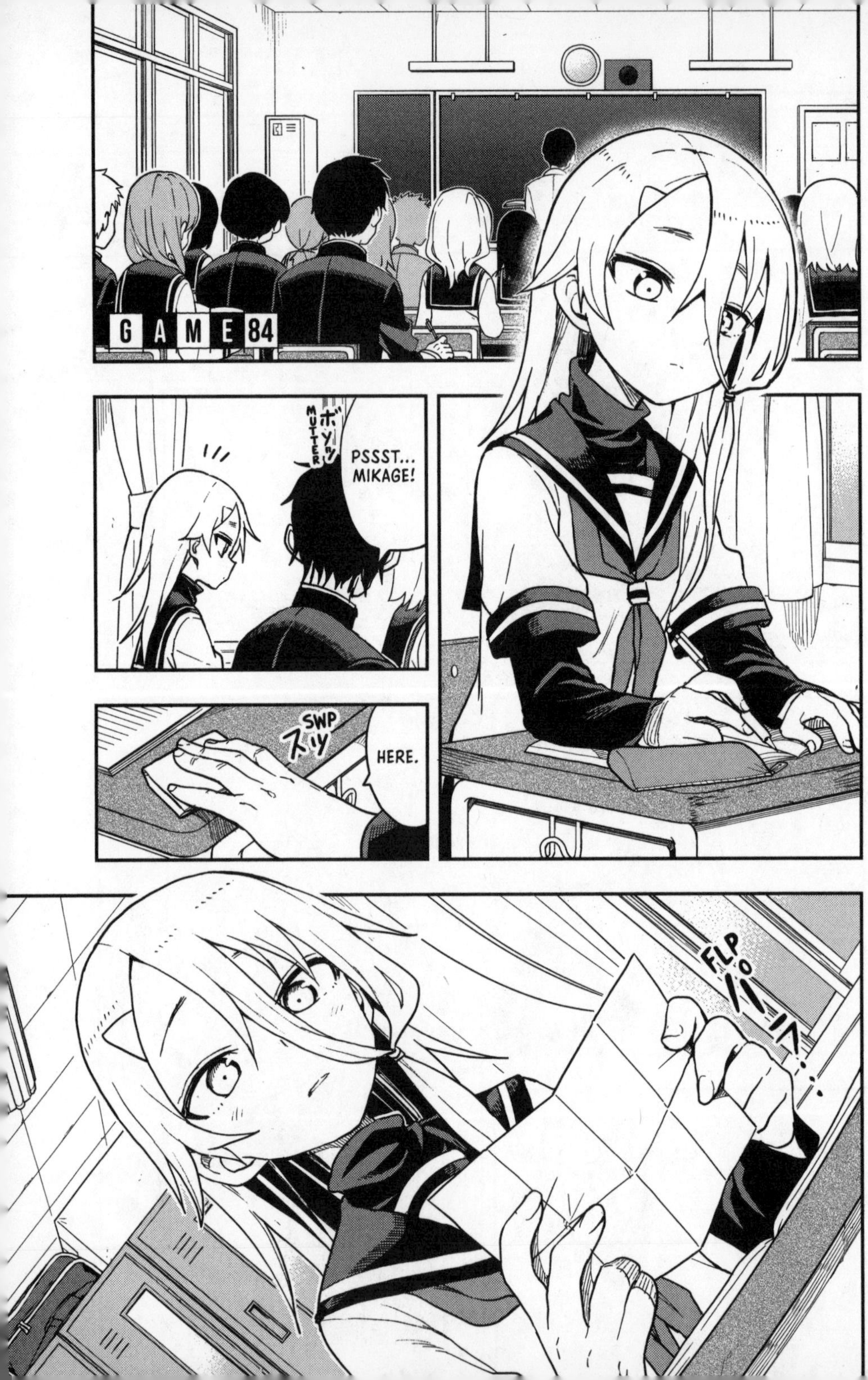
GAME 84
PSSST... MIKAGE!
MUTTER ボソッ
HERE.
SWP スッ
FLP パ...

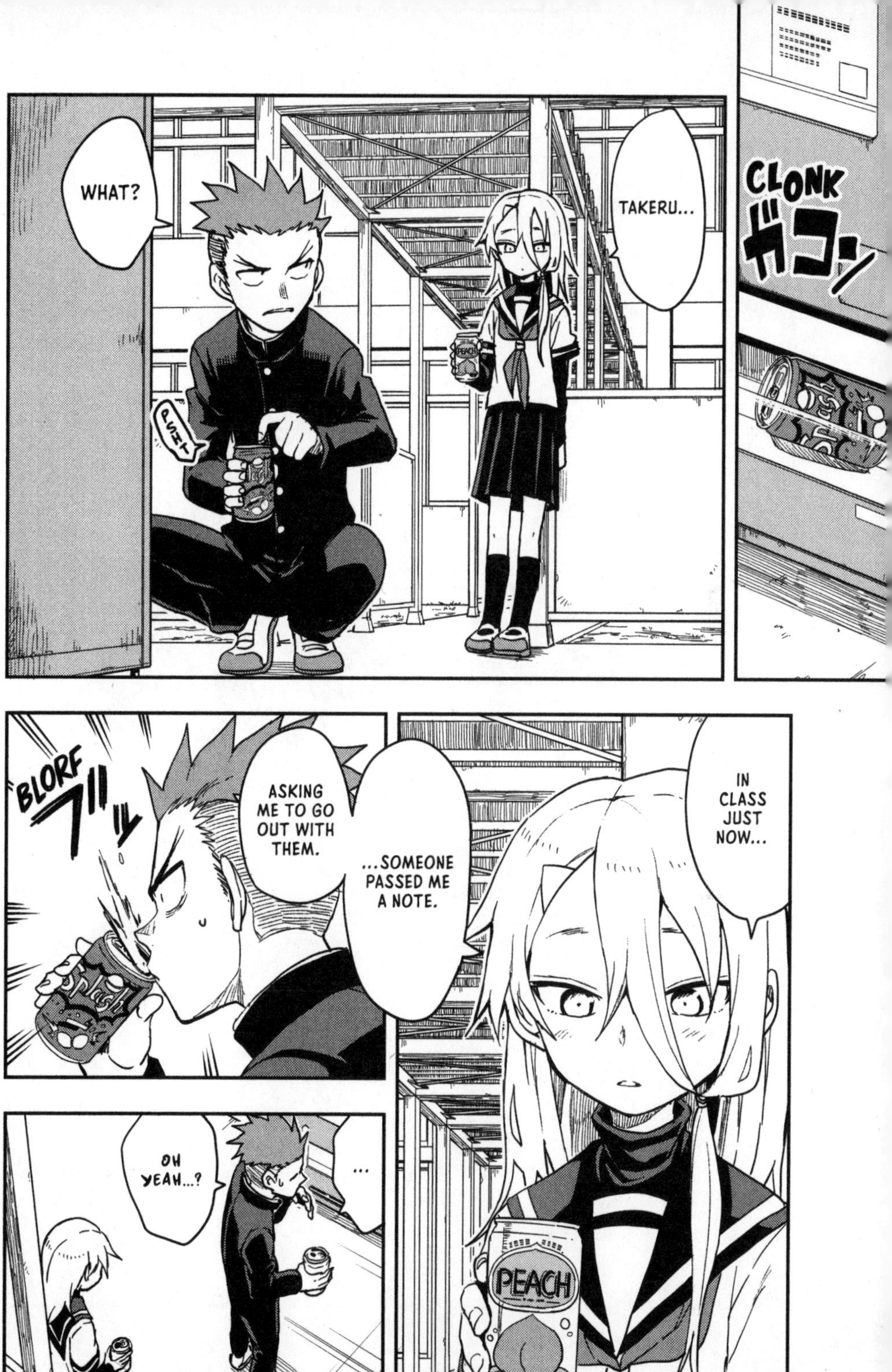
CLONK
ガコン
TAKERU...
WHAT?
PSHT
IN CLASS JUST NOW...
...SOMEONE PASSED ME A NOTE.
ASKING ME TO GO OUT WITH THEM.
BLORF
ブリッ
...
OH YEAH...?

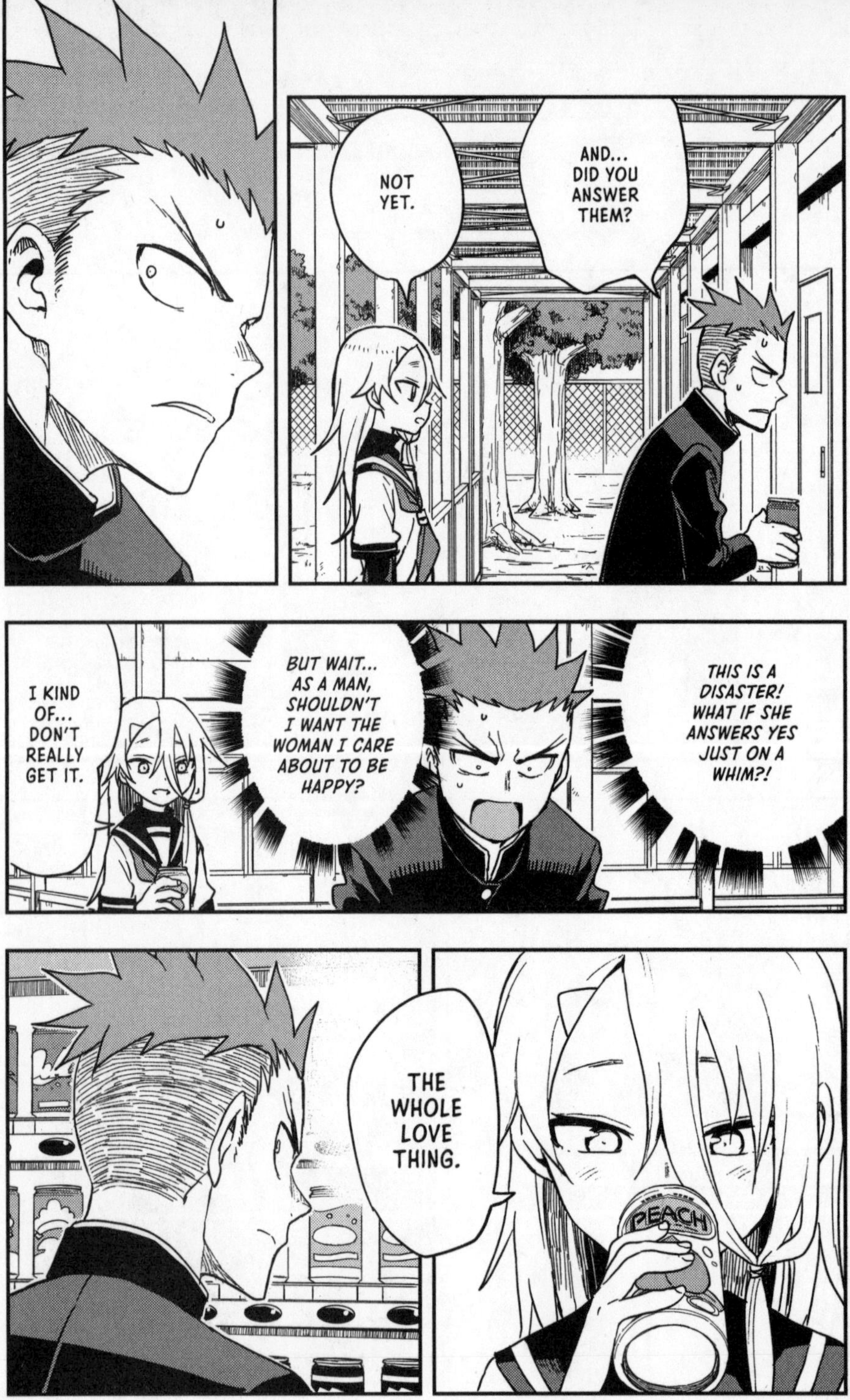
AND... DID YOU ANSWER THEM?
NOT YET.
THIS IS A DISASTER! WHAT IF SHE ANSWERS YES JUST ON A WHIM?!
BUT WAIT... AS A MAN, SHOULDN'T I WANT THE WOMAN I CARE ABOUT TO BE HAPPY?
I KIND OF... DON'T REALLY GET IT.
THE WHOLE LOVE THING.
PEACH

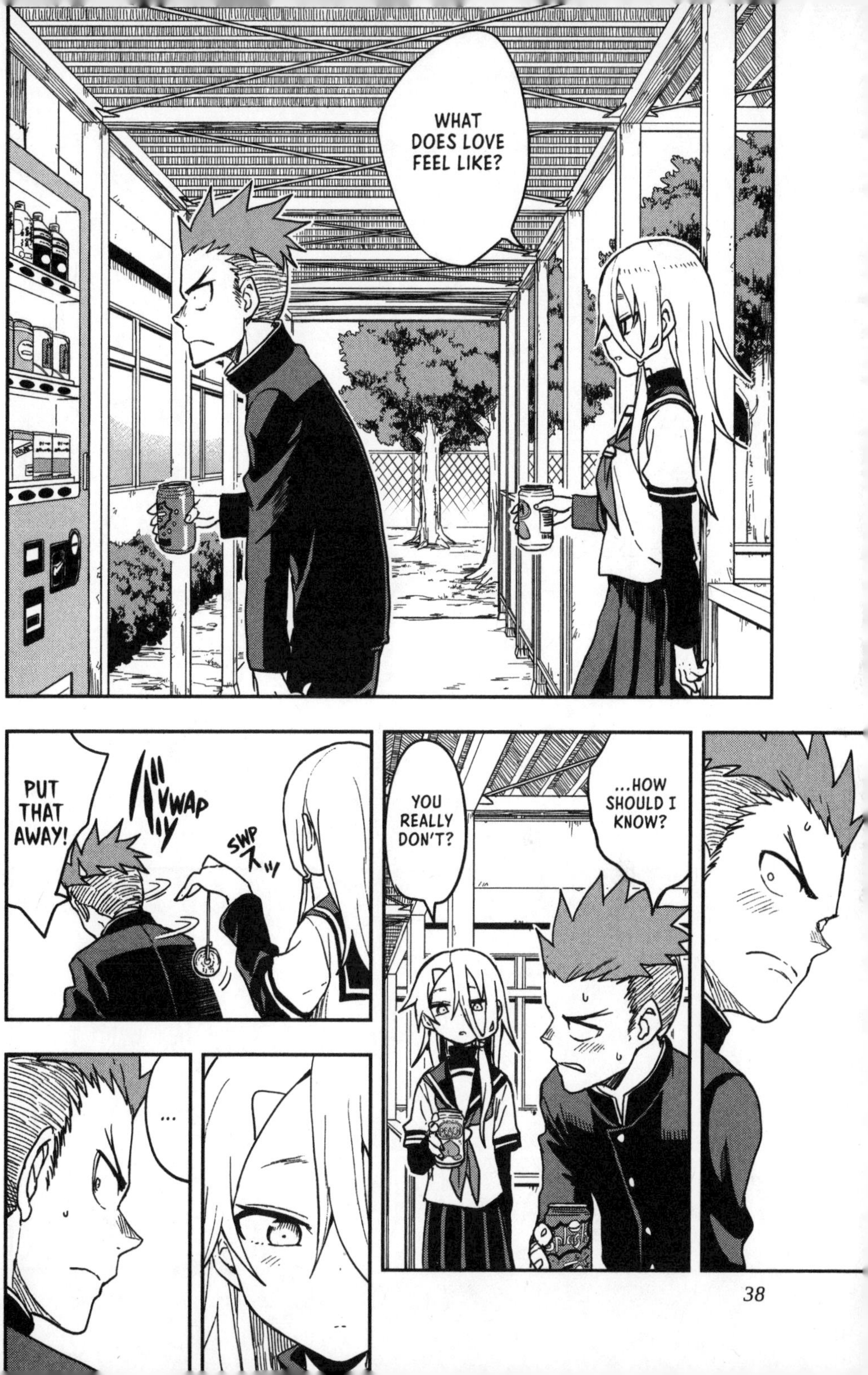
WHAT DOES LOVE FEEL LIKE?
...HOW SHOULD I KNOW?
YOU REALLY DON'T?
PUT THAT AWAY!
VWAP
SWP
...

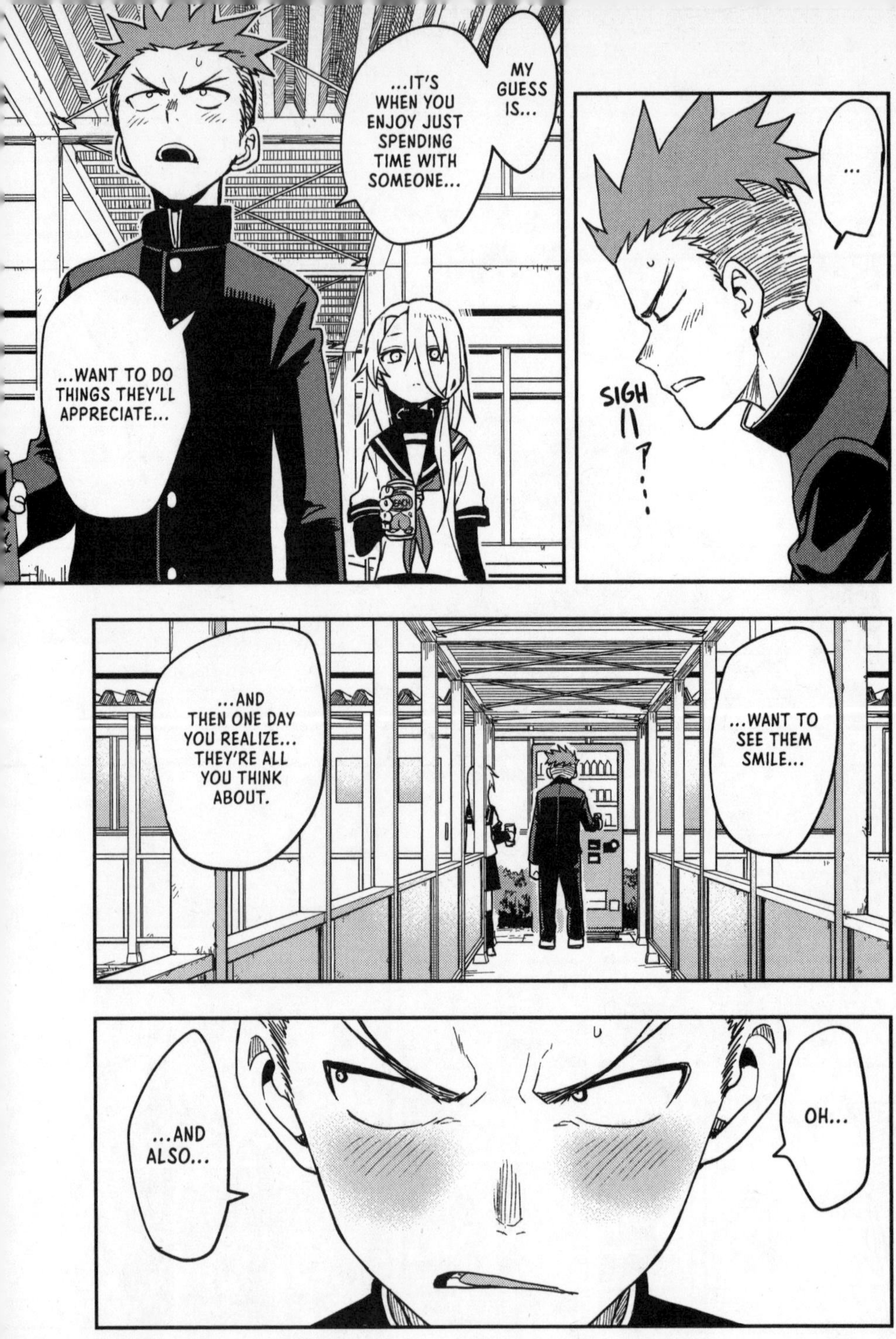
...
SIGH
ハァ…
MY GUESS IS...
...IT'S WHEN YOU ENJOY JUST SPENDING TIME WITH SOMEONE...
...WANT TO DO THINGS THEY'LL APPRECIATE...
...WANT TO SEE THEM SMILE...
...AND THEN ONE DAY YOU REALIZE... THEY'RE ALL YOU THINK ABOUT.
OH...
...AND ALSO...

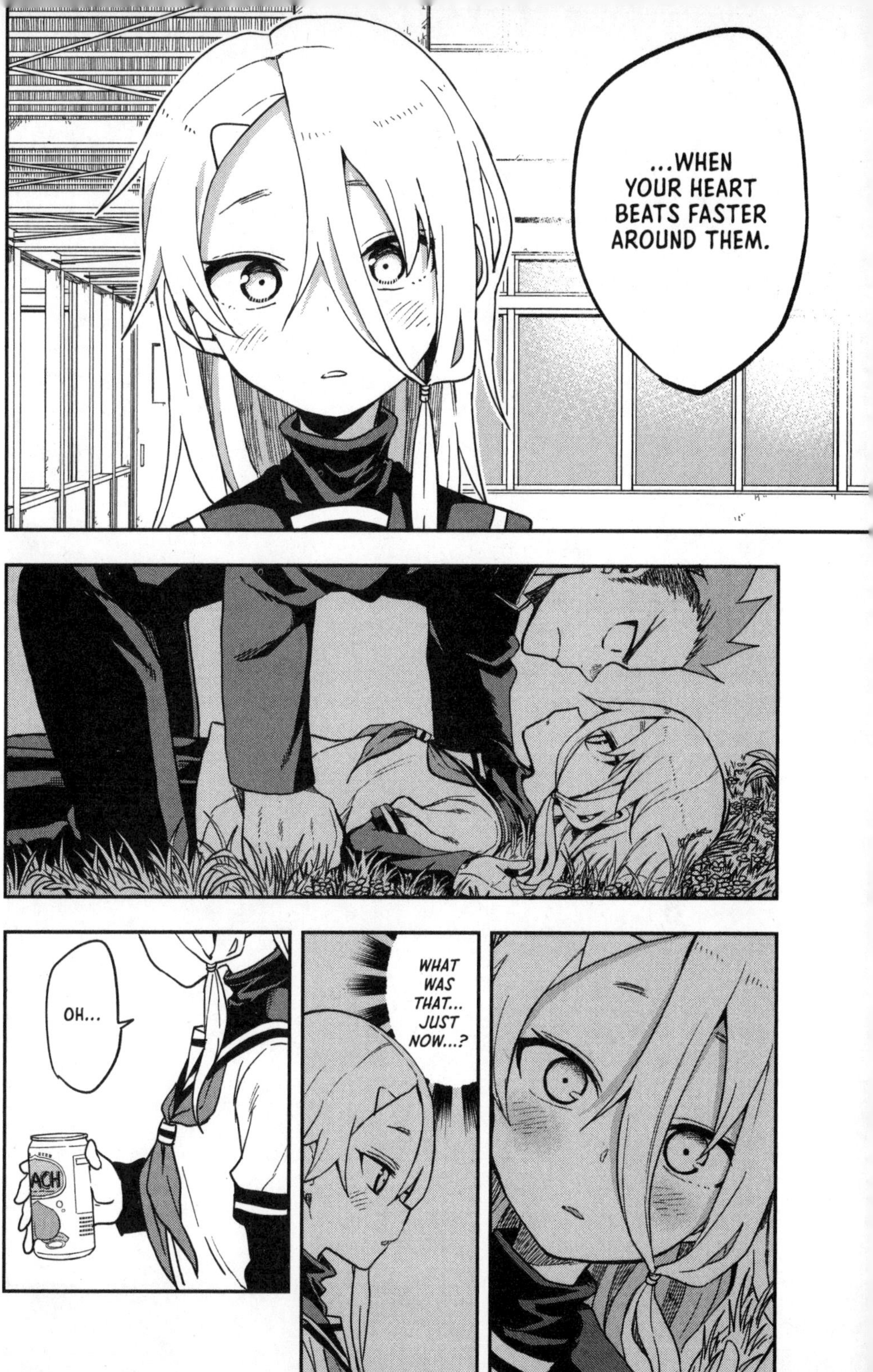
...WHEN YOUR HEART BEATS FASTER AROUND THEM.
WHAT WAS THAT... JUST NOW...?
OH...

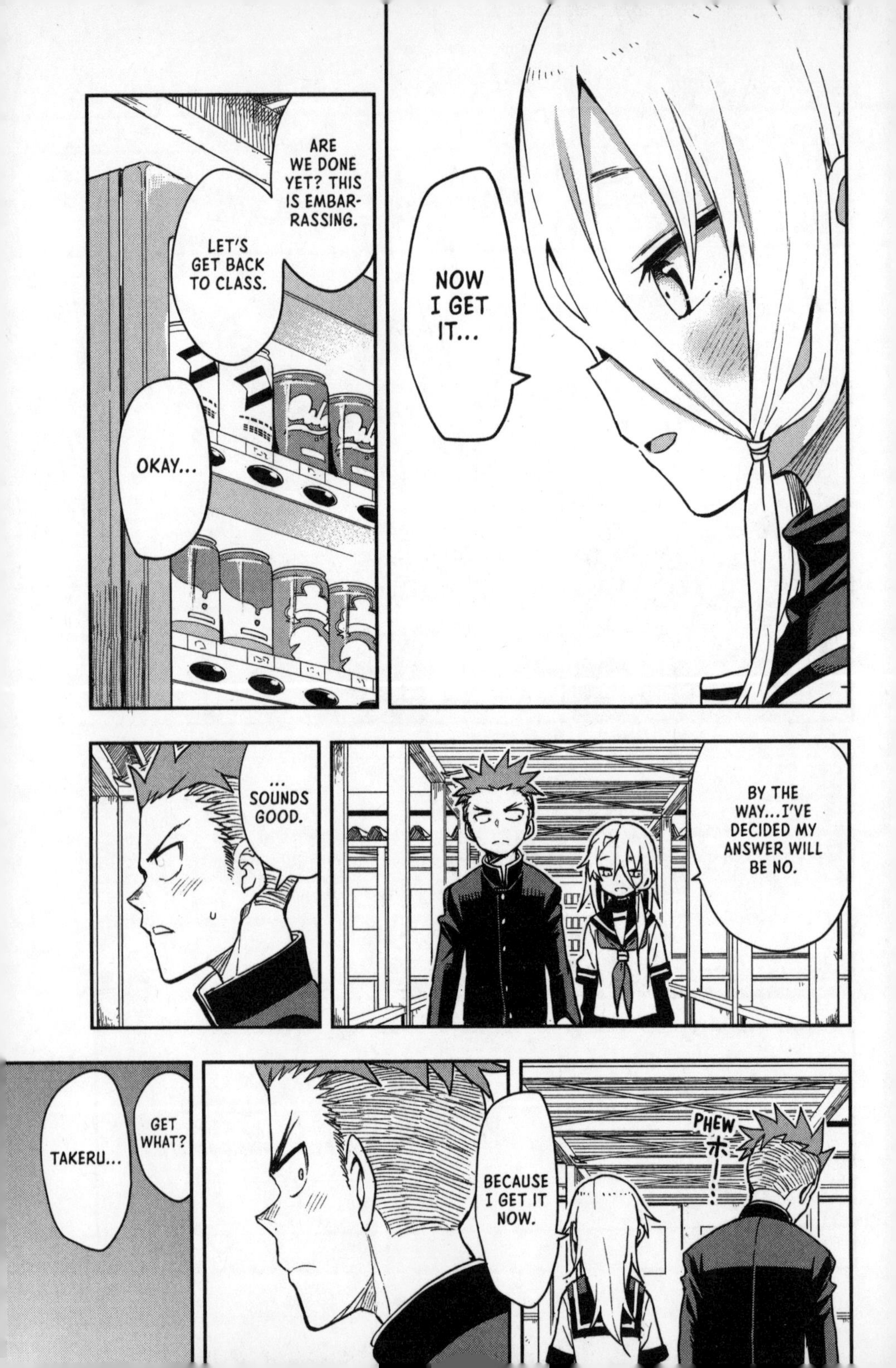
NOW I GET IT...
ARE WE DONE YET? THIS IS EMBARRASSING.
LET'S GET BACK TO CLASS.
OKAY...
BY THE WAY...I'VE DECIDED MY ANSWER WILL BE NO.
... SOUNDS GOOD.
PHEW
BECAUSE I GET IT NOW.
GET WHAT?
TAKERU...

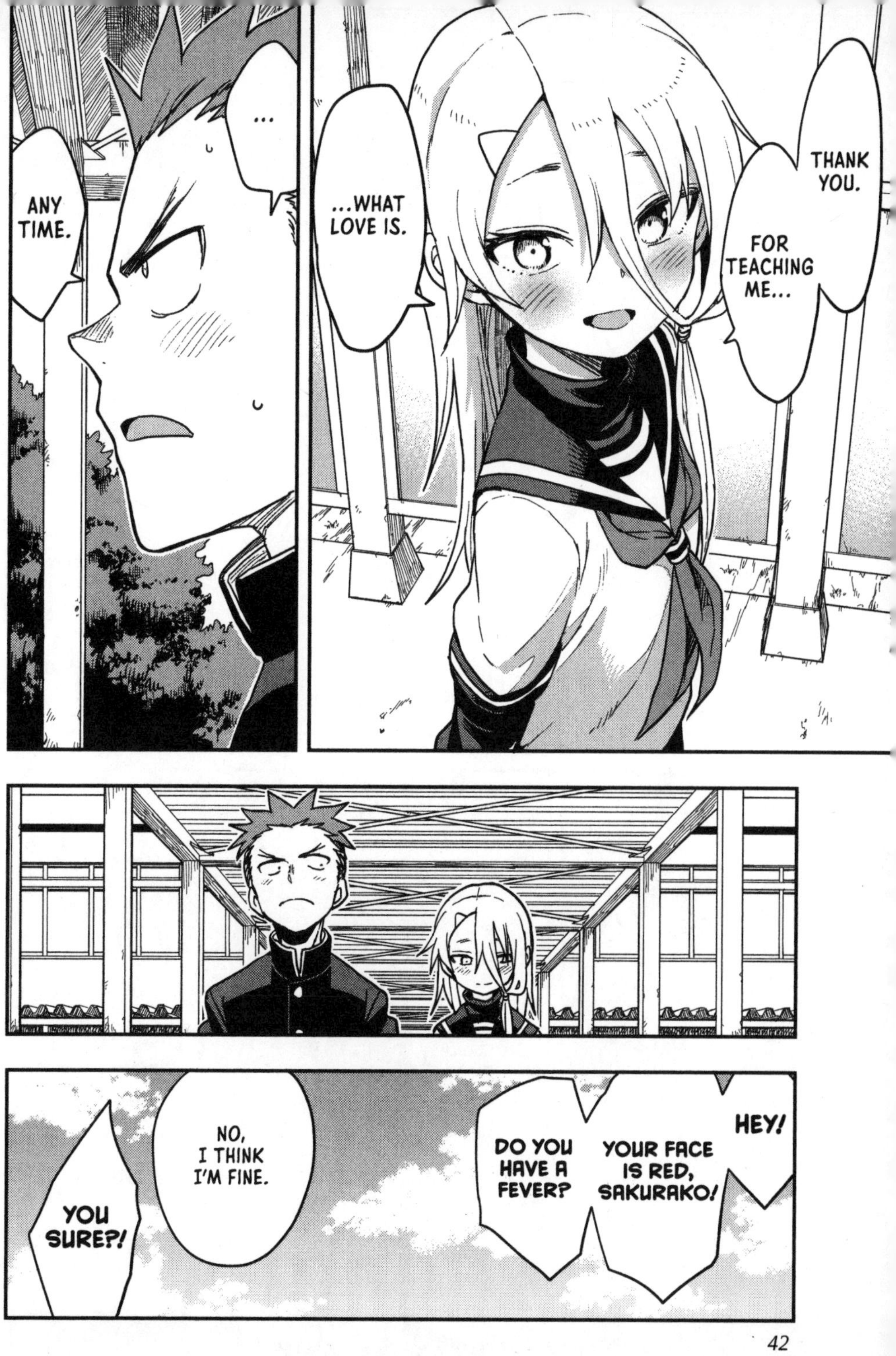
THANK YOU.
FOR TEACHING ME...
...WHAT LOVE IS.
...
ANY TIME.
HEY!
YOUR FACE IS RED, SAKURAKO!
DO YOU HAVE A FEVER?
NO, I THINK I'M FINE.
YOU SURE?!

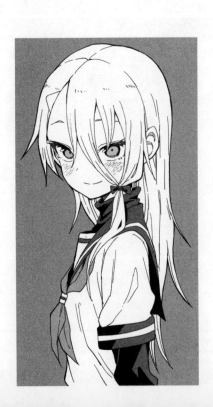

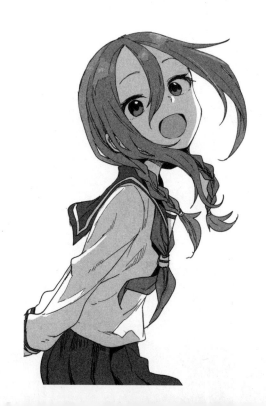

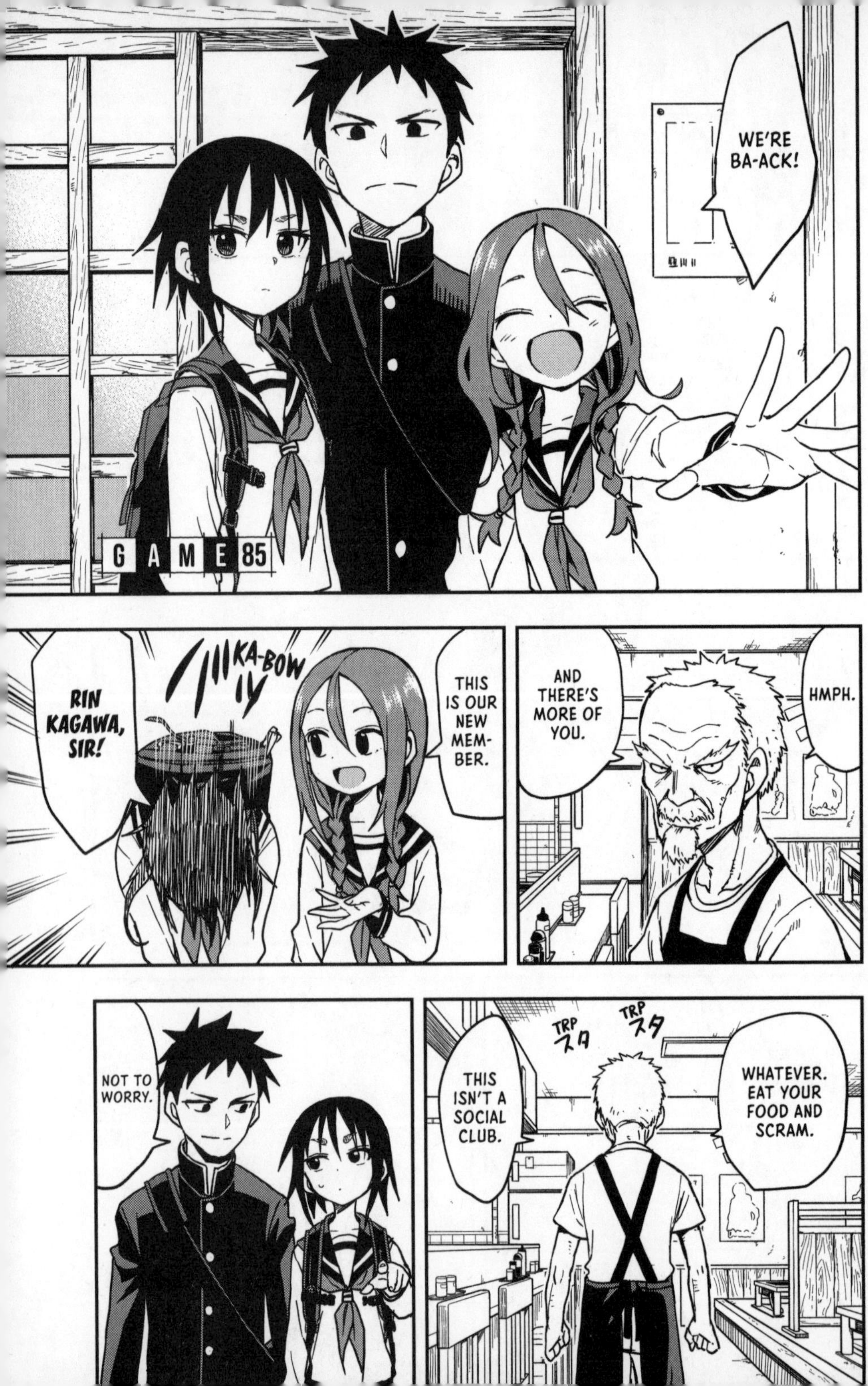
WE'RE BA-ACK!
GAME 85
HMPH.
AND THERE'S MORE OF YOU.
THIS IS OUR NEW MEM-BER.
KA-BOW
RIN KAGAWA, SIR!
WHATEVER. EAT YOUR FOOD AND SCRAM.
TRP スタ
TRP スタ
THIS ISN'T A SOCIAL CLUB.
NOT TO WORRY.

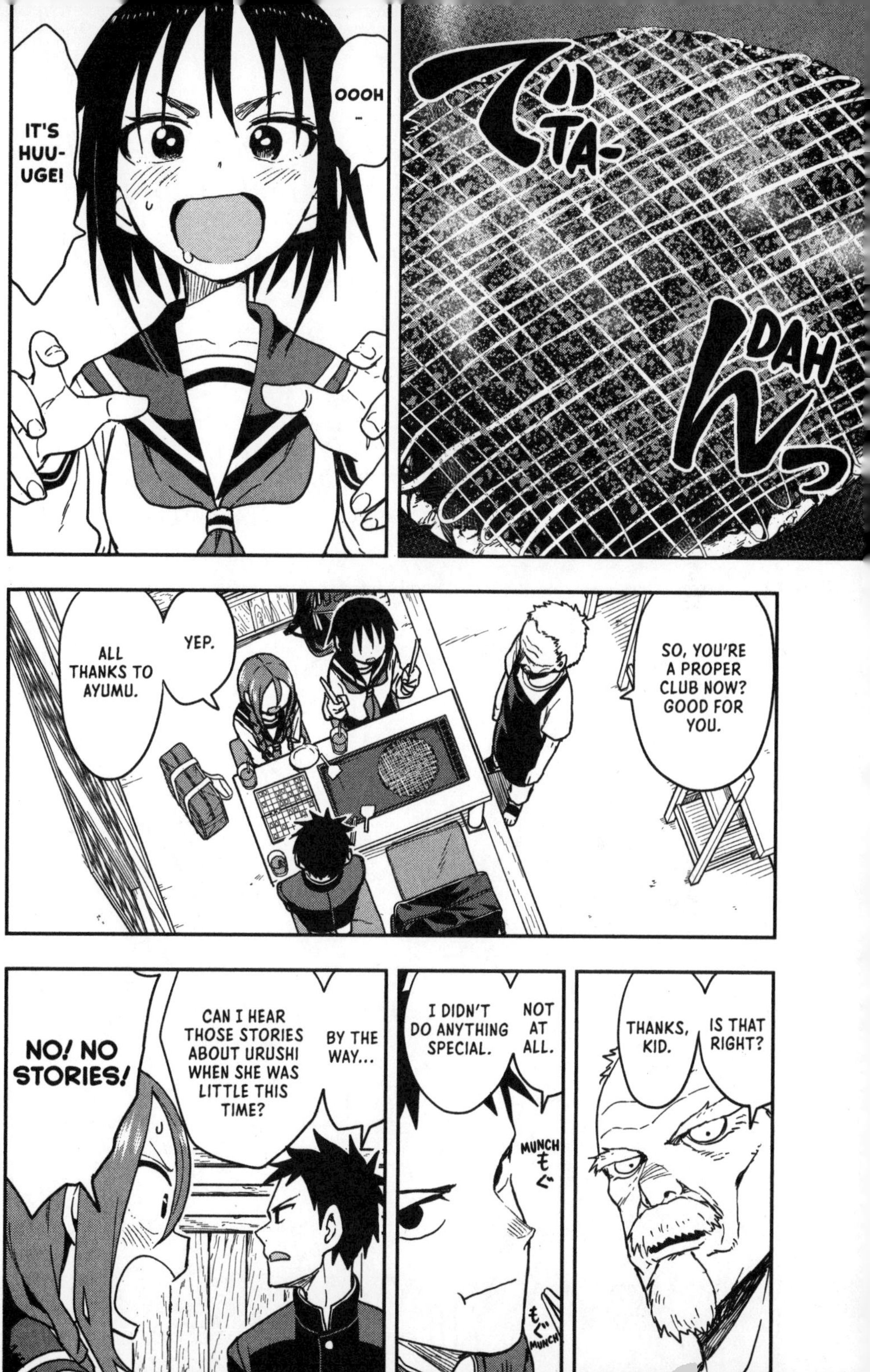
TA-
DAH
OOOH ...
IT'S HUU-UGE!
SO, YOU'RE A PROPER CLUB NOW? GOOD FOR YOU.
YEP.
ALL THANKS TO AYUMU.
IS THAT RIGHT?
THANKS, KID.
NOT AT ALL.
I DIDN'T DO ANYTHING SPECIAL.
MUNCH もぐ
もぐ MUNCH
BY THE WAY...
CAN I HEAR THOSE STORIES ABOUT URUSHI WHEN SHE WAS LITTLE THIS TIME?
NO! NO STORIES!

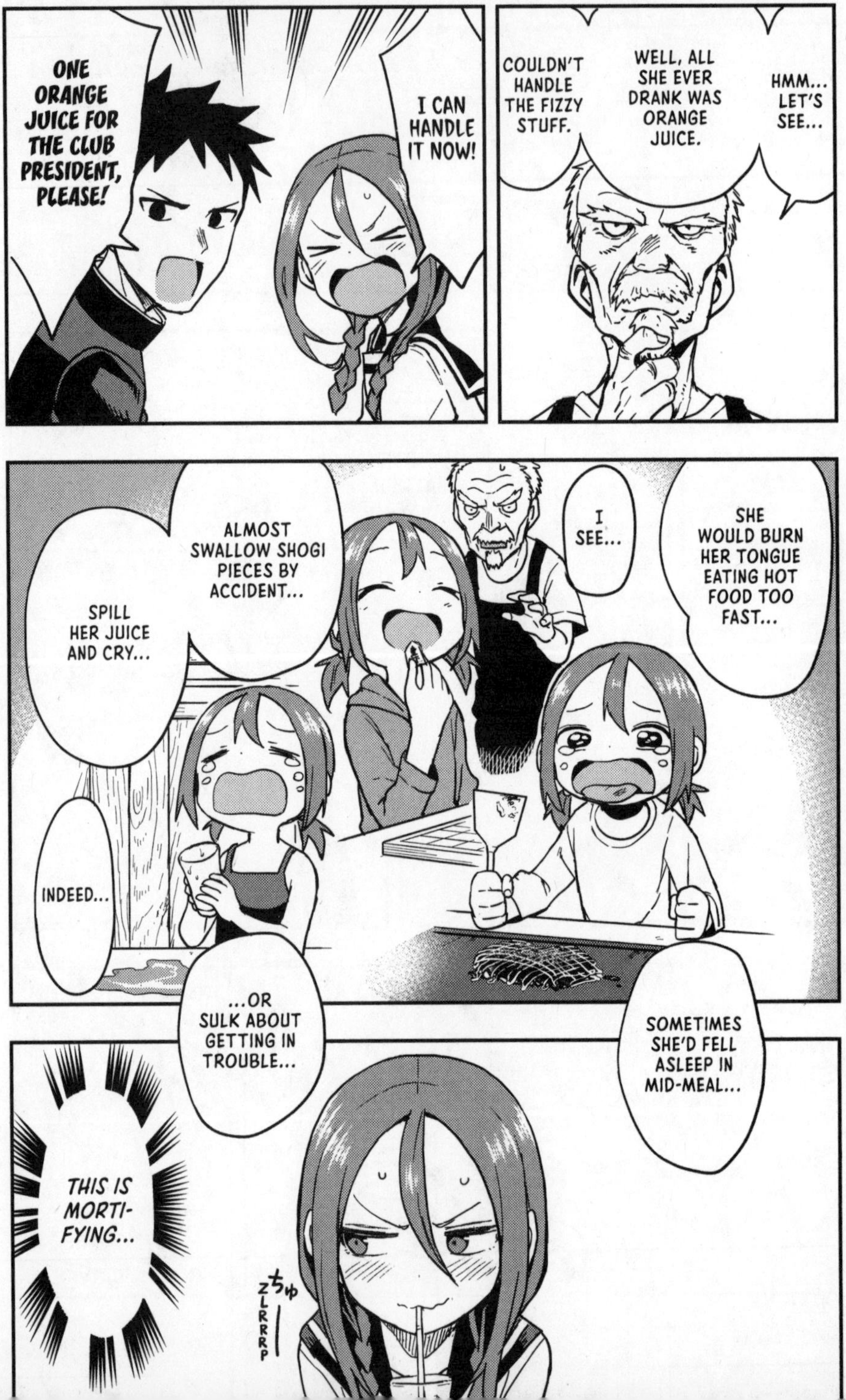
HMM... LET'S SEE...
WELL, ALL SHE EVER DRANK WAS ORANGE JUICE.
COULDN'T HANDLE THE FIZZY STUFF.
I CAN HANDLE IT NOW!
ONE ORANGE JUICE FOR THE CLUB PRESIDENT, PLEASE!
SHE WOULD BURN HER TONGUE EATING HOT FOOD TOO FAST...
I SEE...
ALMOST SWALLOW SHOGI PIECES BY ACCIDENT...
SPILL HER JUICE AND CRY...
INDEED...
SOMETIMES SHE'D FELL ASLEEP IN MID-MEAL...
...OR SULK ABOUT GETTING IN TROUBLE...
THIS IS MORTI-FYING...
ちゅ
ZLRRRP

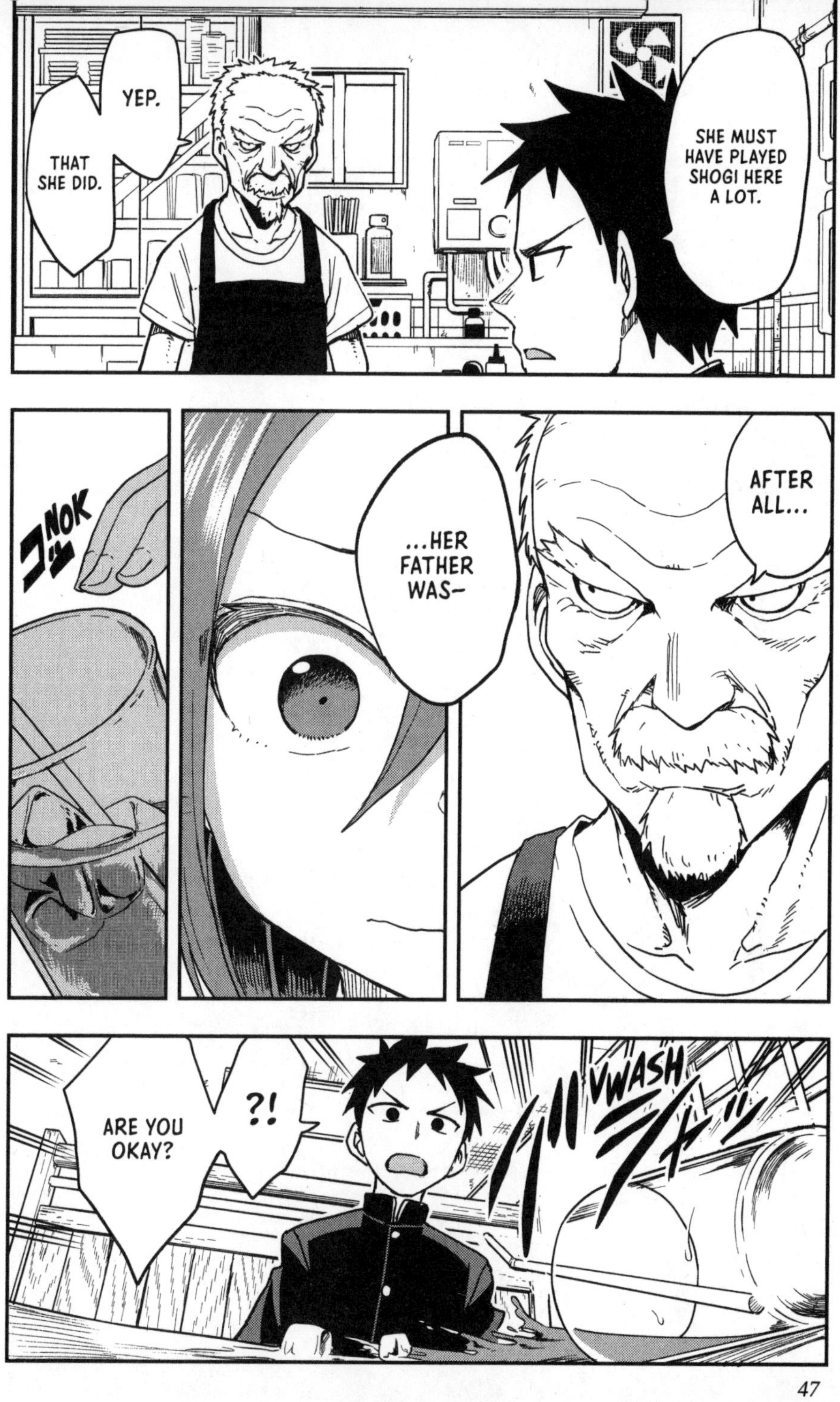
SHE MUST HAVE PLAYED SHOGI HERE A LOT.
YEP.
THAT SHE DID.
AFTER ALL...
...HER FATHER WAS–
NOK
VWASH
?!
ARE YOU OKAY?

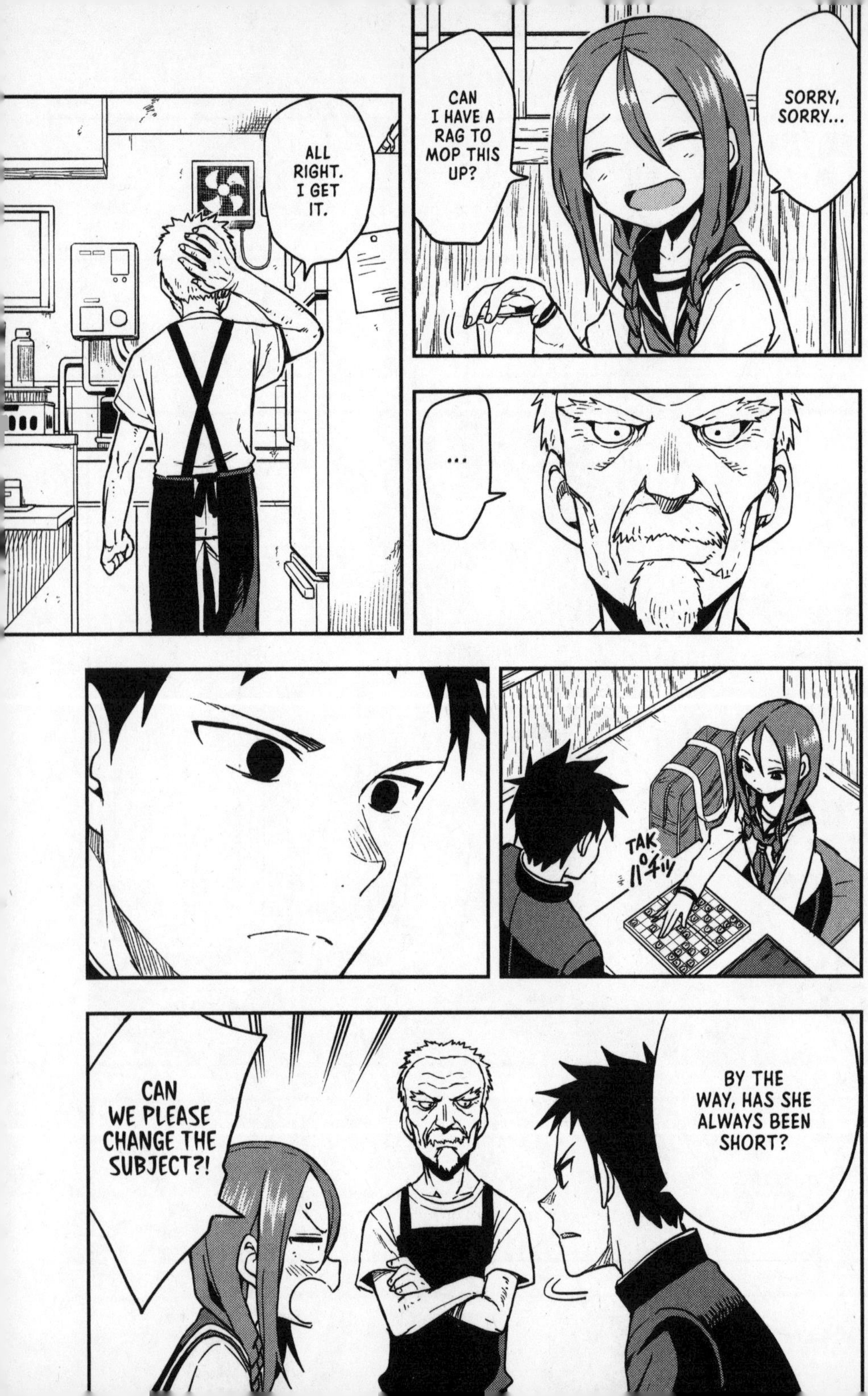
SORRY, SORRY...
CAN I HAVE A RAG TO MOP THIS UP?
...
ALL RIGHT. I GET IT.
TAK
パチッ
BY THE WAY, HAS SHE ALWAYS BEEN SHORT?
CAN WE PLEASE CHANGE THE SUBJECT?!

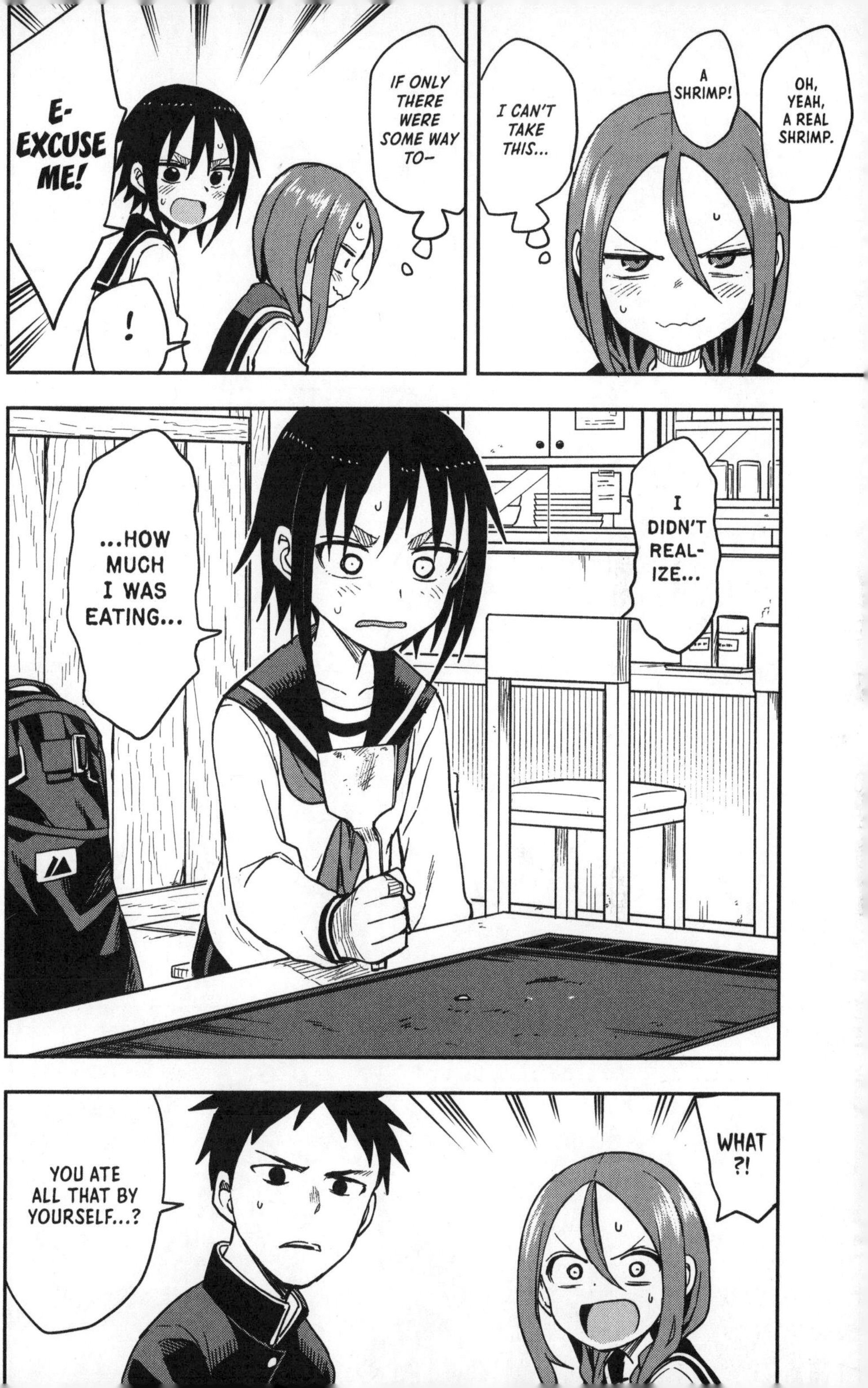
OH, YEAH, A REAL SHRIMP.
A SHRIMP!
I CAN'T TAKE THIS...
IF ONLY THERE WERE SOME WAY TO–
E-EXCUSE ME!
!
I DIDN'T REAL-IZE...
...HOW MUCH I WAS EATING...
WHAT ?!
YOU ATE ALL THAT BY YOURSELF...?

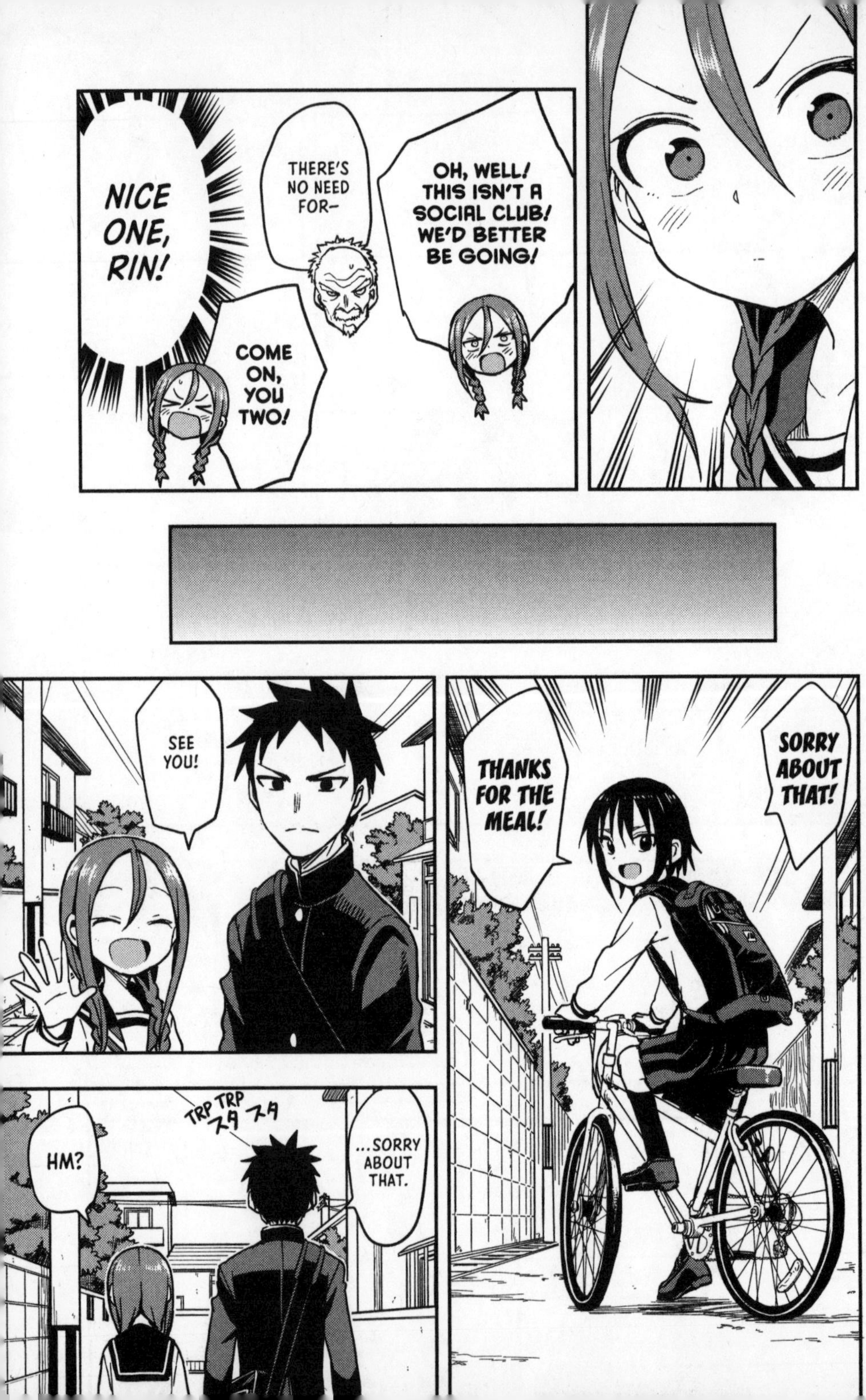
OH, WELL! THIS ISN'T A SOCIAL CLUB! WE'D BETTER BE GOING!
THERE'S NO NEED FOR-
NICE ONE, RIN!
COME ON, YOU TWO!
SORRY ABOUT THAT!
THANKS FOR THE MEAL!
SEE YOU!
...SORRY ABOUT THAT.
TRP TRP スタ スタ
HM?

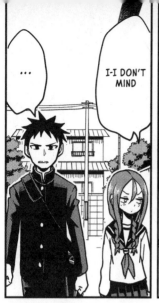

ALL THOSE QUESTIONS I ASKED.
I JUST WANT TO KNOW EVERY-THING ABOUT YOU.
NWHA?!
I-I DON'T MIND
...
AFTER ALL... URUSHI'S FATHER WAS-
SENPAI.
WHAT?
...

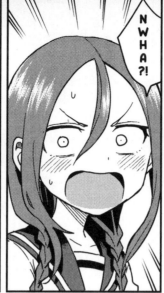

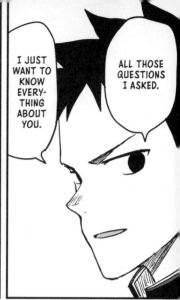

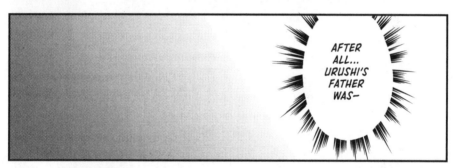

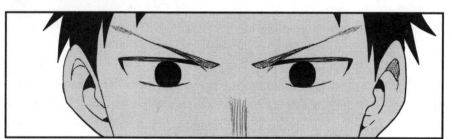

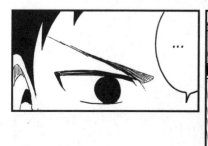

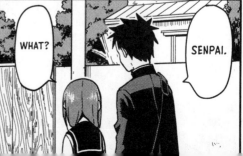

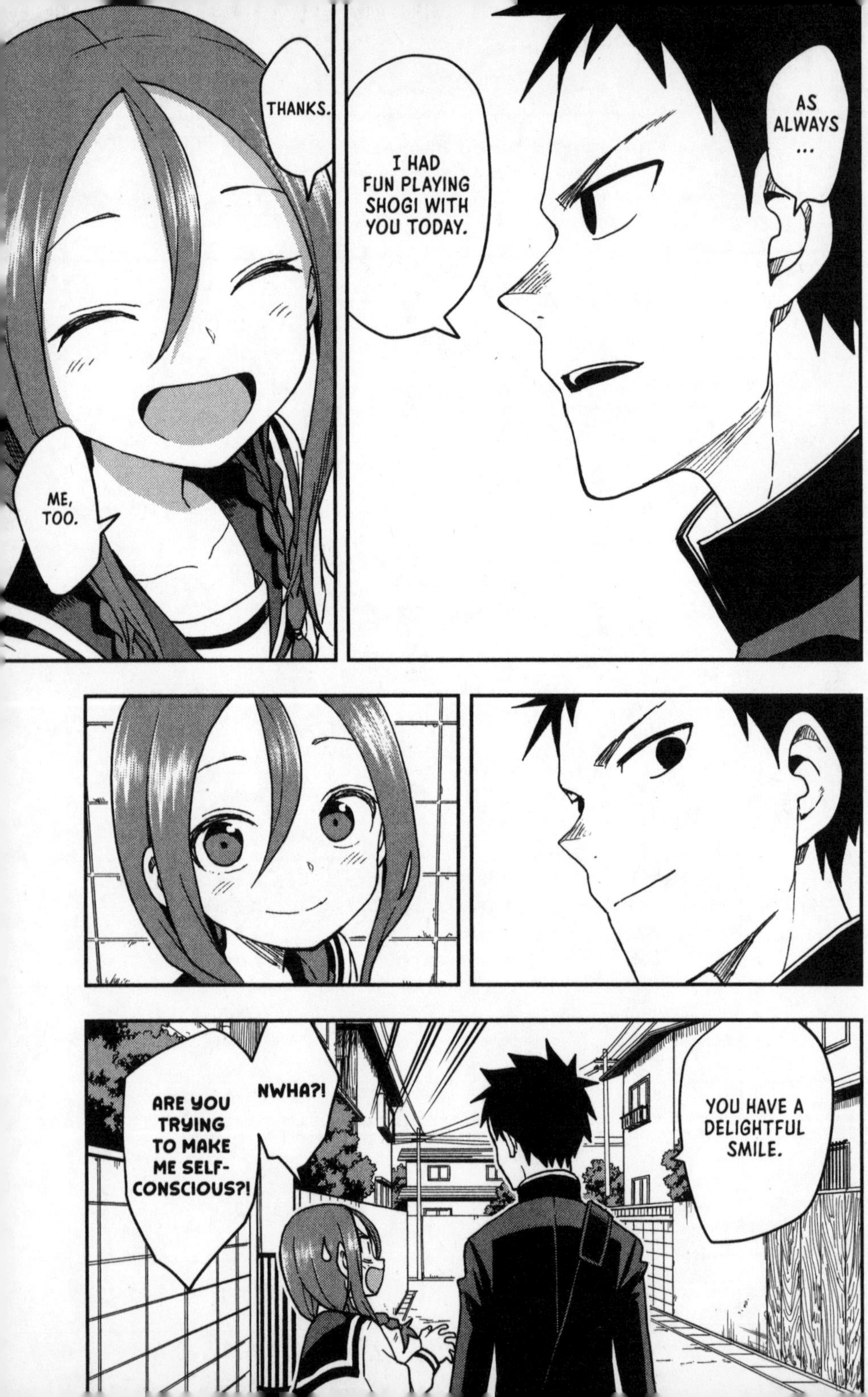
AS ALWAYS ...
I HAD FUN PLAYING SHOGI WITH YOU TODAY.
THANKS.
ME, TOO.
YOU HAVE A DELIGHTFUL SMILE.
NWHA?!
ARE YOU TRYING TO MAKE ME SELF-CONSCIOUS?!

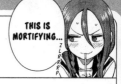

THIS IS MORTIFYING...

GAME 85 RECORD

▲ BLACK (SENTE): AYUMU TANAKA △ WHITE (GOTE): URUSHI YAOTOME

(DIAGRAM SHOWS BOARD AFTER MOVE 74, △ B-4H+)

◁URUSHI:: S, P

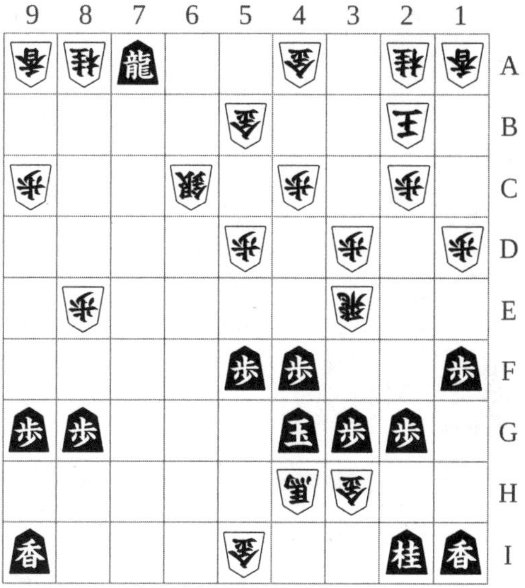

▲AYUMU: AYUMU: B, S×2, N, P×3

	9	8	7	6	5	4	3	2	1	
A	香	桂	龍			金		桂	香	A
B					銀			王		B
C	金			成銀		金		歩		C
D					歩		銀		歩	D
E		歩					馬			E
F					歩	歩			歩	F
G	歩	歩			玉	歩	歩			G
H						金	金			H
I	香				金			桂	香	I

▲ P-7F	△ P-3D	▲ P-5F	△ P-7E	▲ G-5I	△ G×5H
▲ P-6F	△ P-8D	▲ R-7H	△ R-7B	▲ R-7I	△ N-7H+
▲ R-6H	△ P-8E	▲ B-8H	△ P×7F	▲ R×7H	△ B×3I
▲ B-7G	△ S-6B	▲ S×7F	△ P×7E	▲ K-1H	△ G×5I
▲ G6I-5H	△ K-4B	▲ P-6E	△ P×7F	▲ P×6C+	△ G×2H
▲ P-1F	△ P-1D	▲ B×2B+	△ K×2B	▲ K-1G	△ G×3h
▲ S-7H	△ K-3B	▲ P×6D	△ S×6I	▲ K-2F	△ S×6C
▲ S-3H	△ G6A-5B	▲ R-6H	△ S×5H+	▲ R-7A	△ B-5C
▲ P-4F	△ P-5D	▲ G-5H	△ P-7G+	▲ K-3F	△ B×7A
▲ S-6G	△ S-4B	▲ N×7G	△ R×7G+	▲ R×7A+	△ R×3E
▲ K-4H	△ S4B-5C	▲ B×6F	△ +R×6F	▲ K-4G	△ B-4H+
▲ K-3I	△ P-7D	▲ R×6F	△ B×7E	(URUSHI WINS AT MOVE 74)	
▲ K-2H	△ S-6D	▲ R-6I	△ N×6F		

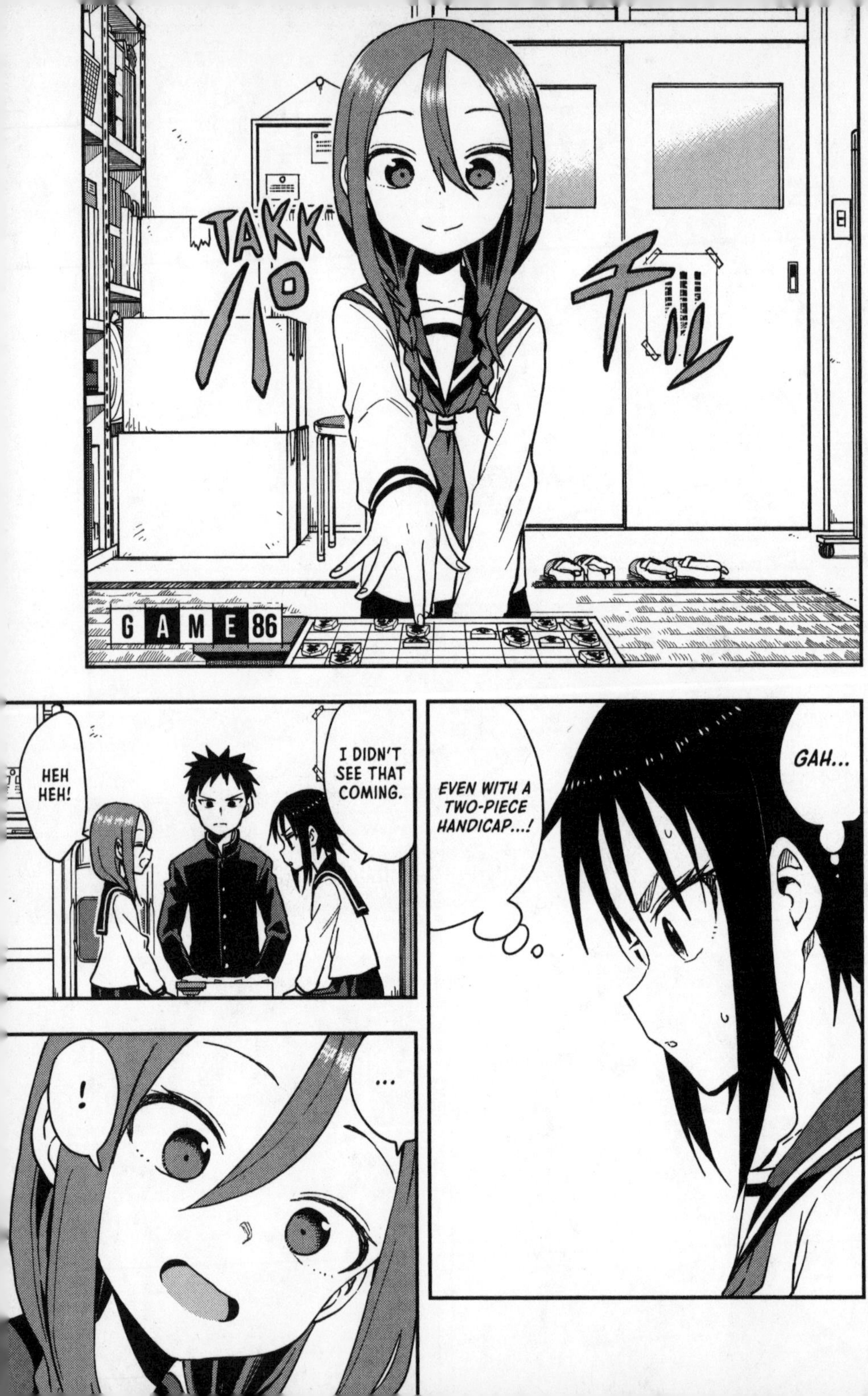
TAKK
GAME 86
GAH...
EVEN WITH A TWO-PIECE HANDICAP...!
I DIDN'T SEE THAT COMING.
HEH HEH!
...
!

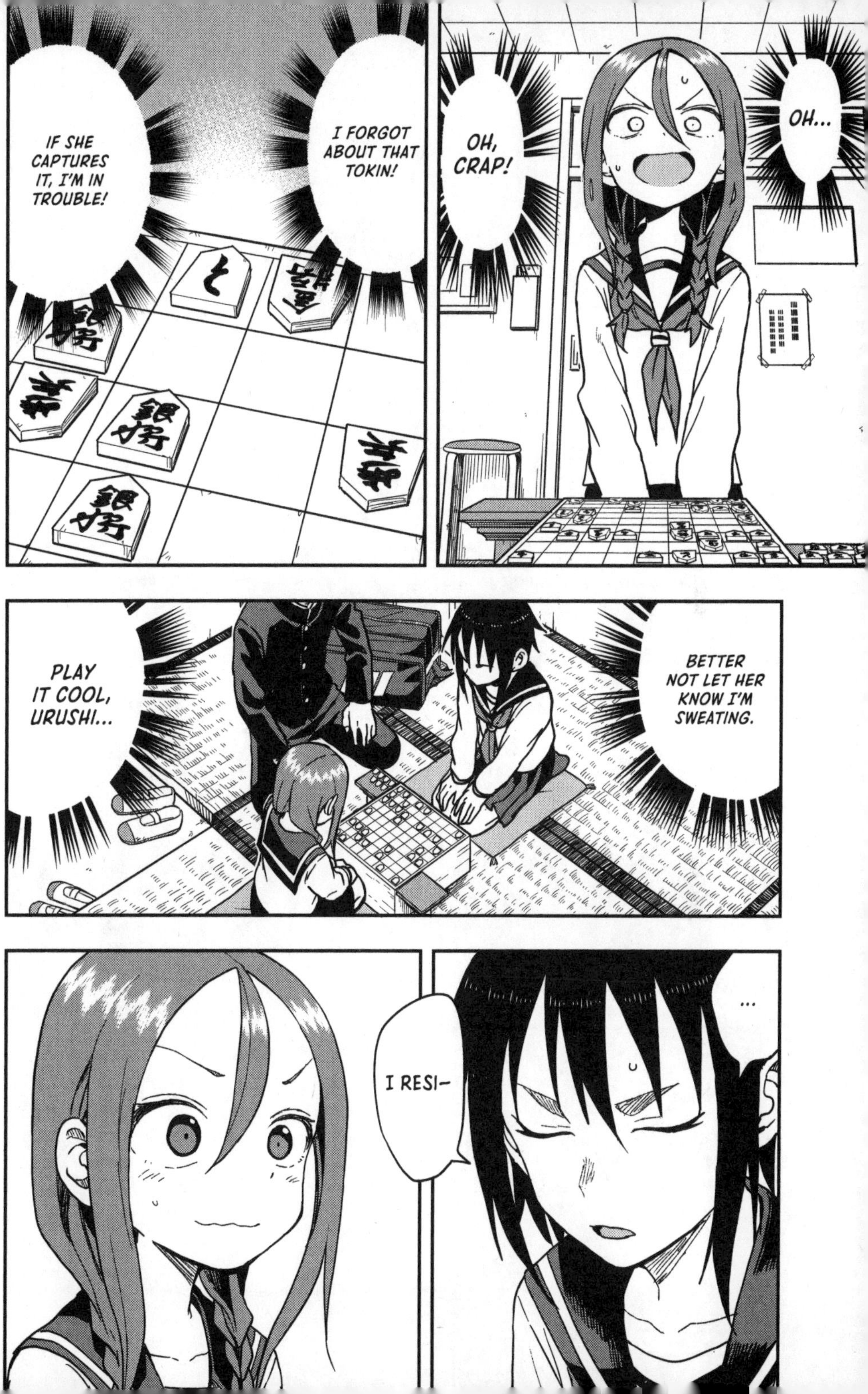
OH...
OH, CRAP!
I FORGOT ABOUT THAT TOKIN!
IF SHE CAPTURES IT, I'M IN TROUBLE!
BETTER NOT LET HER KNOW I'M SWEATING.
PLAY IT COOL, URUSHI...
...
I RESI–

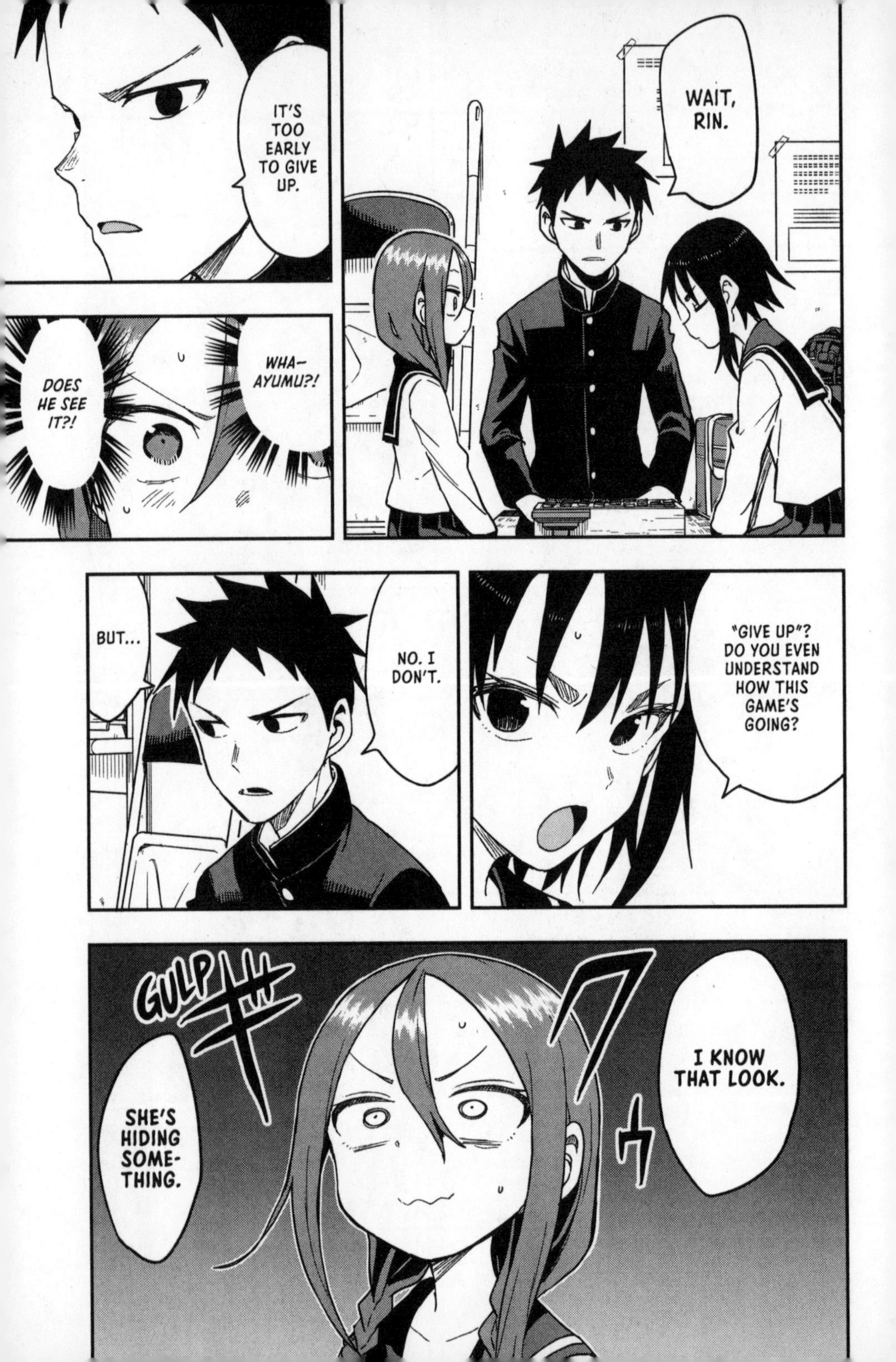
WAIT, RIN.
IT'S TOO EARLY TO GIVE UP.
WHA- AYUMU?!
DOES HE SEE IT?!
"GIVE UP"? DO YOU EVEN UNDERSTAND HOW THIS GAME'S GOING?
NO. I DON'T.
BUT...
I KNOW THAT LOOK.
GULP
SHE'S HIDING SOME-THING.

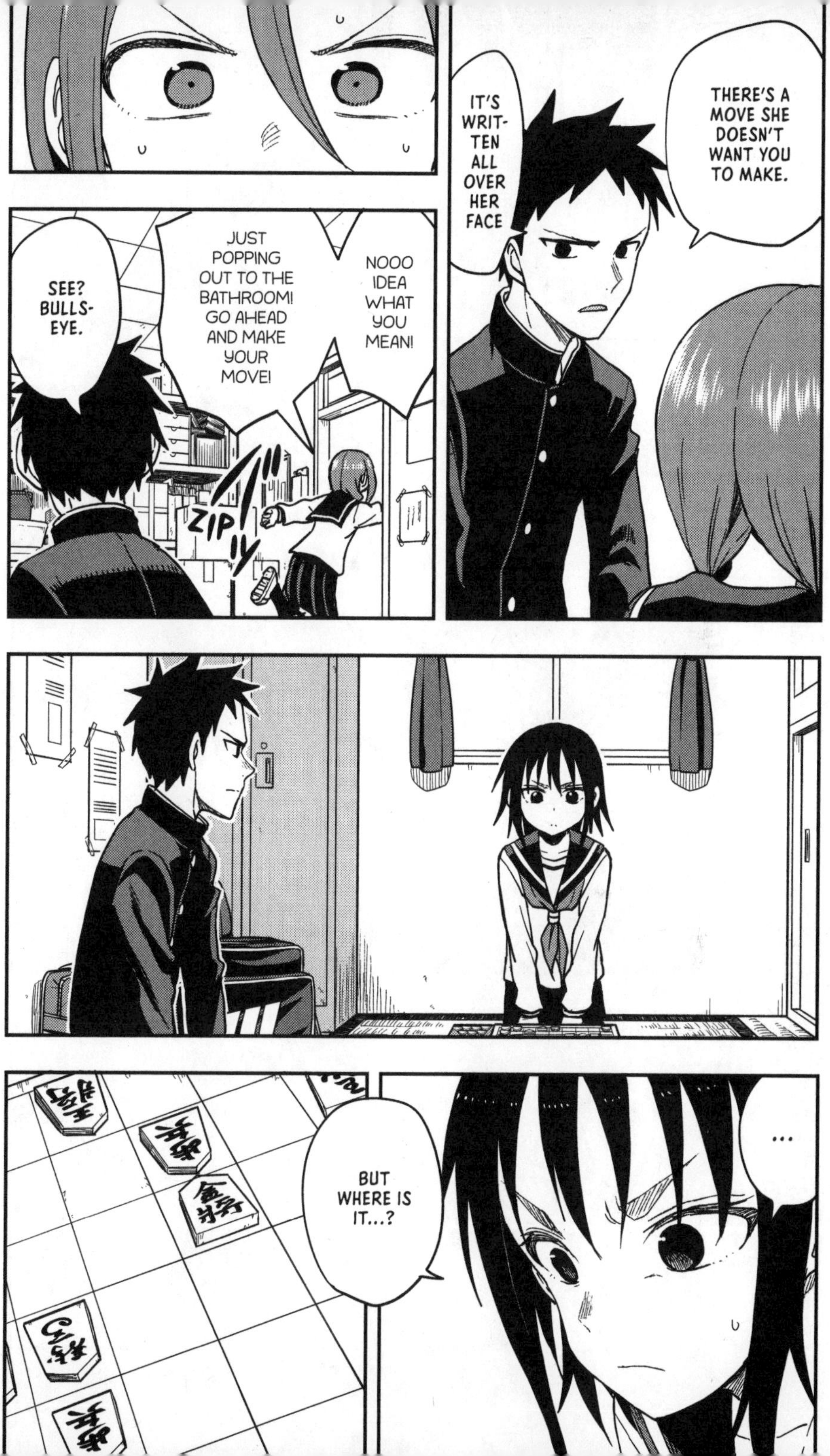
THERE'S A MOVE SHE DOESN'T WANT YOU TO MAKE.
IT'S WRIT-TEN ALL OVER HER FACE
NOOO IDEA WHAT YOU MEAN!
JUST POPPING OUT TO THE BATHROOM! GO AHEAD AND MAKE YOUR MOVE!
ZIP
SEE? BULLS-EYE.
...
BUT WHERE IS IT...?

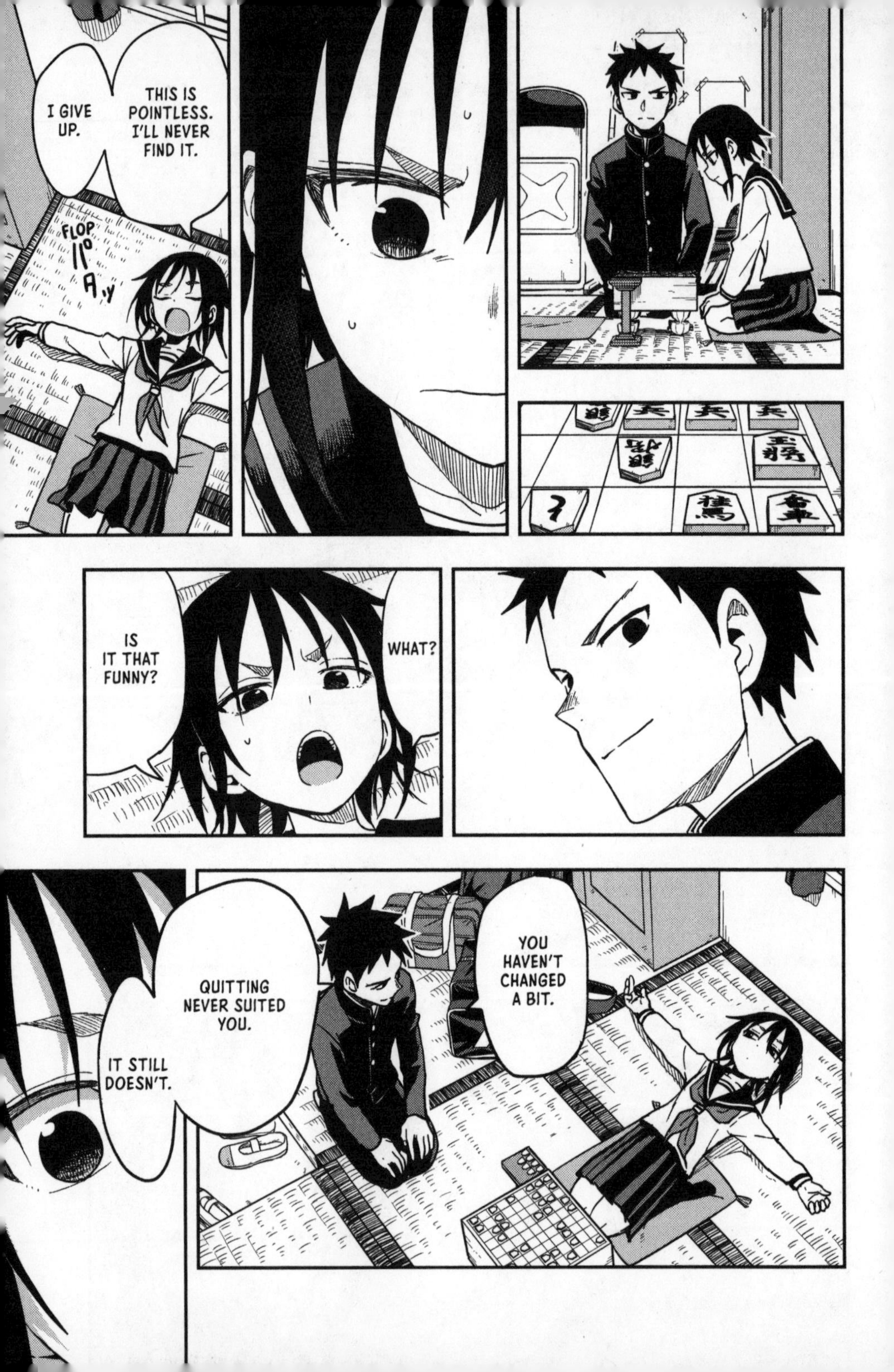

THIS IS POINTLESS. I'LL NEVER FIND IT.
I GIVE UP.
FLOP
WHAT?
IS IT THAT FUNNY?
YOU HAVEN'T CHANGED A BIT.
QUITTING NEVER SUITED YOU.
IT STILL DOESN'T.

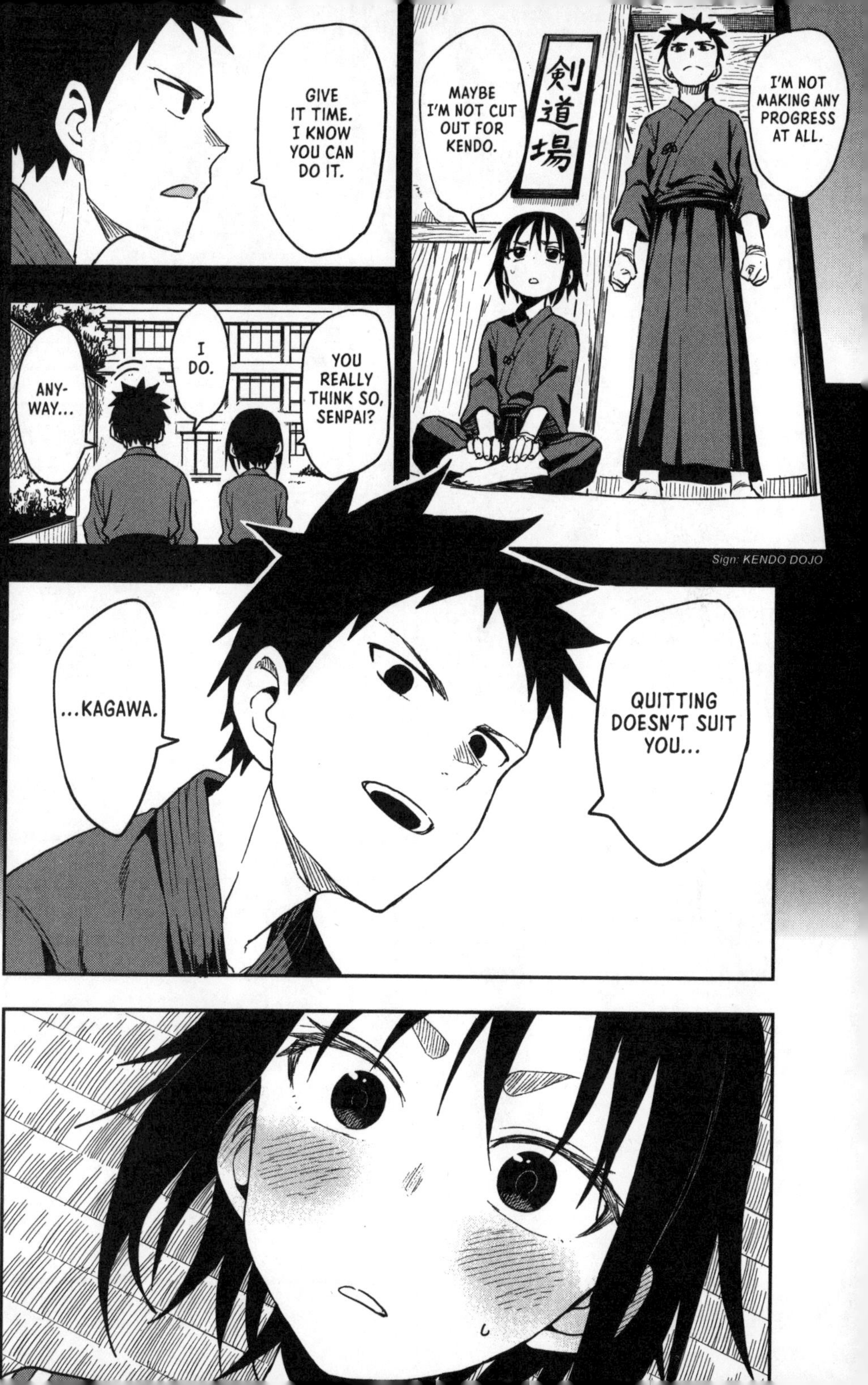
I'M NOT MAKING ANY PROGRESS AT ALL.
MAYBE I'M NOT CUT OUT FOR KENDO.
剣道場
GIVE IT TIME. I KNOW YOU CAN DO IT.
YOU REALLY THINK SO, SENPAI?
I DO.
ANY-WAY...
QUITTING DOESN'T SUIT YOU...
...KAGAWA.
Sign: KENDO DOJO

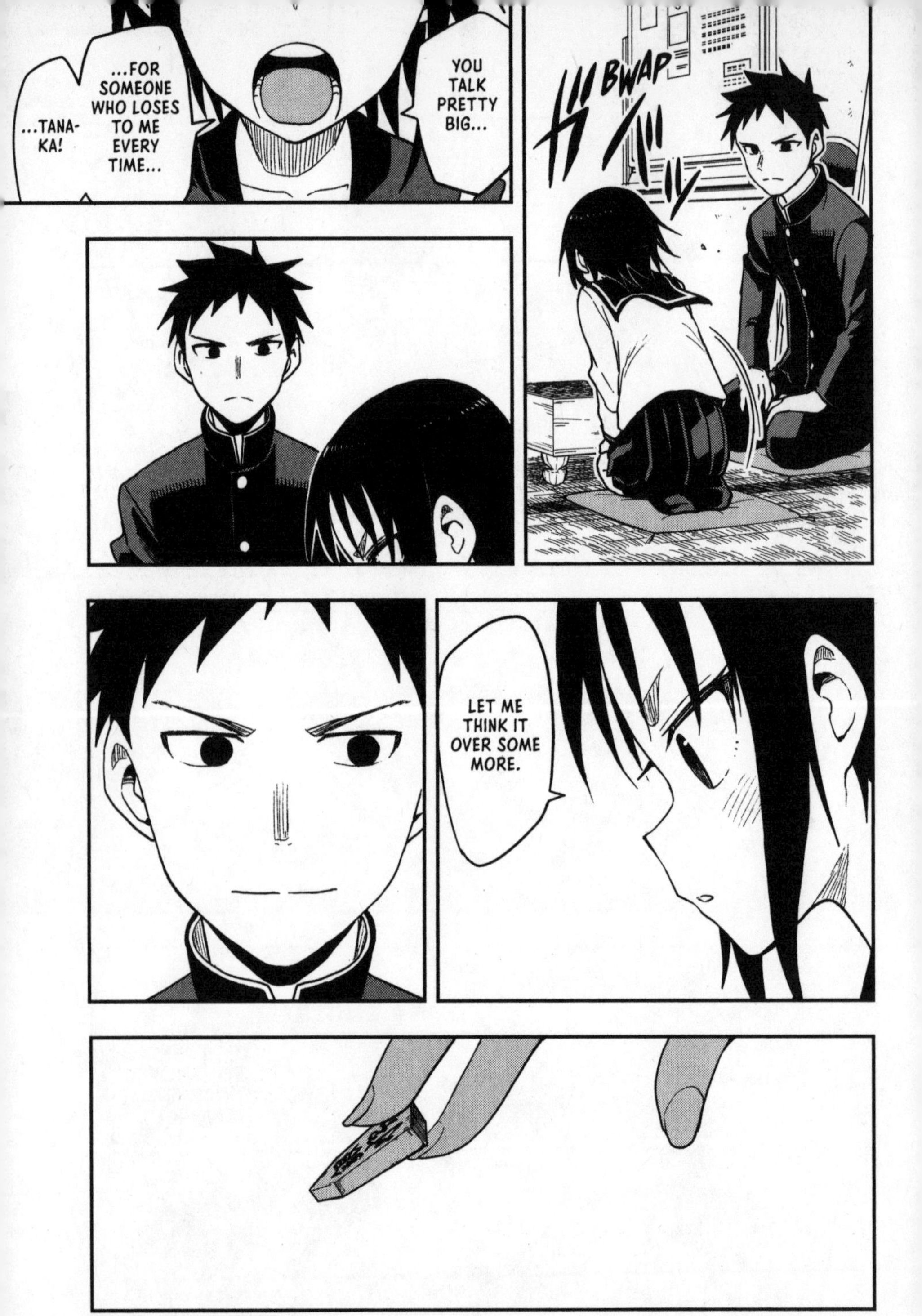
BWAP
YOU TALK PRETTY BIG...
...FOR SOMEONE WHO LOSES TO ME EVERY TIME...
...TANAKA!
LET ME THINK IT OVER SOME MORE.

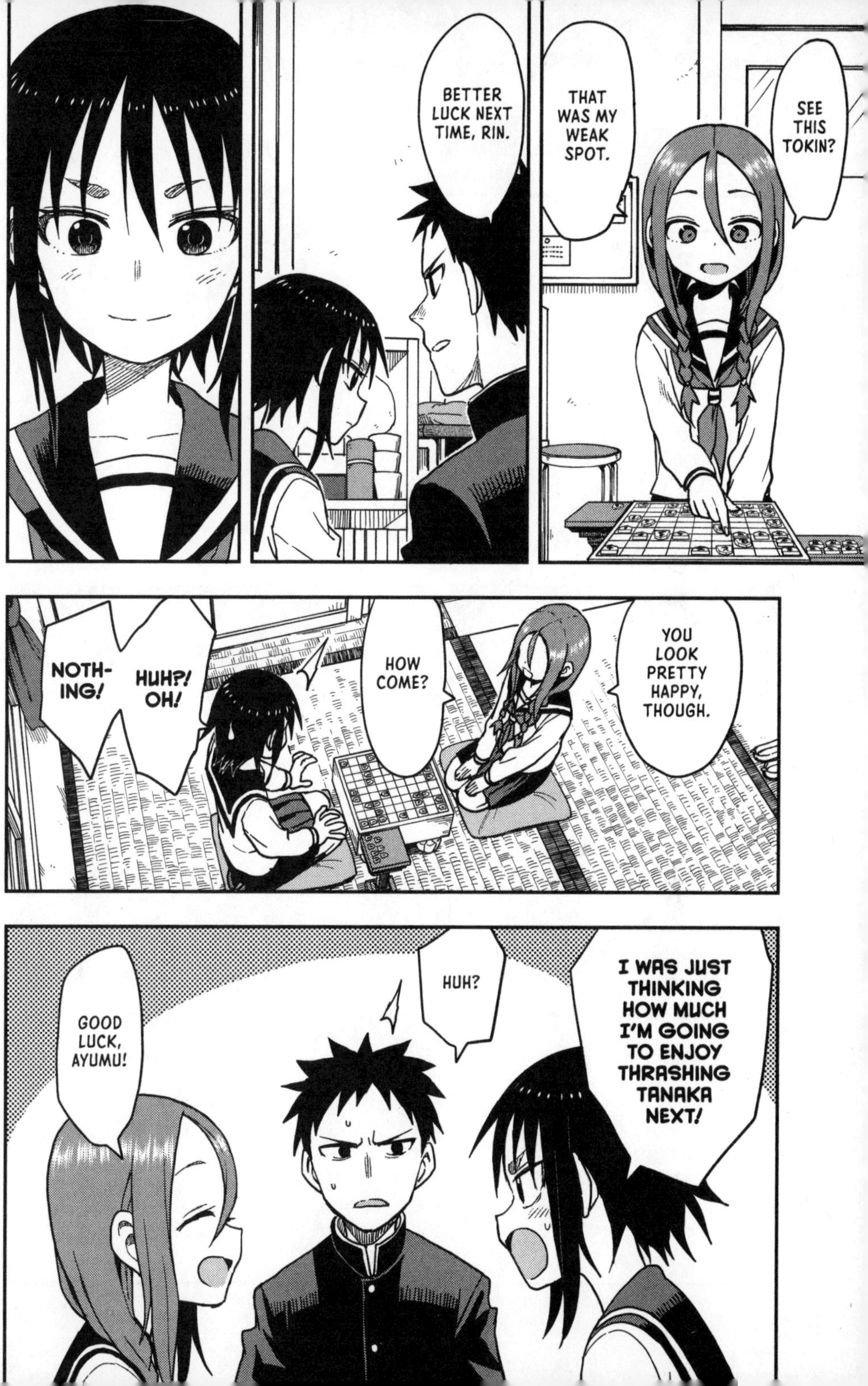
SEE THIS TOKIN?
THAT WAS MY WEAK SPOT.
BETTER LUCK NEXT TIME, RIN.
YOU LOOK PRETTY HAPPY, THOUGH.
HOW COME?
HUH?! OH!
NOTH-ING!
I WAS JUST THINKING HOW MUCH I'M GOING TO ENJOY THRASHING TANAKA NEXT!
HUH?
GOOD LUCK, AYUMU!

GAME 86 RECORD

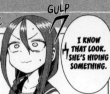

GULP

I KNOW THAT LOOK. SHE'S HIDING SOMETHING.

▽URUSHI: S

▲RIN: S, P×6

△ S-6B	▲ P-7F	△ P-7E	▲ R-2F	△ G-6B	▲ +P×6B
△ P-5D	▲ P-7E	△ N-8E	▲ N×8E	△ K×6B	▲ S-4E
△ S-4B	▲ R-7H	△ P×8E	▲ B-8H	△ S6D-5E	▲ S×4D
△ S4B-5C	▲ S-6H	△ P-5E	▲ S-4H	△ P×4D	▲ G×5D
△ G-7B	▲ P-7D	△ G-7D	▲ P-4F	△ S×4F	▲ R×4D
△ P×7D	▲ R×7D	△ P-7F	▲ S-4G	△ S×4G	▲ K-3I
△ P×7C	▲ R-7F	△ G-6E	▲ K-4H	△ P×4H	▲ G-5I
△ K-4B	▲ S-7G	△ S-4D	▲ S-3F	△ S×3H	▲ K-2H
△ K-3B	▲ S-6F	△ P-5F	▲ P×5F	△ B×3I	▲ K-1H
△ S-6D	▲ N-7G	△ G×5F	▲ G6I-5H	△ P-4I+	▲ R-4C+
△ P-8D	▲ P-9F	△ P×5G	▲ G×5G	△ B-8D+	▲ G-6C
△ G-8C	▲ B-9G	△ G×5G	▲ K×5G	△ K-7A	▲ +R-4B
△ P-9D	▲ S-6E	△ P-7G+	▲ B×7G	△ P×6B	▲ S×7C
△ G-5B	▲ S×6D	△ N×6E	▲ K-4H	△ S×2I=	▲ K×2I
△ P×6D	▲ B×6D	△ N×7G+	▲ N×1E	△ S-3H+	▲ K-1H
△ S-5C	▲ B-9G	△ G×2D	▲ S×4A	△ +B×7C	▲ +R-5A
△ S×6D	▲ P×7B	△ K×4A	▲ N×2C+	△ N×6A	
△ P-7D	▲ P-7A+	△ G-1E	▲ G×3B	(URUSHI WINS AT MOVE	
△ N-9C	▲ +P-7B	△ K-5A	▲ R-2D	109)	

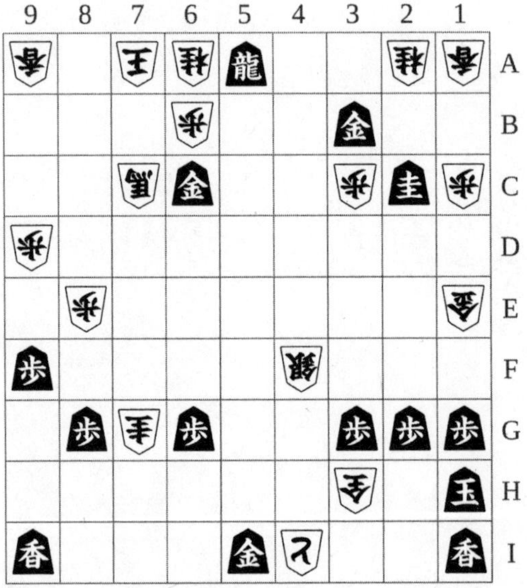

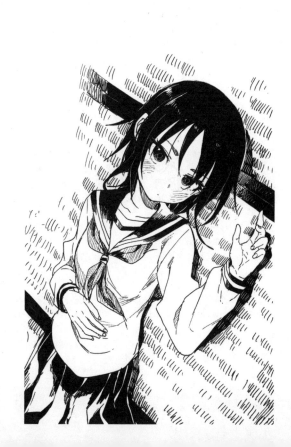

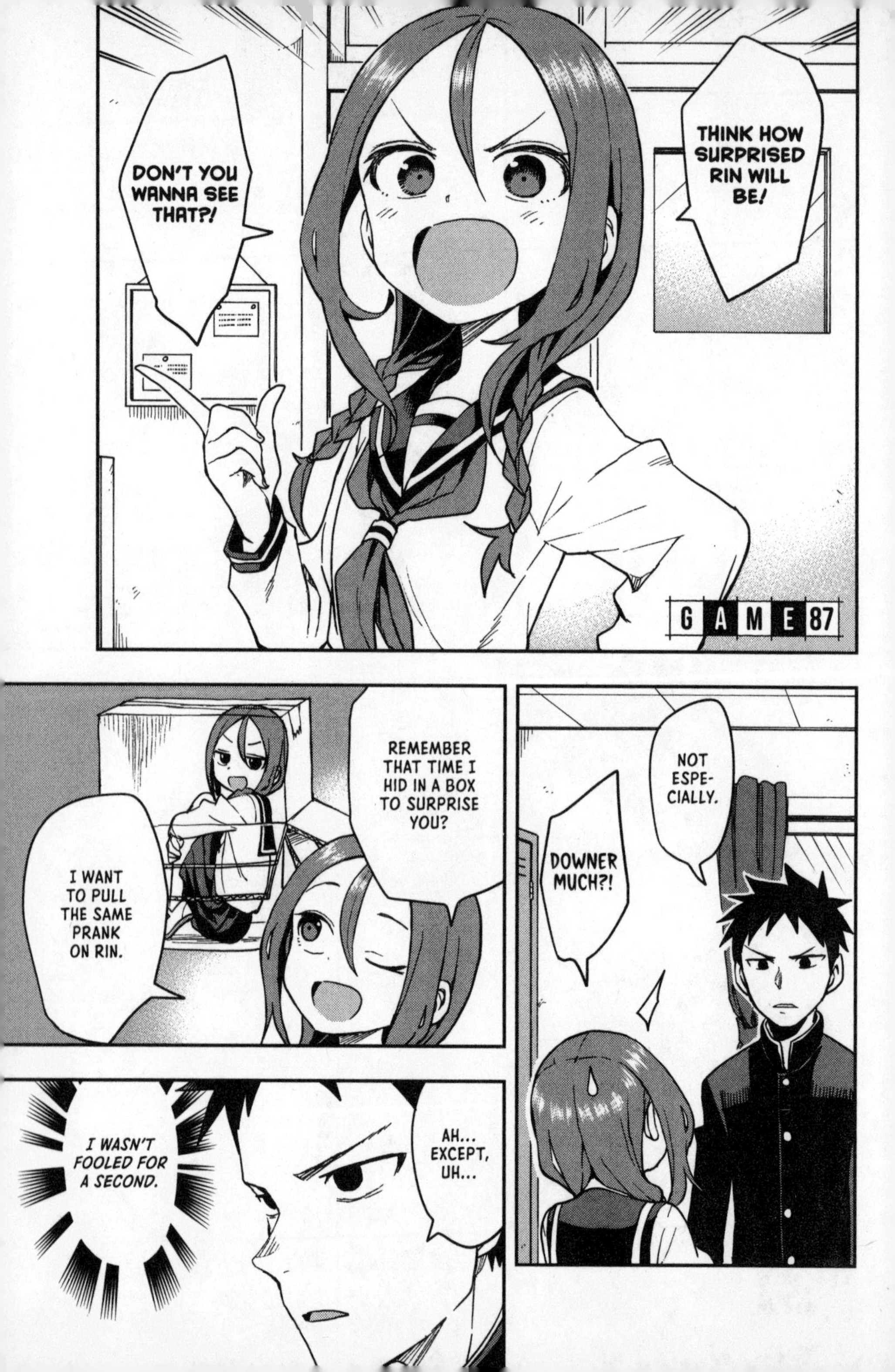
THINK HOW SURPRISED RIN WILL BE!
DON'T YOU WANNA SEE THAT?!
GAME 87
NOT ESPE-CIALLY.
DOWNER MUCH?!
REMEMBER THAT TIME I HID IN A BOX TO SURPRISE YOU?
I WANT TO PULL THE SAME PRANK ON RIN.
AH... EXCEPT, UH...
I WASN'T FOOLED FOR A SECOND.

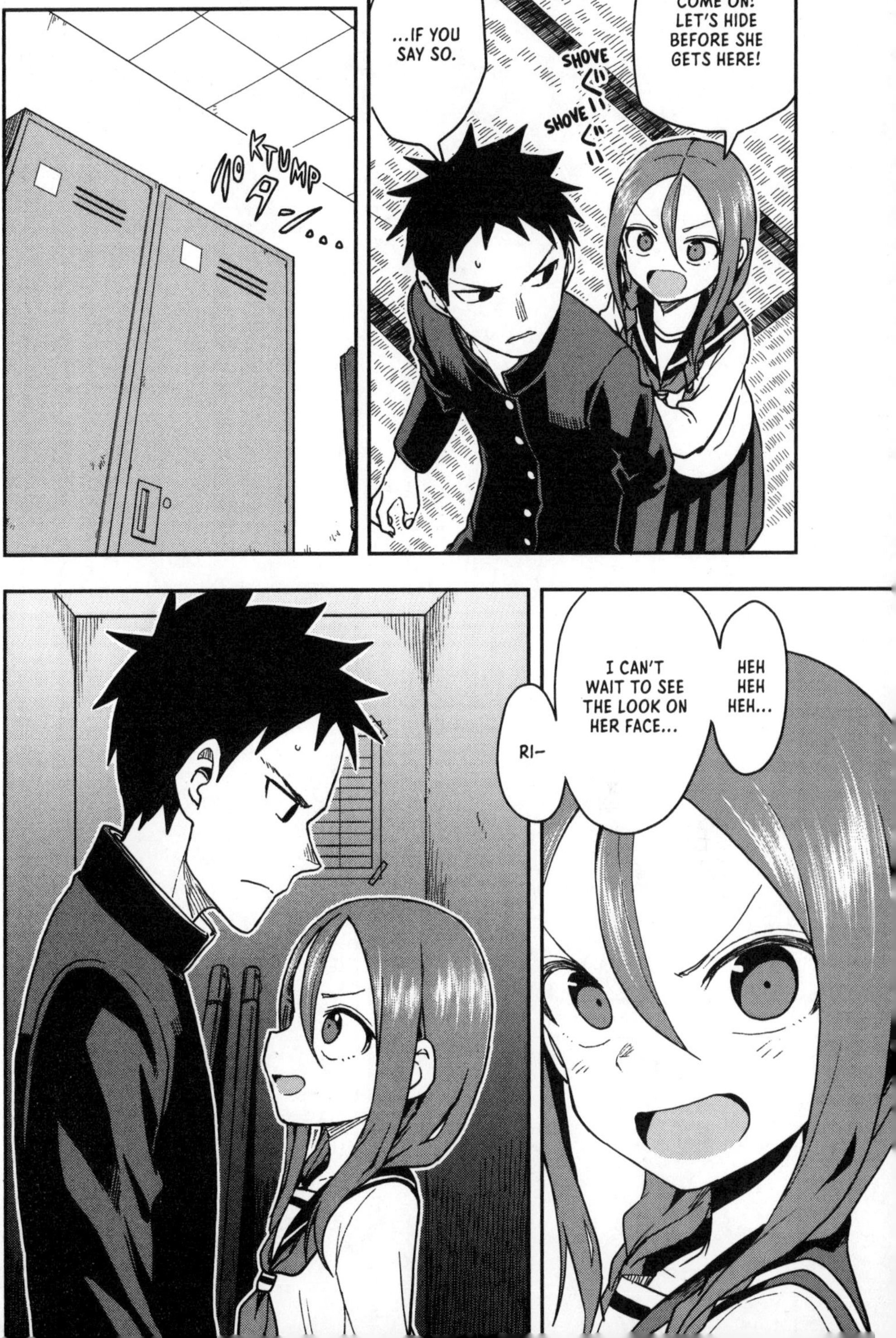
COME ON! LET'S HIDE BEFORE SHE GETS HERE!
SHOVE
SHOVE
...IF YOU SAY SO.
KTUMP
HEH HEH HEH...
I CAN'T WAIT TO SEE THE LOOK ON HER FACE...
RI–

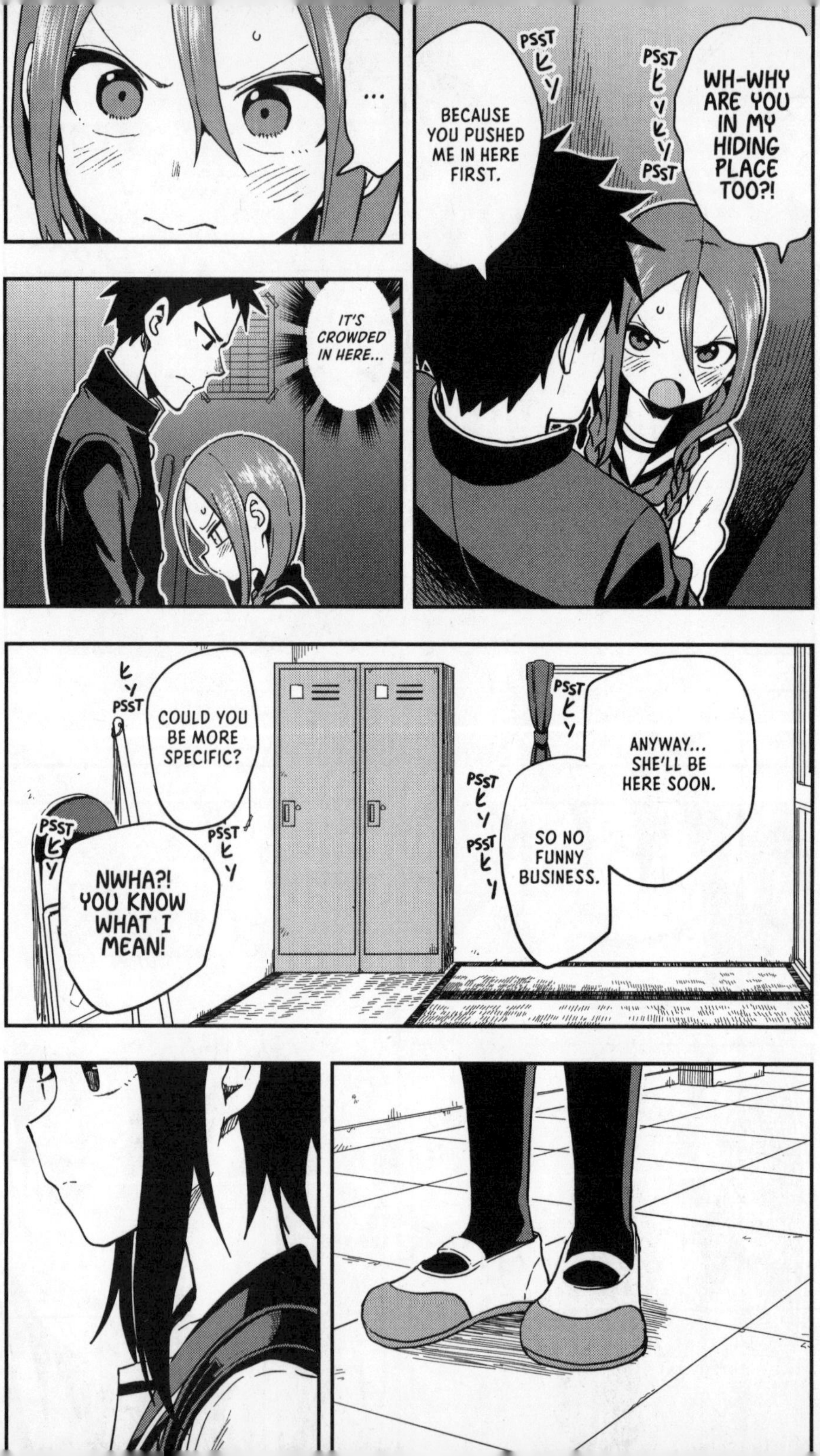
PSST ヒソ ヒソ PSST
WH-WHY ARE YOU IN MY HIDING PLACE TOO?!
PSST ヒソ
BECAUSE YOU PUSHED ME IN HERE FIRST.
...
IT'S CROWDED IN HERE...
PSST ヒソ
ANYWAY... SHE'LL BE HERE SOON.
PSST ヒソ PSST ヒソ
SO NO FUNNY BUSINESS.
ヒソ PSST
COULD YOU BE MORE SPECIFIC?
PSST ヒソ
PSST ヒソ
NWHA?! YOU KNOW WHAT I MEAN!

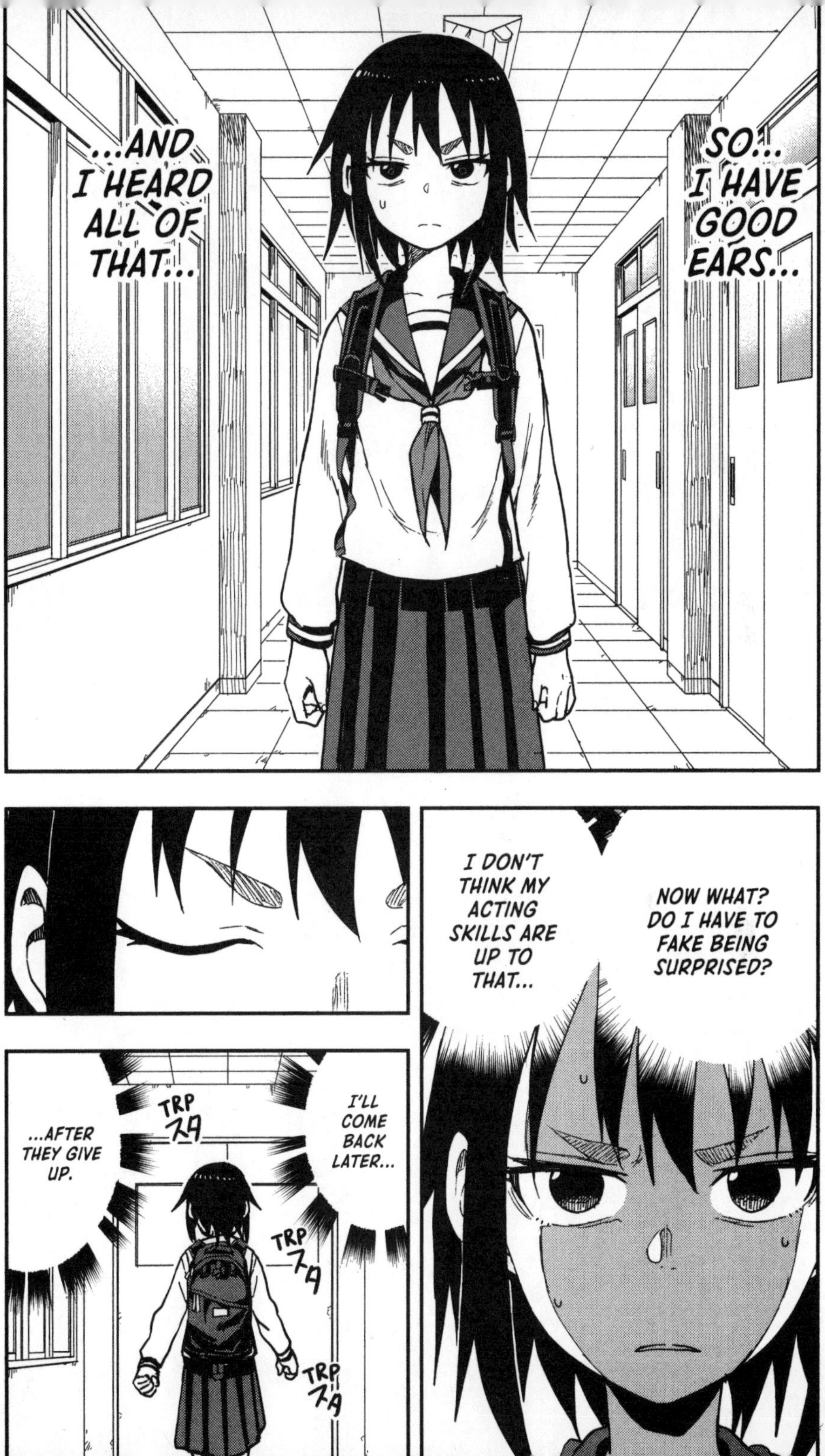
SO... I HAVE GOOD EARS...
...AND I HEARD ALL OF THAT...
NOW WHAT? DO I HAVE TO FAKE BEING SURPRISED?
I DON'T THINK MY ACTING SKILLS ARE UP TO THAT...
I'LL COME BACK LATER...
...AFTER THEY GIVE UP.
TRP スタ
TRP スタ
TRP スタ

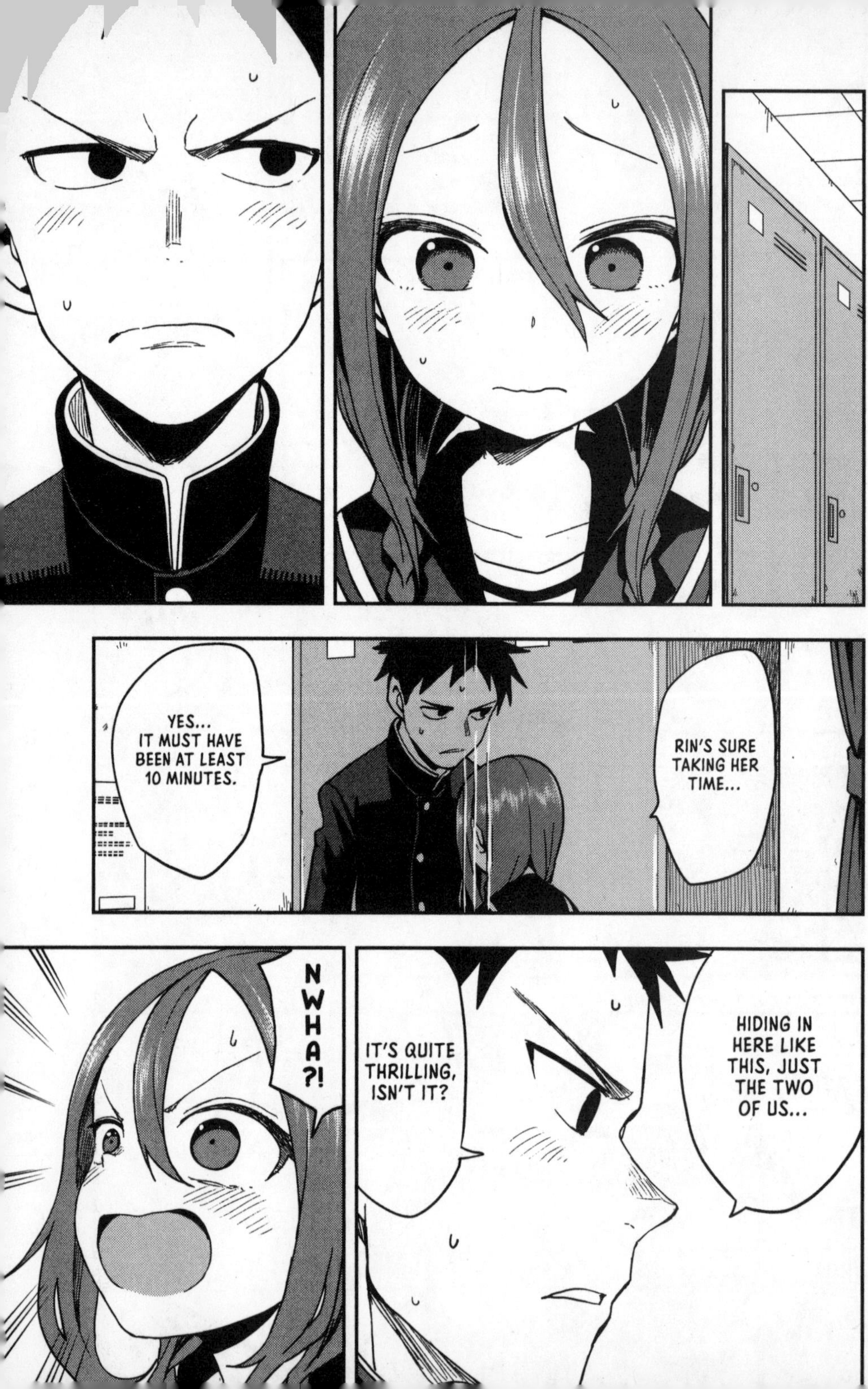
RIN'S SURE TAKING HER TIME...
YES... IT MUST HAVE BEEN AT LEAST 10 MINUTES.
HIDING IN HERE LIKE THIS, JUST THE TWO OF US...
IT'S QUITE THRILLING, ISN'T IT?
NWHA?!

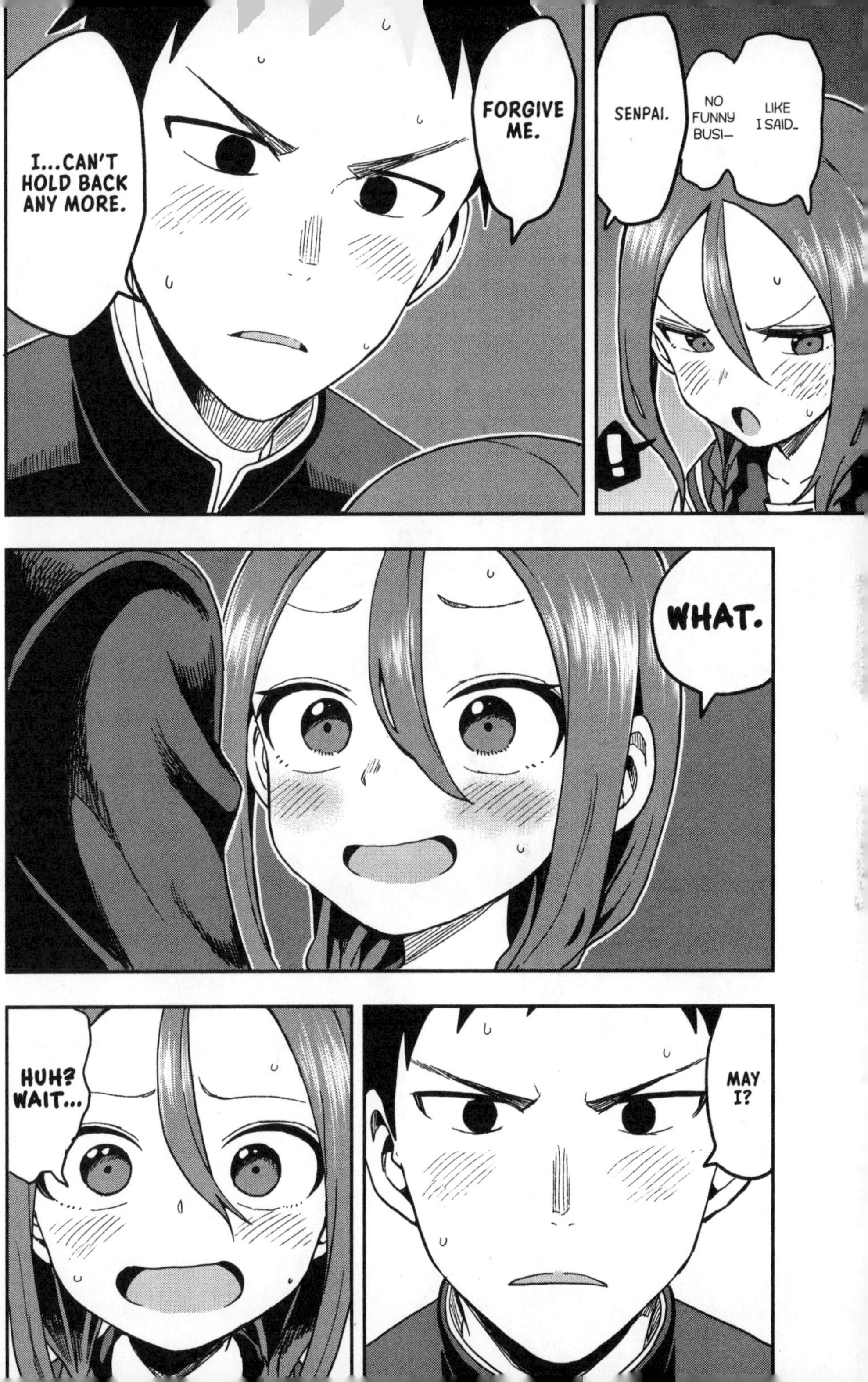
LIKE I SAID_
NO FUNNY BUSI—
SENPAI.
!
FORGIVE ME.
I...CAN'T HOLD BACK ANY MORE.
WHAT.
MAY I?
HUH? WAIT...

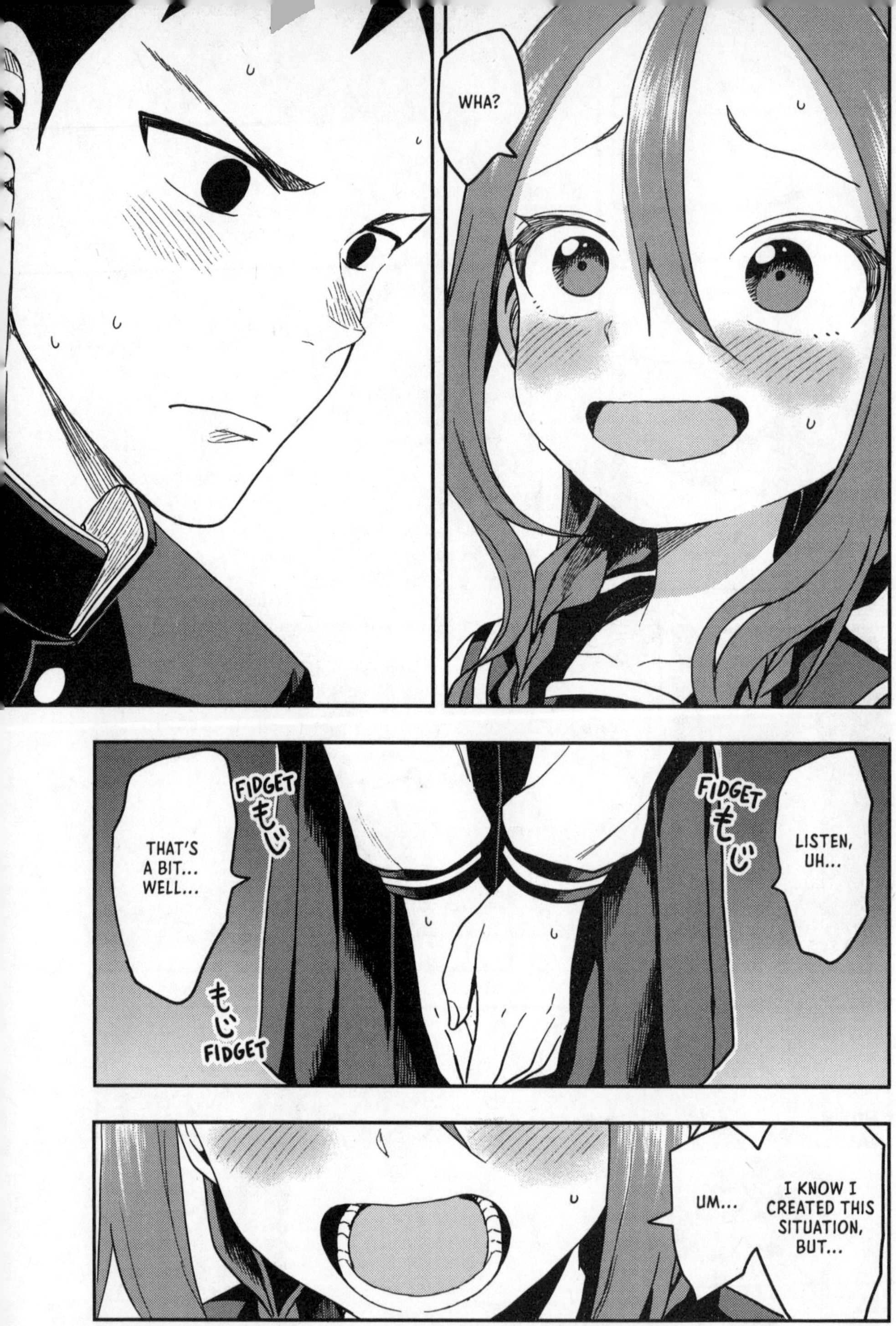

WHA?
LISTEN, UH...
FIDGET もじ
THAT'S A BIT... WELL...
FIDGET もじ
もじ FIDGET
I KNOW I CREATED THIS SITUATION, BUT...
UM...

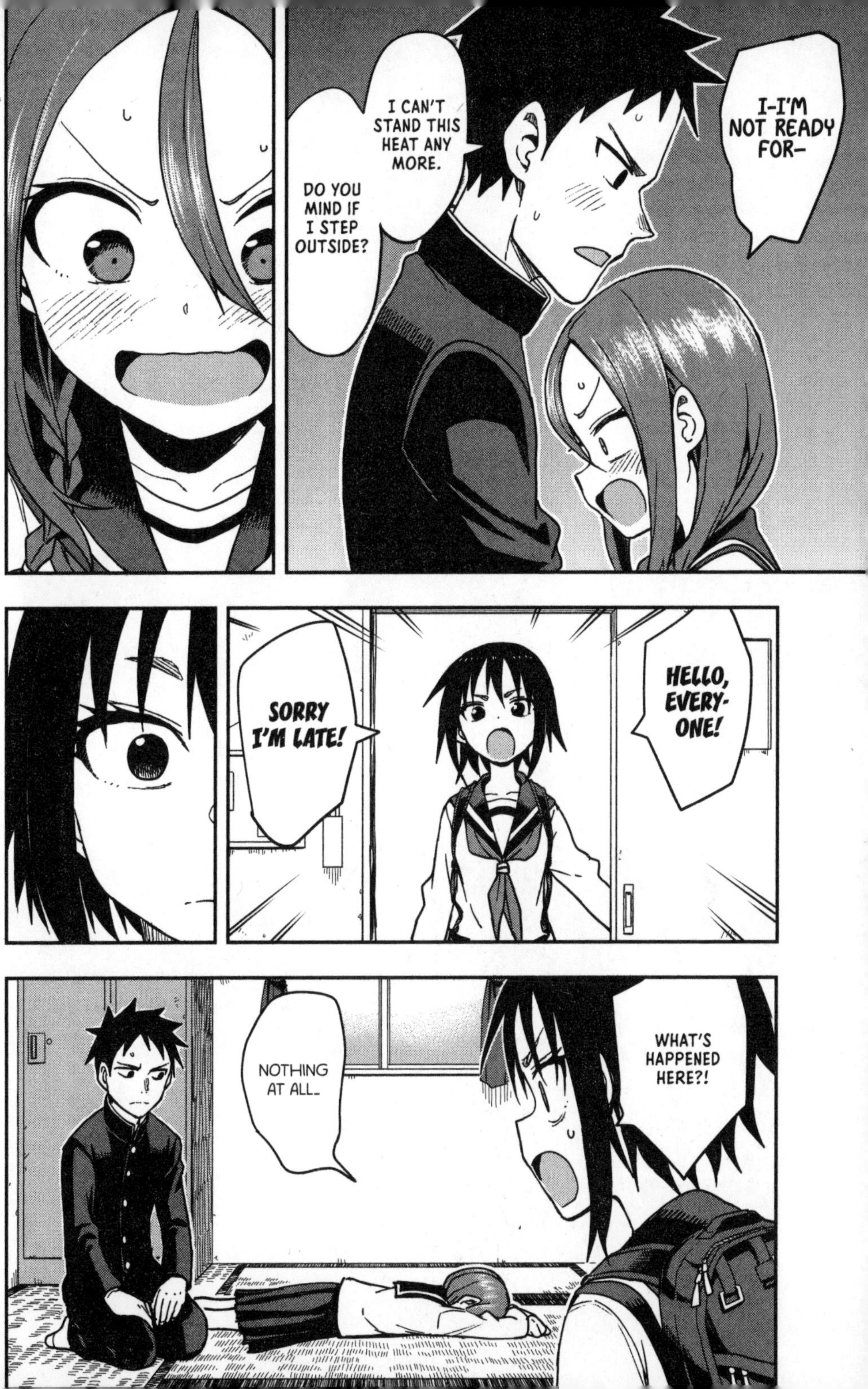
I-I'M NOT READY FOR–
I CAN'T STAND THIS HEAT ANY MORE.
DO YOU MIND IF I STEP OUTSIDE?
HELLO, EVERY-ONE!
SORRY I'M LATE!
WHAT'S HAPPENED HERE?!
NOTHING AT ALL…

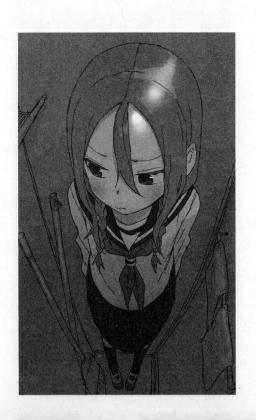

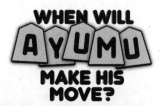

WHEN WILL
AYUMU
MAKE HIS
MOVE?

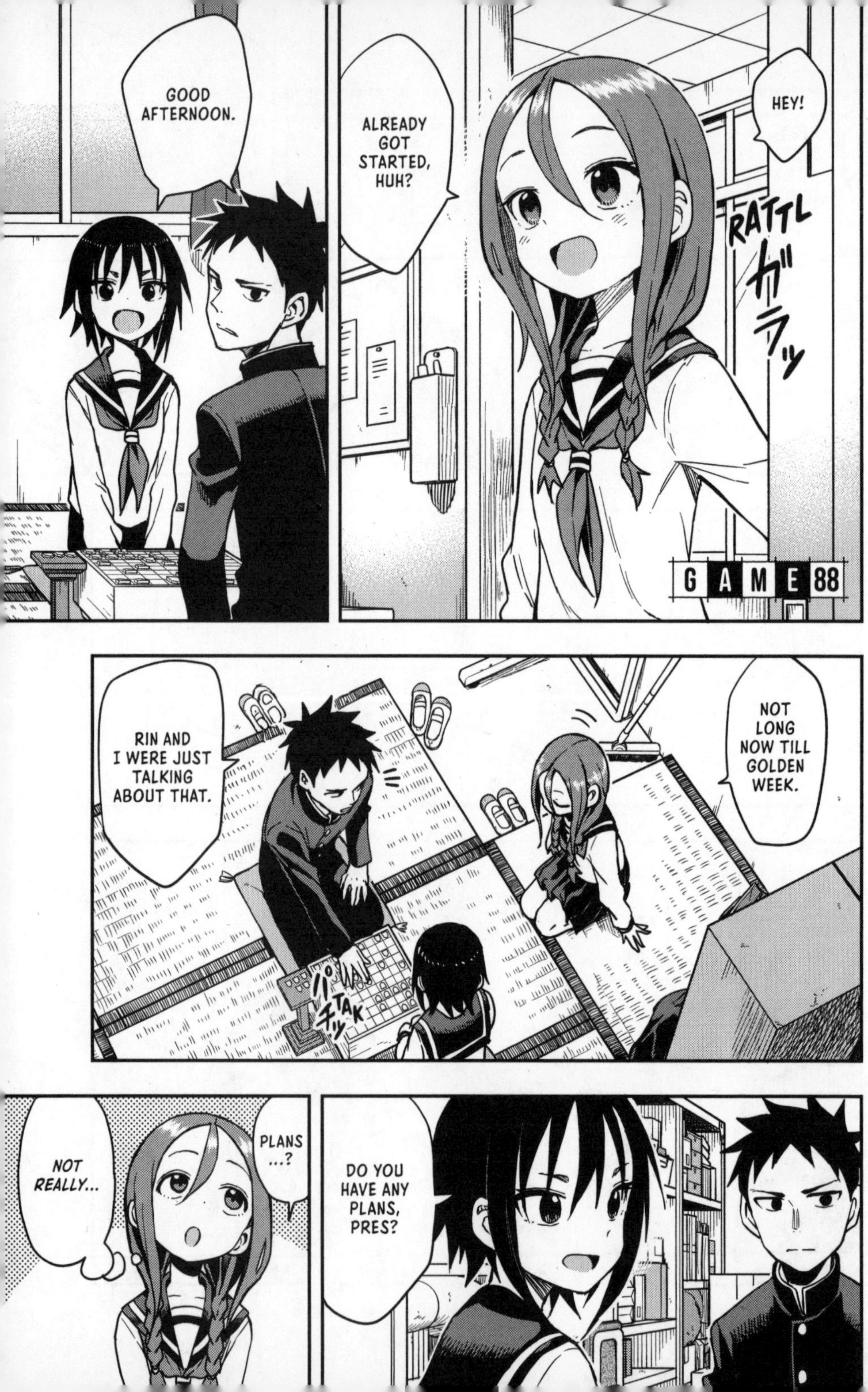
HEY!
RATTL
ガラッ
ALREADY GOT STARTED, HUH?
GAME 88
GOOD AFTERNOON.
NOT LONG NOW TILL GOLDEN WEEK.
RIN AND I WERE JUST TALKING ABOUT THAT.
パチッ
TAK
DO YOU HAVE ANY PLANS, PRES?
PLANS ...?
NOT REALLY...

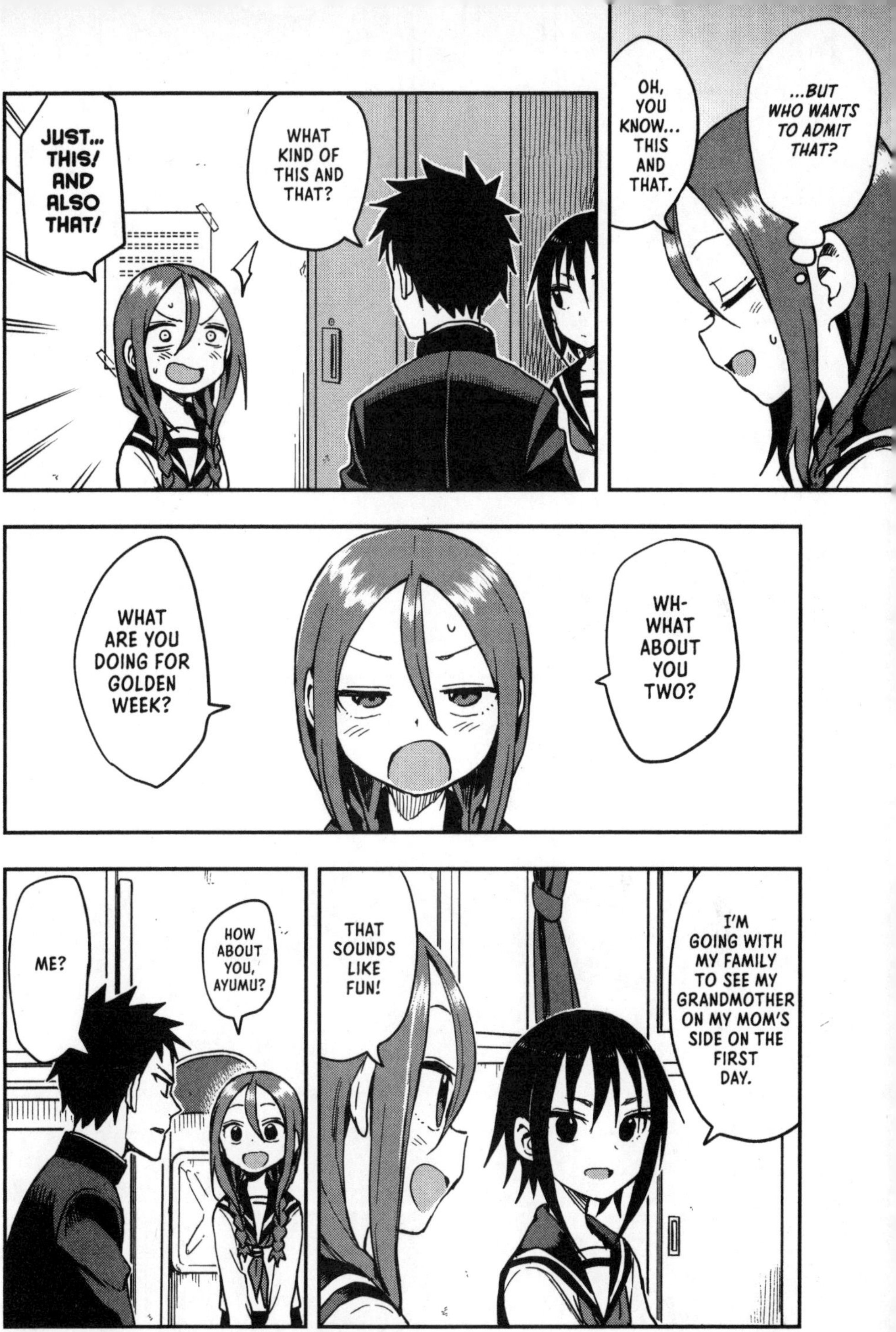

OH, YOU KNOW... THIS AND THAT.
...BUT WHO WANTS TO ADMIT THAT?
WHAT KIND OF THIS AND THAT?
JUST... THIS! AND ALSO THAT!
WH- WHAT ABOUT YOU TWO?
WHAT ARE YOU DOING FOR GOLDEN WEEK?
I'M GOING WITH MY FAMILY TO SEE MY GRANDMOTHER ON MY MOM'S SIDE ON THE FIRST DAY.
THAT SOUNDS LIKE FUN!
HOW ABOUT YOU, AYUMU?
ME?

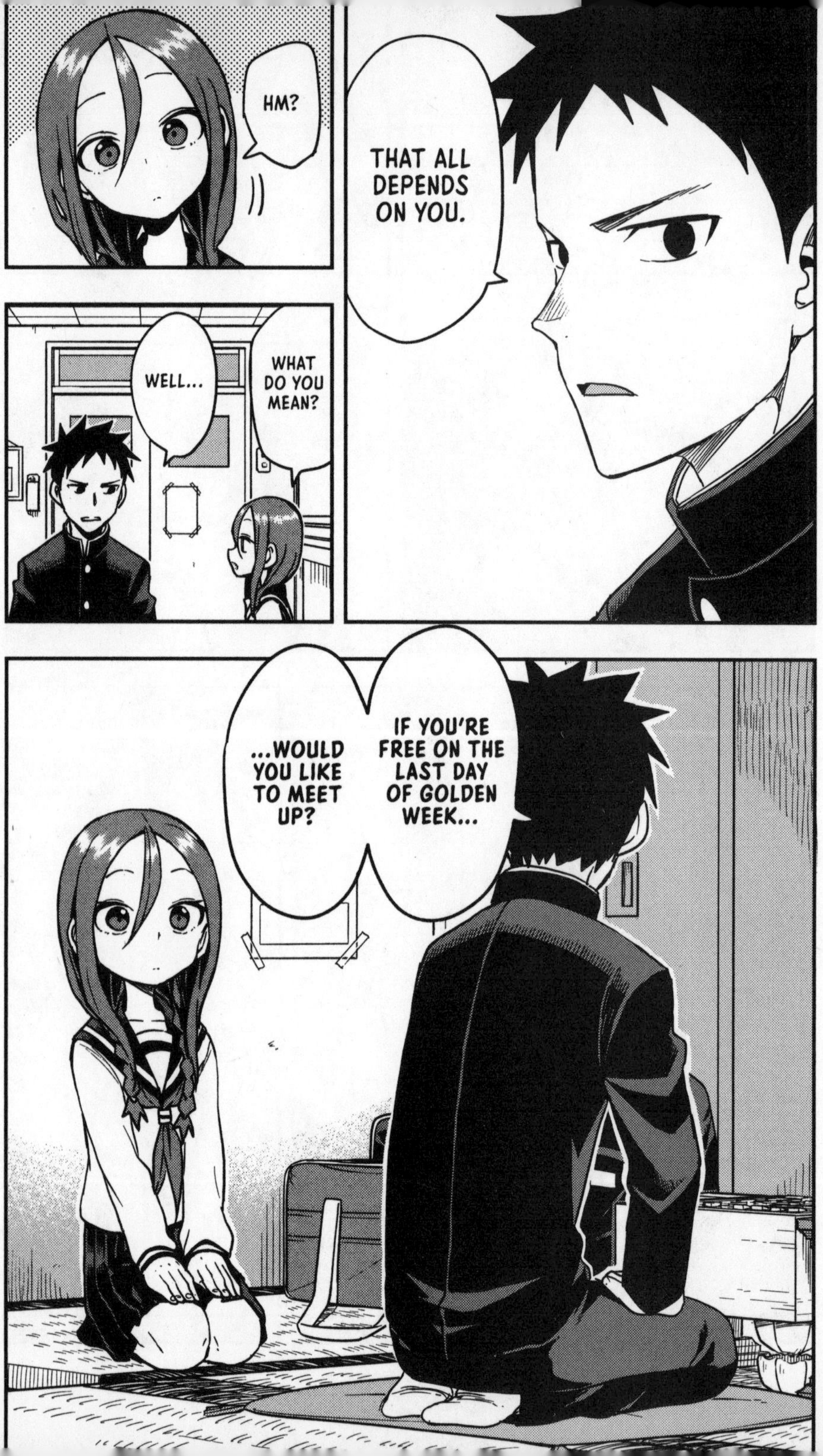
THAT ALL DEPENDS ON YOU.
HM?
WHAT DO YOU MEAN?
WELL...
IF YOU'RE FREE ON THE LAST DAY OF GOLDEN WEEK...
...WOULD YOU LIKE TO MEET UP?

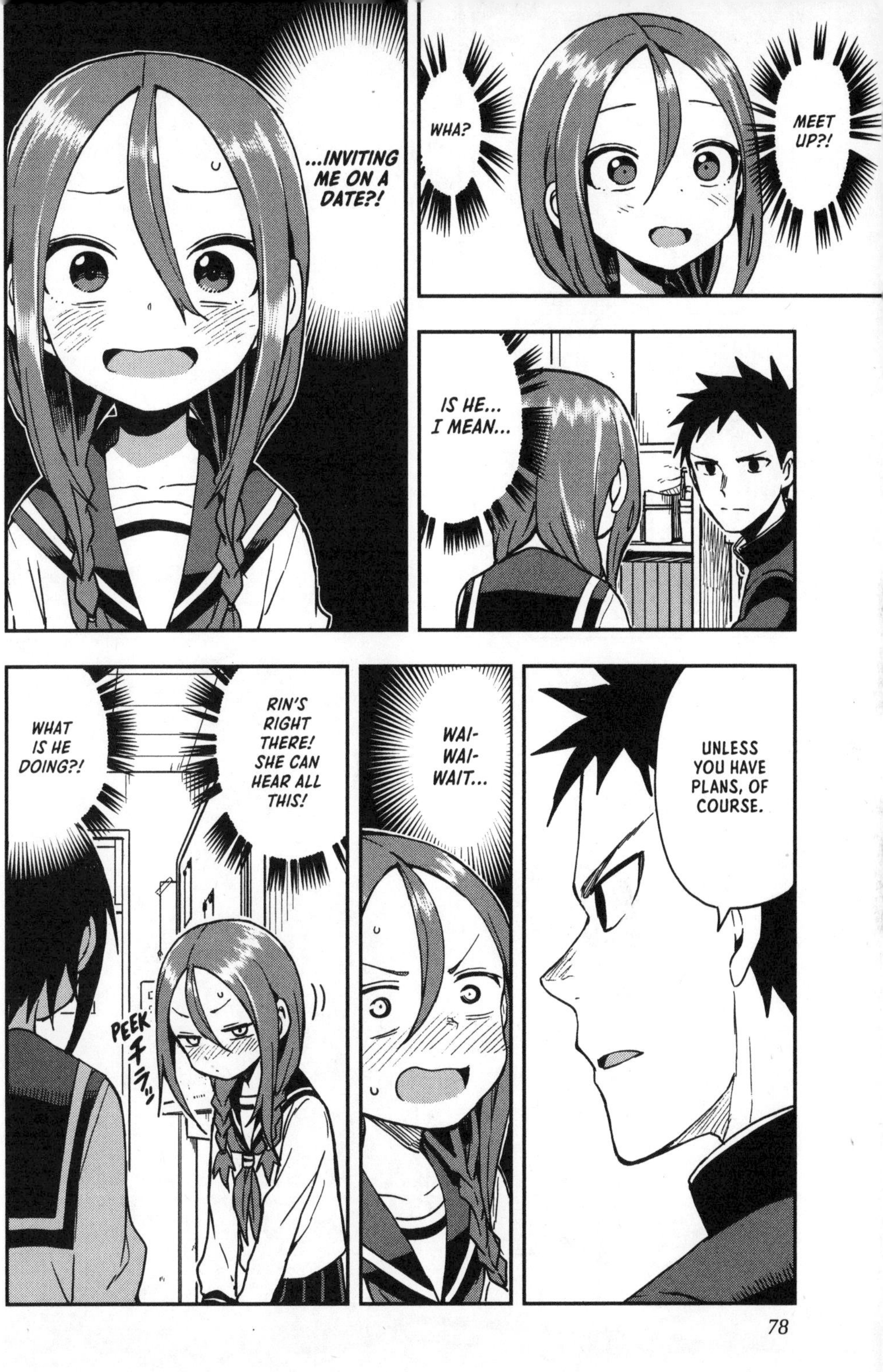
MEET UP?!
WHA?
IS HE... I MEAN...
...INVITING ME ON A DATE?!
UNLESS YOU HAVE PLANS, OF COURSE.
WAI-WAI-WAIT...
RIN'S RIGHT THERE! SHE CAN HEAR ALL THIS!
WHAT IS HE DOING?!
PEEK
チラッ

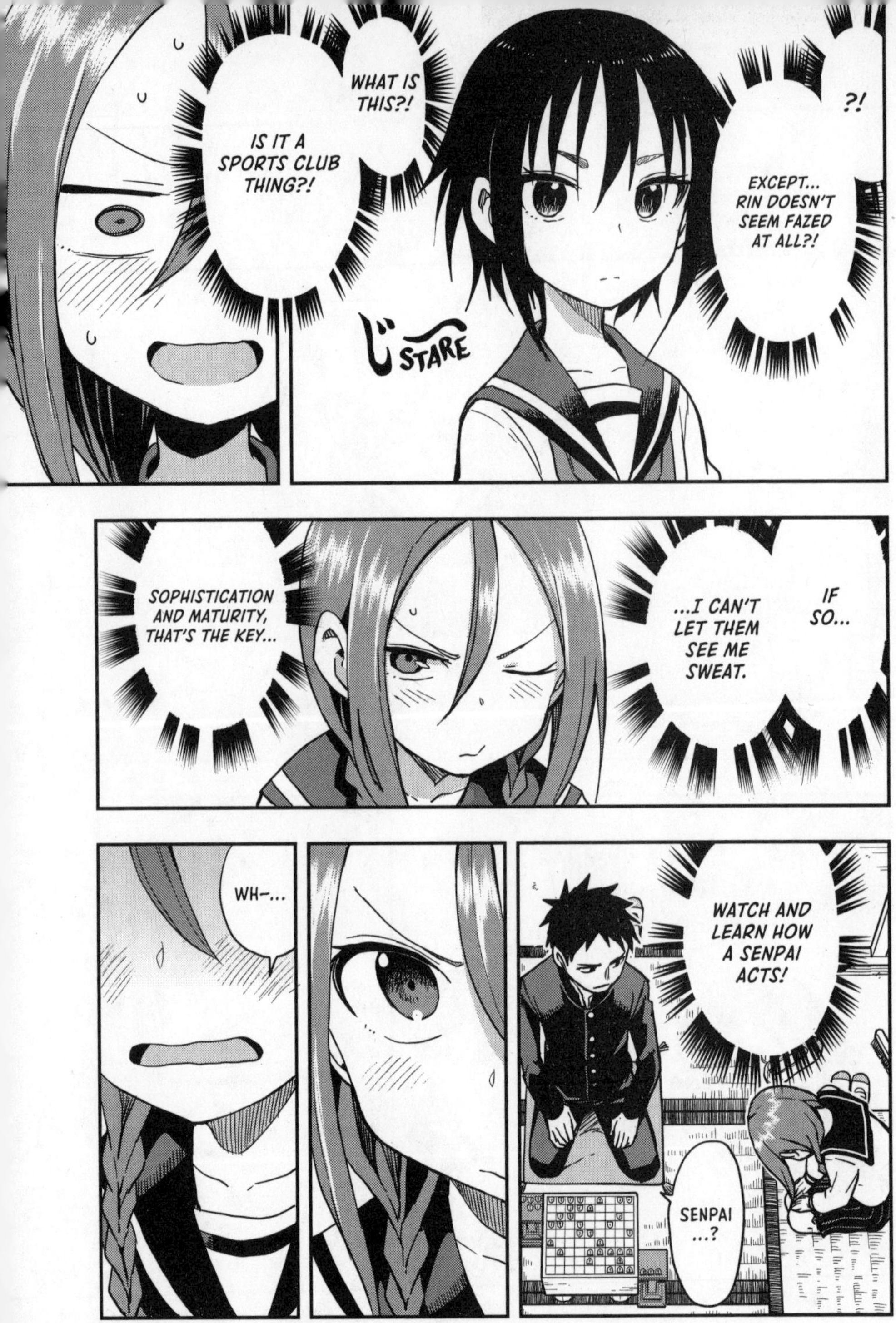
?!
EXCEPT... RIN DOESN'T SEEM FAZED AT ALL?!
じ STARE
WHAT IS THIS?!
IS IT A SPORTS CLUB THING?!
IF SO...
...I CAN'T LET THEM SEE ME SWEAT.
SOPHISTICATION AND MATURITY, THAT'S THE KEY...
WATCH AND LEARN HOW A SENPAI ACTS!
SENPAI ...?
WH-...

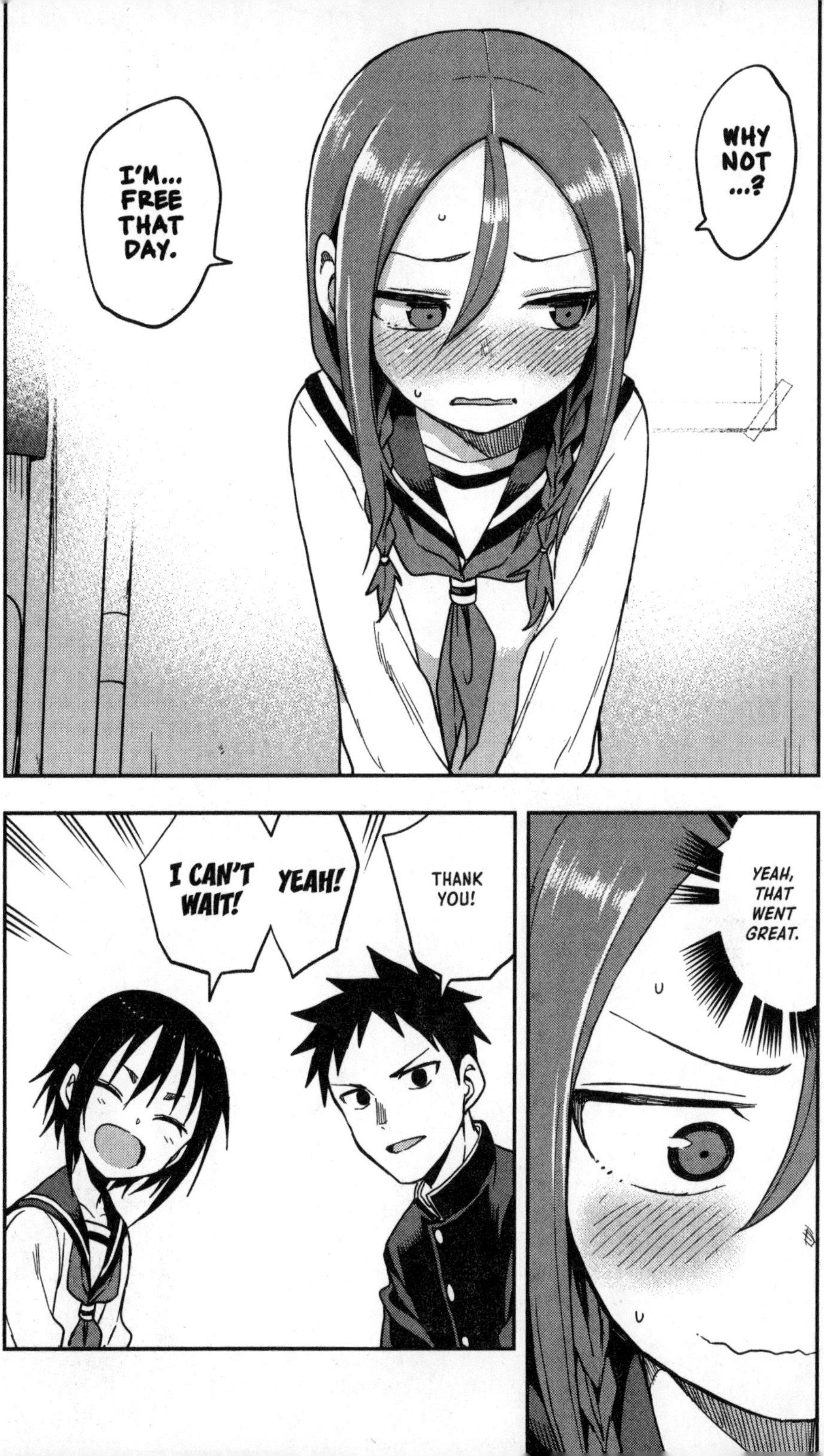
WHY NOT ...?
I'M... FREE THAT DAY.
YEAH, THAT WENT GREAT.
THANK YOU!
YEAH!
I CAN'T WAIT!

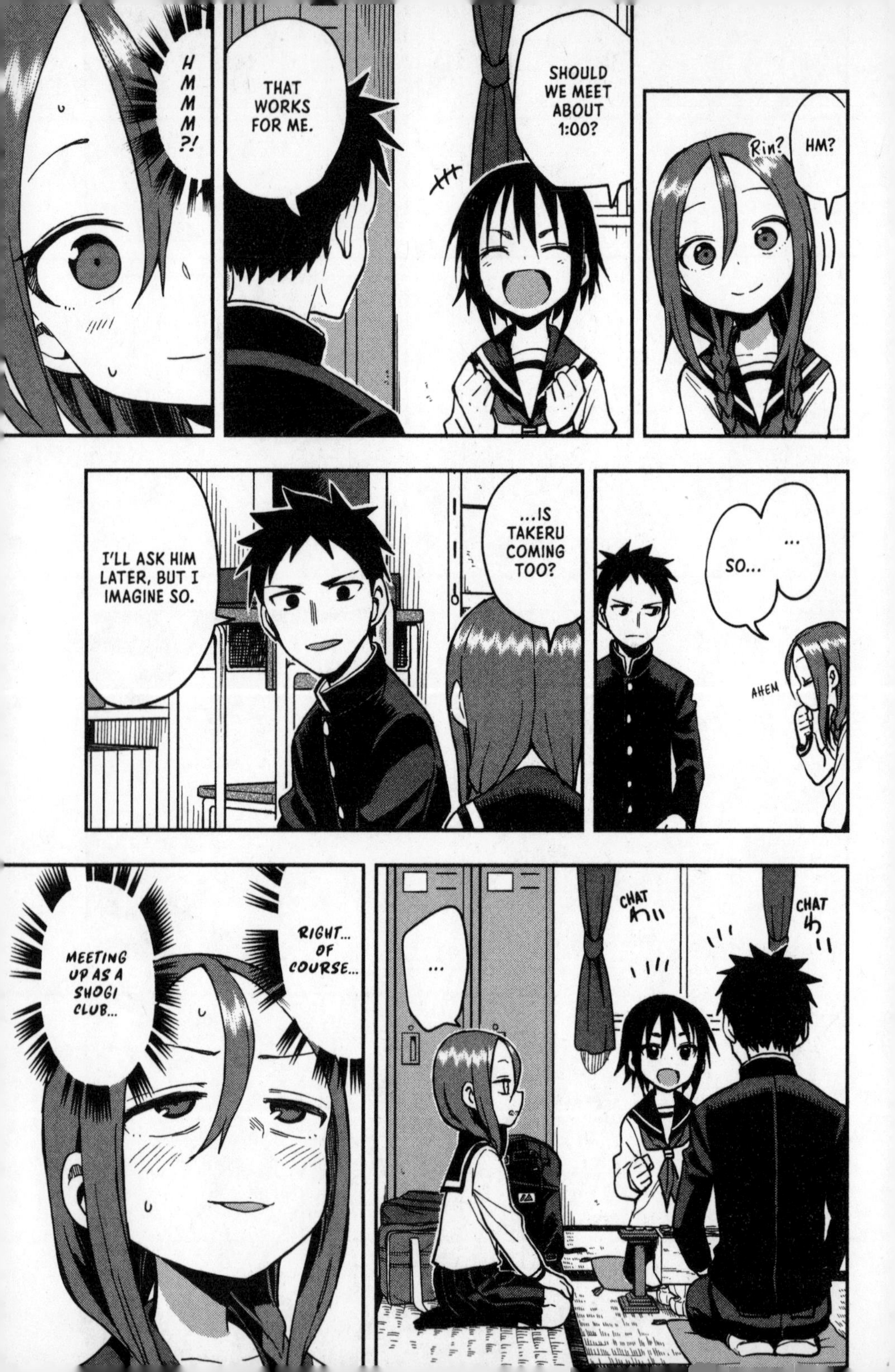

HM?
Rin?
SHOULD WE MEET ABOUT 1:00?
THAT WORKS FOR ME.
HMMMM?!
...
SO...
AHEM
...IS TAKERU COMING TOO?
I'LL ASK HIM LATER, BUT I IMAGINE SO.
CHAT
CHAT
...
RIGHT... OF COURSE...
MEETING UP AS A SHOGI CLUB...

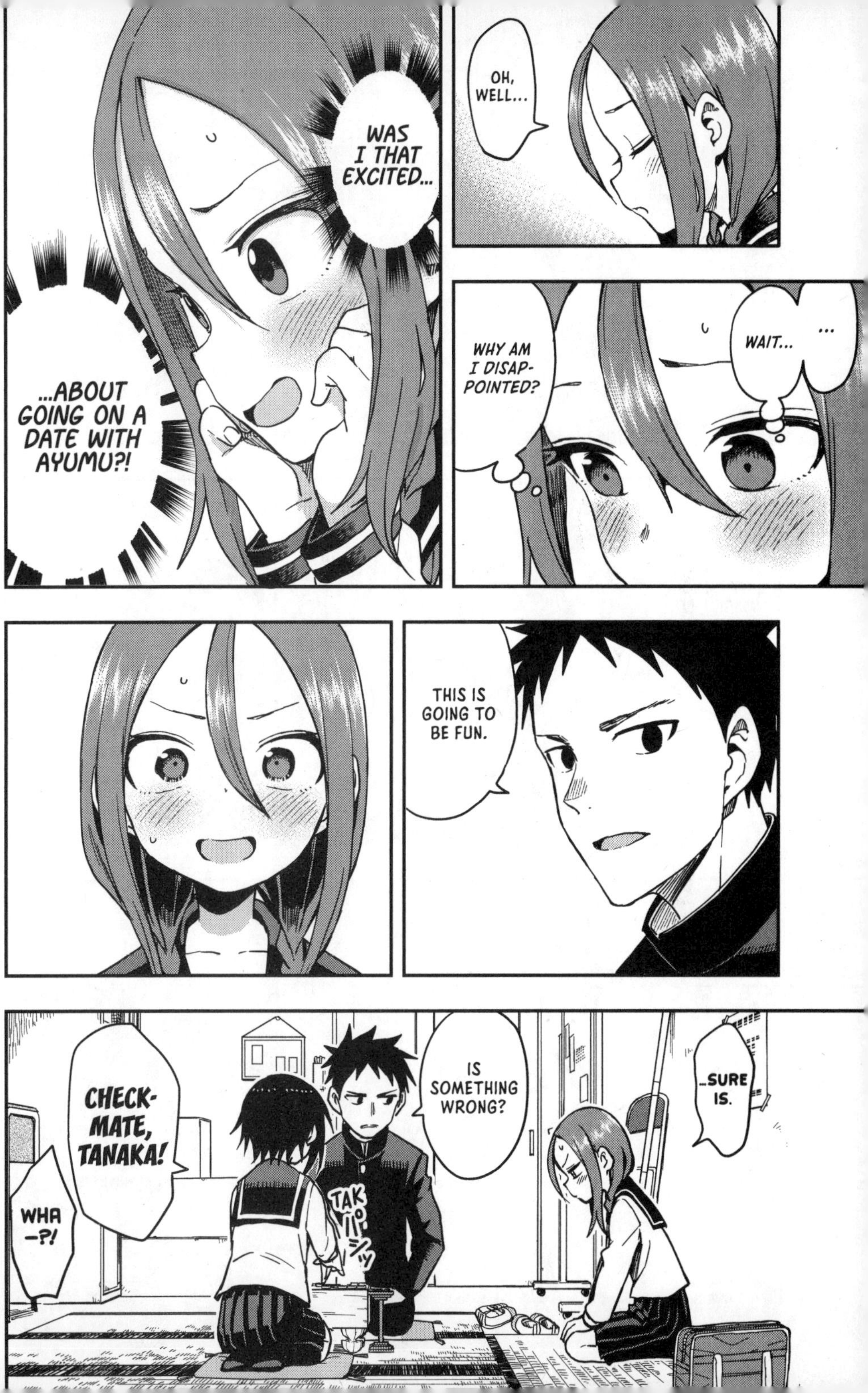
OH, WELL...
...
WAIT...
WHY AM I DISAP-POINTED?
WAS I THAT EXCITED...
...ABOUT GOING ON A DATE WITH AYUMU?!
THIS IS GOING TO BE FUN.
...SURE IS.
IS SOMETHING WRONG?
TAK
CHECK-MATE, TANAKA!
WHA-?!

GAME 88 RECORD

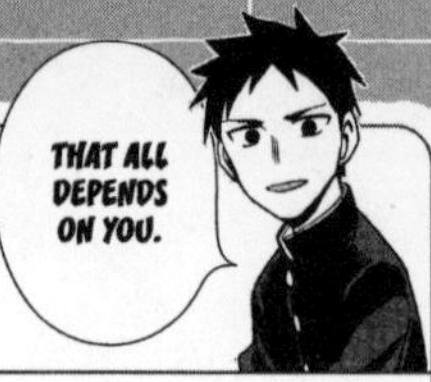
THAT ALL DEPENDS ON YOU.

▲ BLACK (SENTE): AYUMU TANAKA △ WHITE (GOTE): RIN KAGAWA

(DIAGRAM SHOWS BOARD AFTER MOVE 98, △ G-2A)

◁RIN: G, S, P

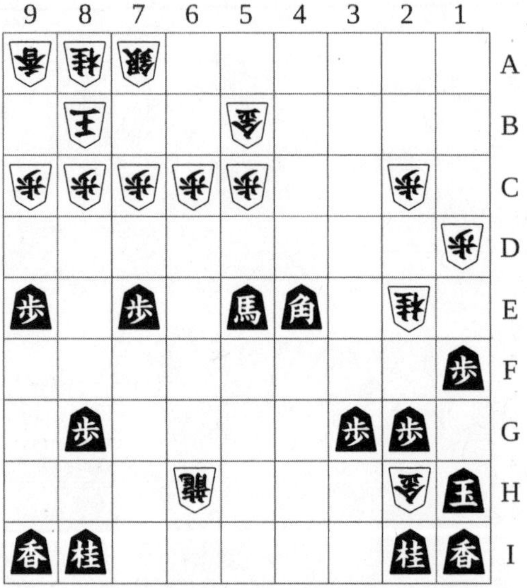

▲AYUMU: R, G, S×2, L, P×4

▲ P-7F	△ P-3D	▲ G-4G	△ P-4E	▲ N×6D	△ K-8B
▲ P-6F	△ P-3E	▲ P×4E	△ P×4F	▲ N×5B+	△ G×5B
▲ R-6H	△ R-3B	▲ G4G-4H	△ S×4E	▲ P-6D	△ R×6D
▲ K-4H	△ K-6B	▲ S×4E	△ N×4E	▲ +B-5E	△ R-6H+
▲ S-3H	△ K-7B	▲ B×1A+	△ P-4G+	▲ P-7E	△ P×4G
▲ G6I-5H	△ G4A-5B	▲ S×4G	△ N×5G+	▲ G×4G	△ S×4G+
▲ K-3I	△ S-4B	▲ G×5G	△ B×5G+	▲ S4H×4G	△ +R×4I
▲ S-7H	△ P-4D	▲ R-4H	△ +B×4H	▲ K-2H	△ N×2E
▲ S-6G	△ S-4C	▲ G×4H	△ R×7I	▲ G×3I	△ +R×3I
▲ S-5F	△ S-5D	▲ P×4I	△ P×4F	▲ K×3I	△ G×4H
▲ P-6E	△ P-3F	▲ S-5H	△ S×4G	▲ K-2H	△ G×3H
▲ P×3F	△ R×3F	▲ S×4G	△ P×4G+	▲ S×3H	△ S×3I
▲ P×3G	△ R-3D	▲ G×4G	△ P×4F	▲ K×3I	△ G×4H
▲ P-9F	△ G6A-6B	▲ G×4F	△ S×5H	▲ K-2H	△ G×3H
▲ P-9E	△ P-1D	▲ S×3H	△ R-5I+	▲ K-1H	△ G-2H
▲ P-1F	△ N-3C	▲ S×4H	△ +R-6I	(RIN WINS AT MOVE 98)	
▲ P-4F	△ B-1C	▲ B×4E	△ R-2D		

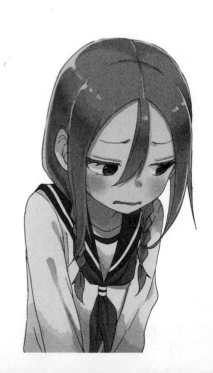

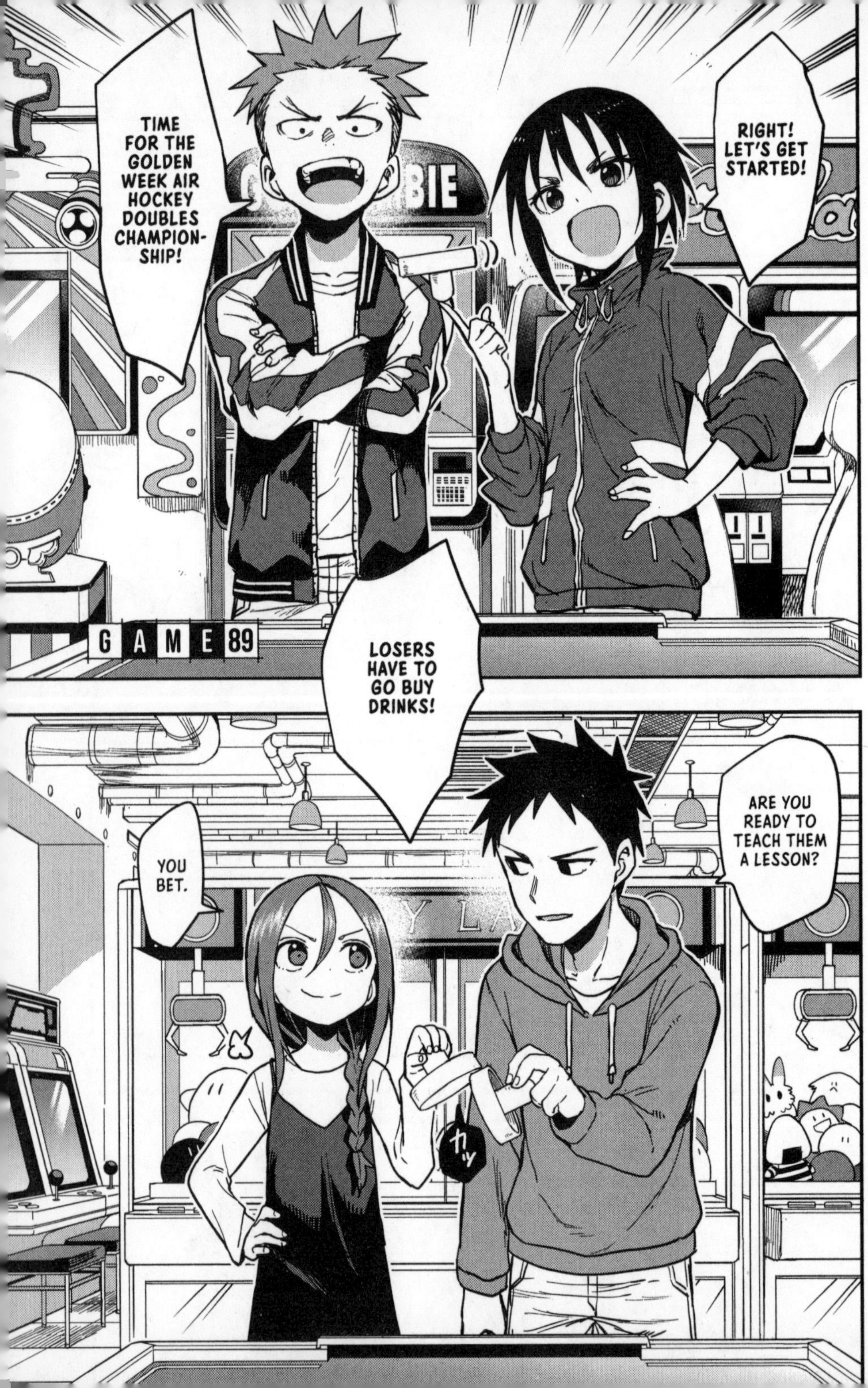
RIGHT! LET'S GET STARTED!
TIME FOR THE GOLDEN WEEK AIR HOCKEY DOUBLES CHAMPION-SHIP!
GAME 89
LOSERS HAVE TO GO BUY DRINKS!
ARE YOU READY TO TEACH THEM A LESSON?
カッ
YOU BET.

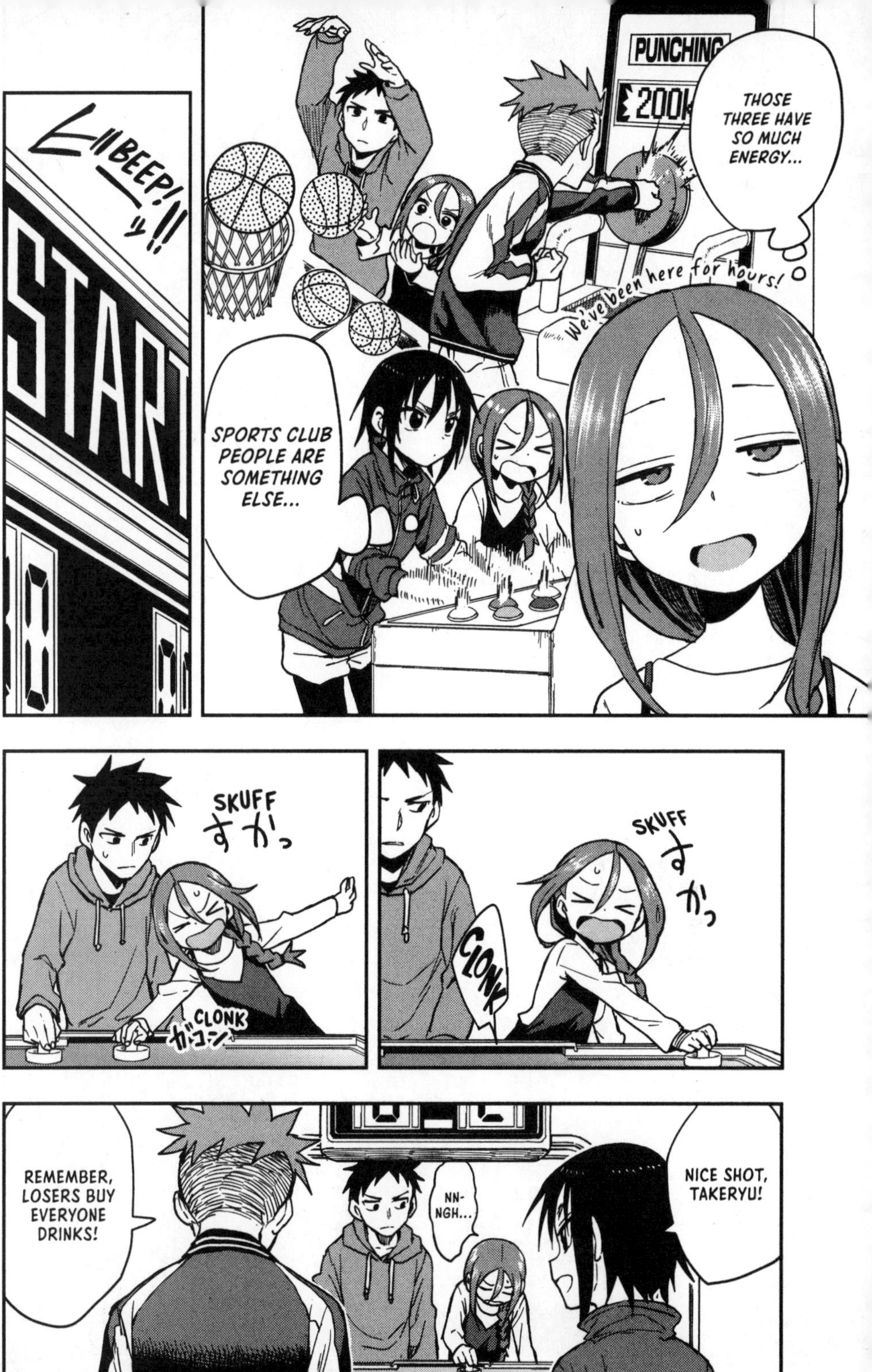
PUNCHING
THOSE THREE HAVE SO MUCH ENERGY...
We've been here for hours!
SPORTS CLUB PEOPLE ARE SOMETHING ELSE...
BEEP!!
START
SKUFF すかっ
CLONK
SKUFF すかっ
CLONK ガコン
NICE SHOT, TAKERYU!
NN-NGH...
REMEMBER, LOSERS BUY EVERYONE DRINKS!

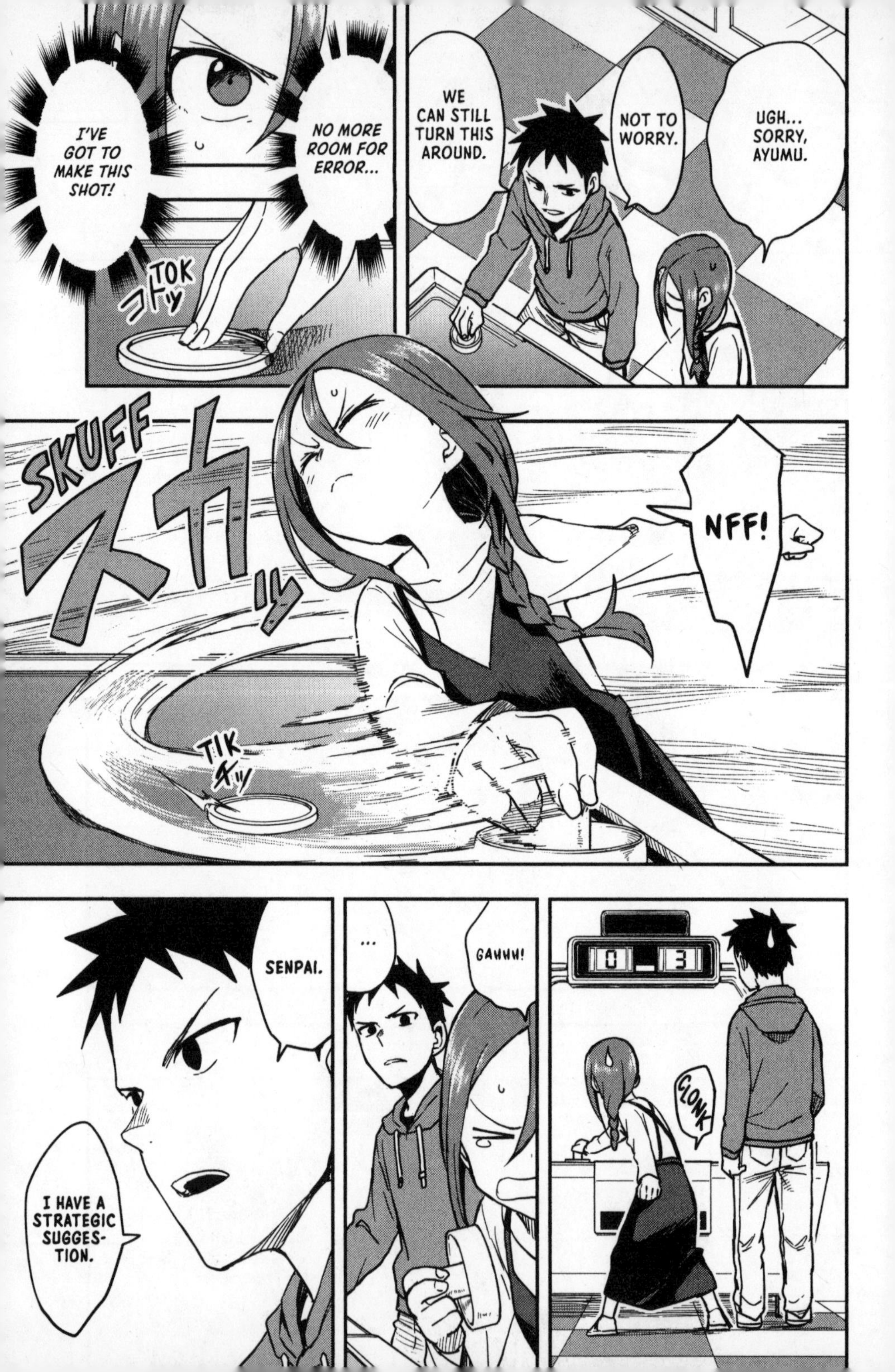

UGH... SORRY, AYUMU.
NOT TO WORRY.
WE CAN STILL TURN THIS AROUND.
NO MORE ROOM FOR ERROR...
I'VE GOT TO MAKE THIS SHOT!
TOK
コトッ
NFF!
SKUFF
スカッ
TIK
0 3
CLONK
...
GAHHH!
SENPAI.
I HAVE A STRATEGIC SUGGES-TION.

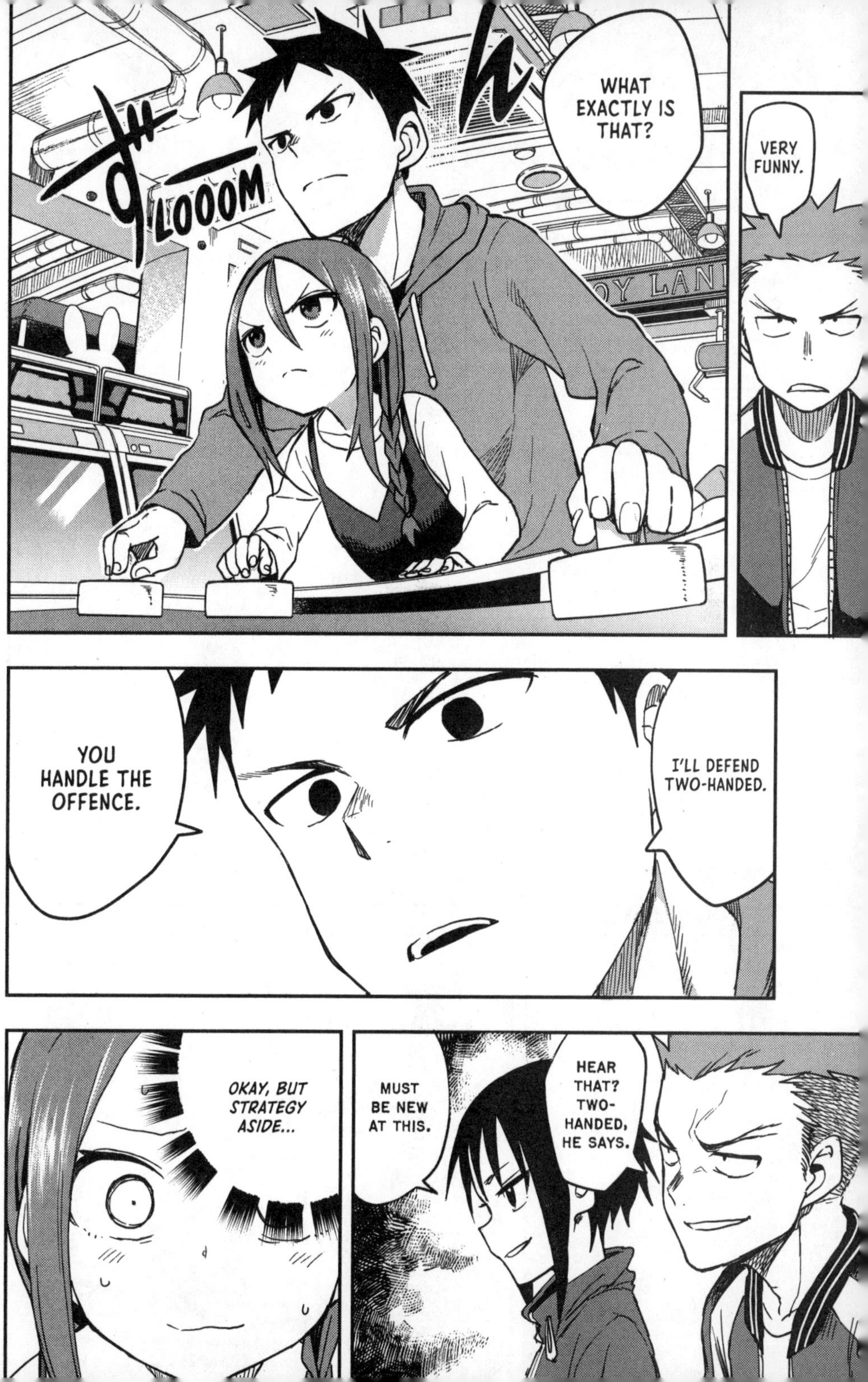
VERY FUNNY.
WHAT EXACTLY IS THAT?
I'LL DEFEND TWO-HANDED.
YOU HANDLE THE OFFENCE.
HEAR THAT? TWO-HANDED, HE SAYS.
MUST BE NEW AT THIS.
OKAY, BUT STRATEGY ASIDE...

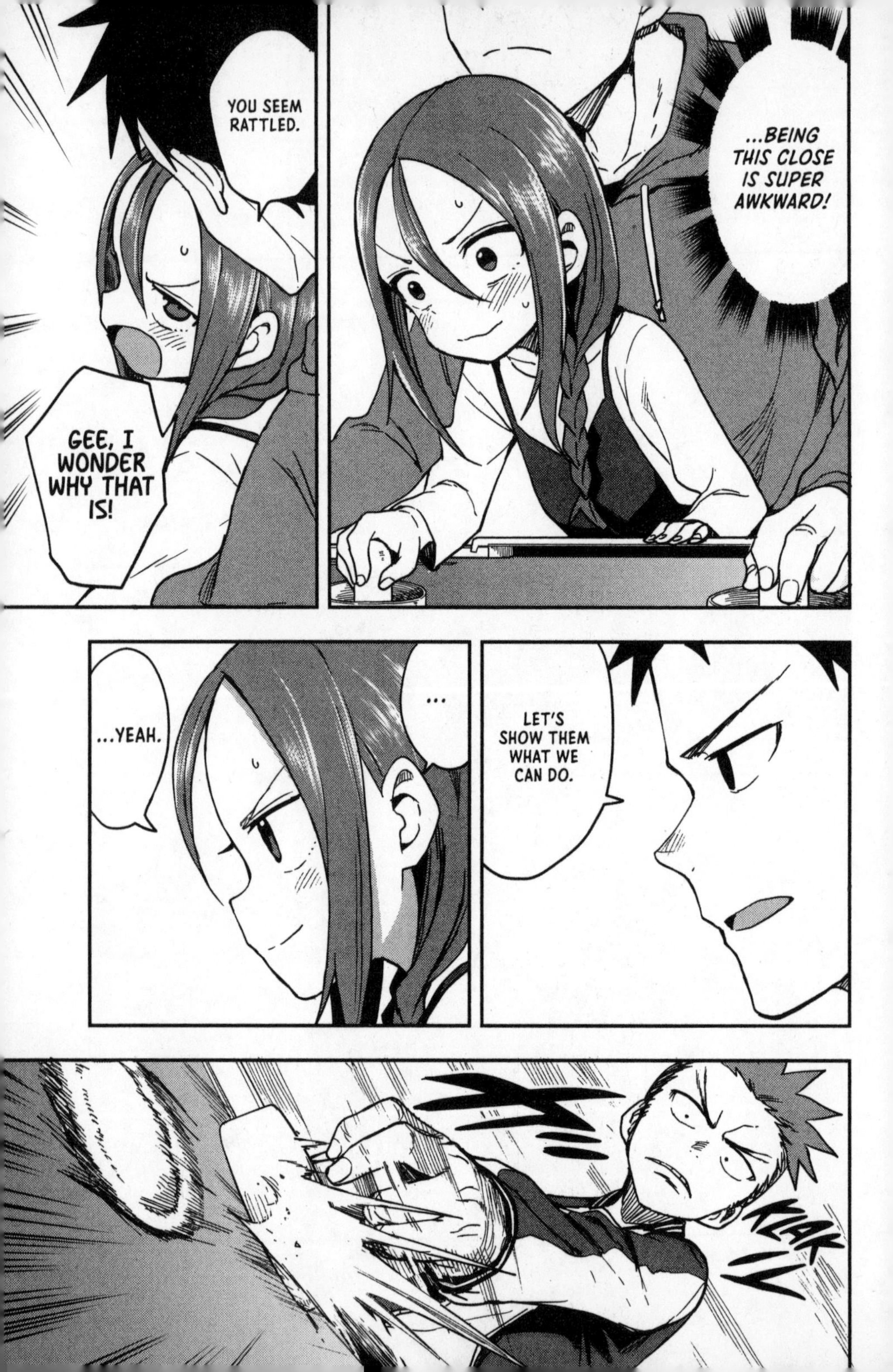
...BEING THIS CLOSE IS SUPER AWKWARD!
YOU SEEM RATTLED.
GEE, I WONDER WHY THAT IS!
LET'S SHOW THEM WHAT WE CAN DO.
...
...YEAH.
KLAK

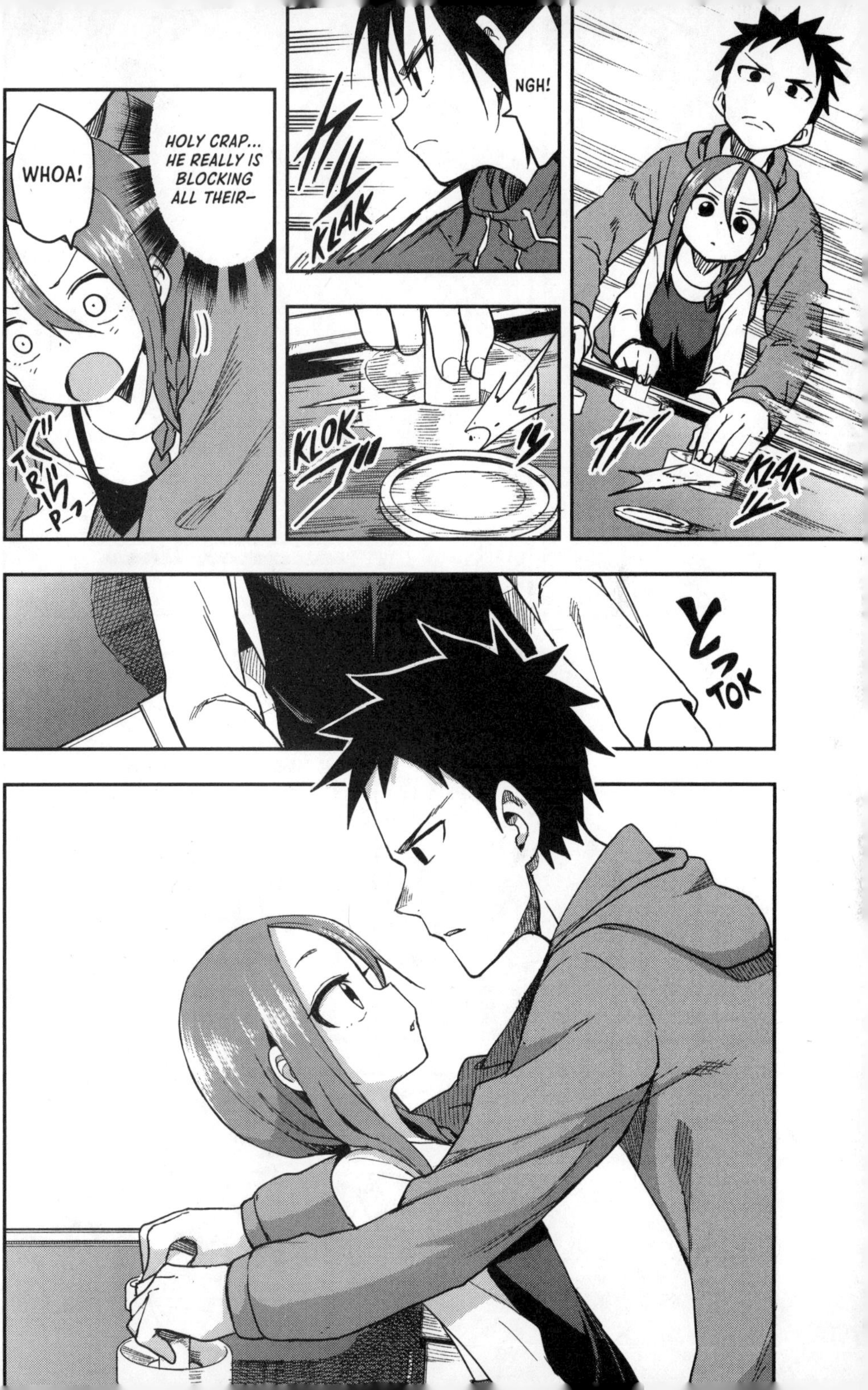
KLAK
NGH!
KLAK
KLOK
WHOA!
HOLY CRAP... HE REALLY IS BLOCKING ALL THEIR–
TRIP
とっ
TOK

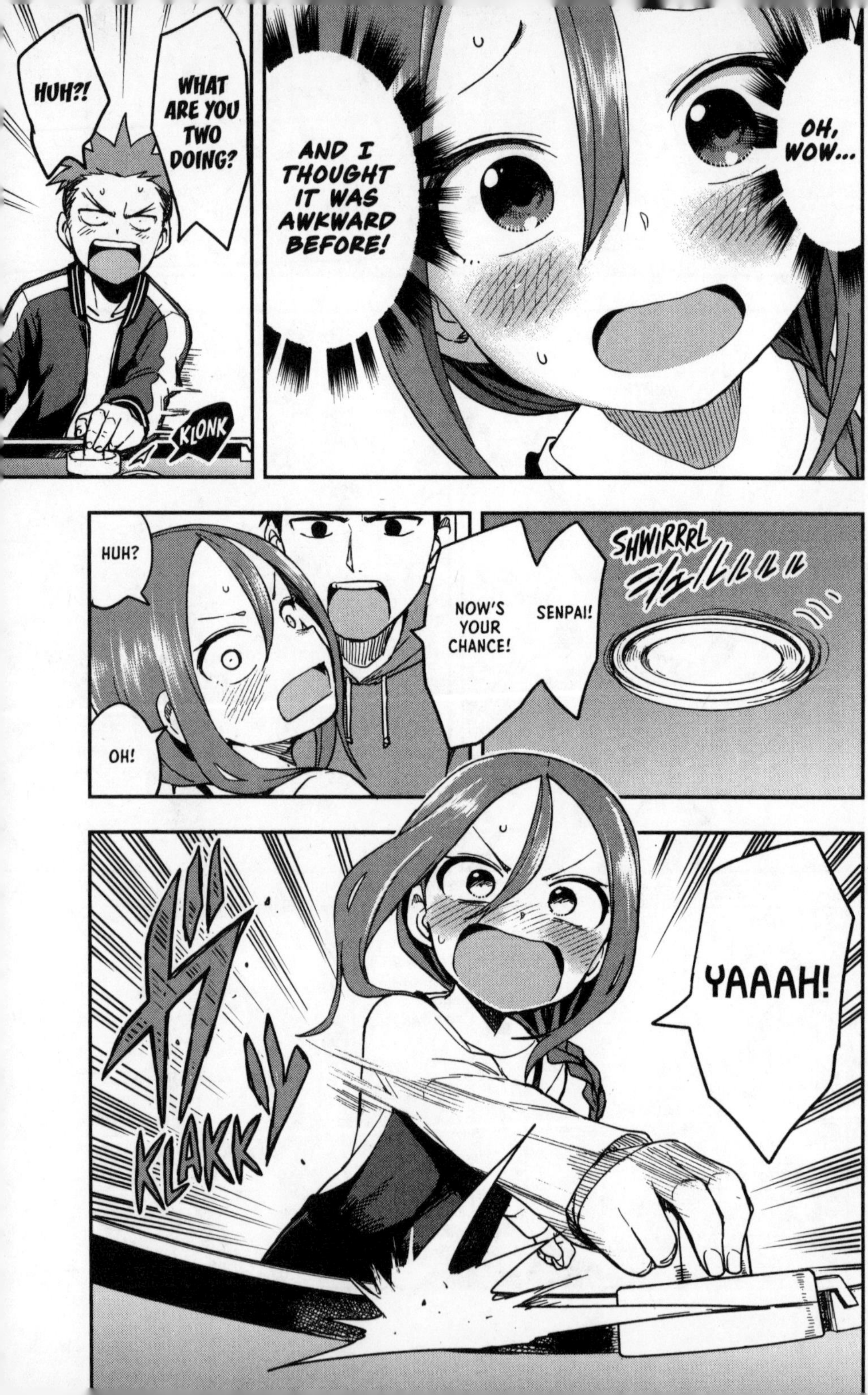
OH, WOW...
AND I THOUGHT IT WAS AWKWARD BEFORE!
WHAT ARE YOU TWO DOING?
HUH?!
KLONK
SHWIRRRL
SENPAI!
NOW'S YOUR CHANCE!
HUH?
OH!
YAAAH!
KLAKK

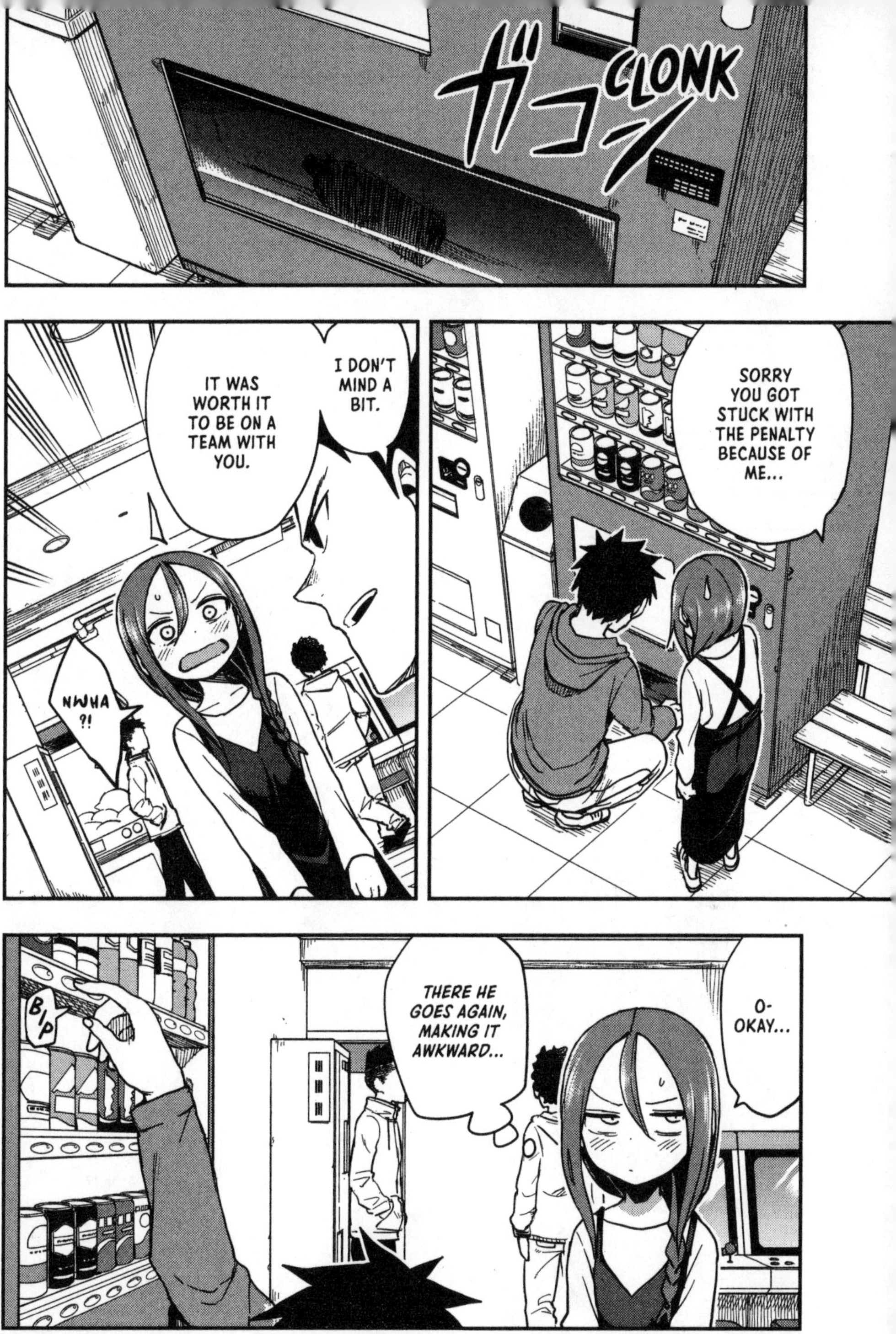
ガコン
CLONK
SORRY YOU GOT STUCK WITH THE PENALTY BECAUSE OF ME...
I DON'T MIND A BIT.
IT WAS WORTH IT TO BE ON A TEAM WITH YOU.
NWHA ?!
O-OKAY...
THERE HE GOES AGAIN, MAKING IT AWKWARD...
BIP

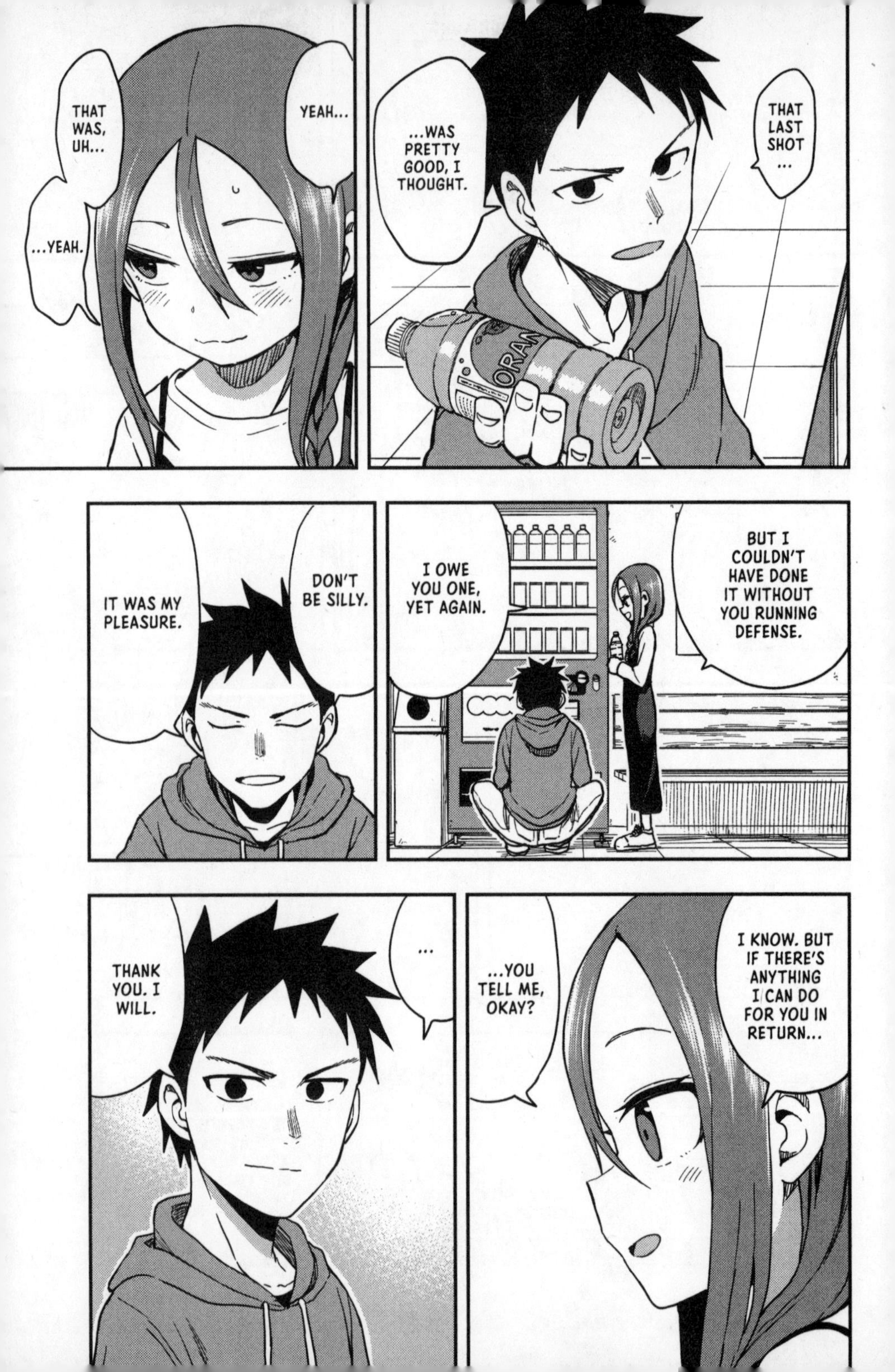

THAT LAST SHOT ...
...WAS PRETTY GOOD, I THOUGHT.
YEAH...
THAT WAS, UH...
...YEAH.
BUT I COULDN'T HAVE DONE IT WITHOUT YOU RUNNING DEFENSE.
I OWE YOU ONE, YET AGAIN.
DON'T BE SILLY.
IT WAS MY PLEASURE.
I KNOW. BUT IF THERE'S ANYTHING I CAN DO FOR YOU IN RETURN...
...YOU TELL ME, OKAY?
...
THANK YOU. I WILL.

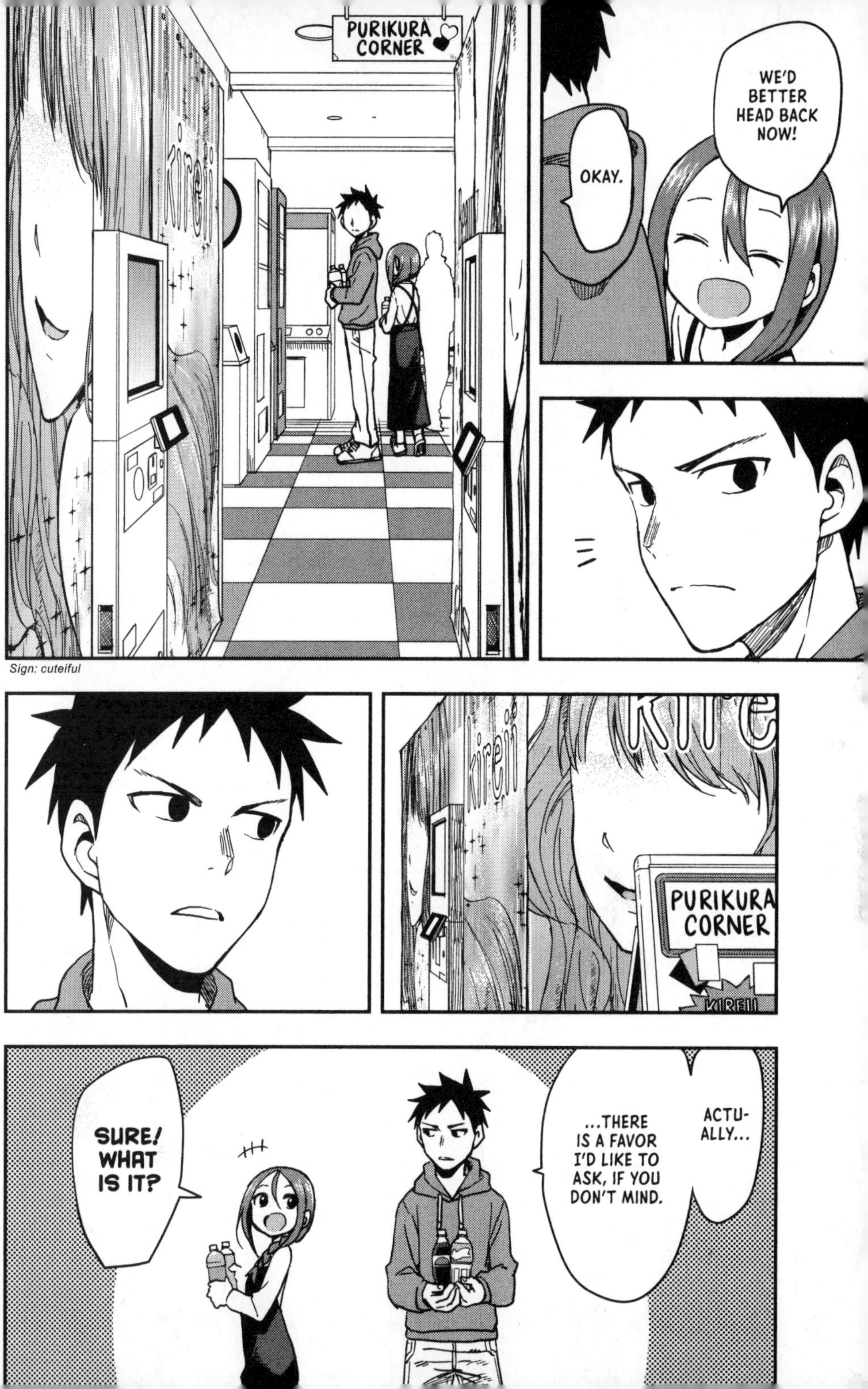
WE'D BETTER HEAD BACK NOW!
OKAY.
PURIKURA CORNER
kirei!
kirei!
PURIKURA CORNER
ACTU-ALLY...
...THERE IS A FAVOR I'D LIKE TO ASK, IF YOU DON'T MIND.
SURE! WHAT IS IT?
Sign: cuteiful

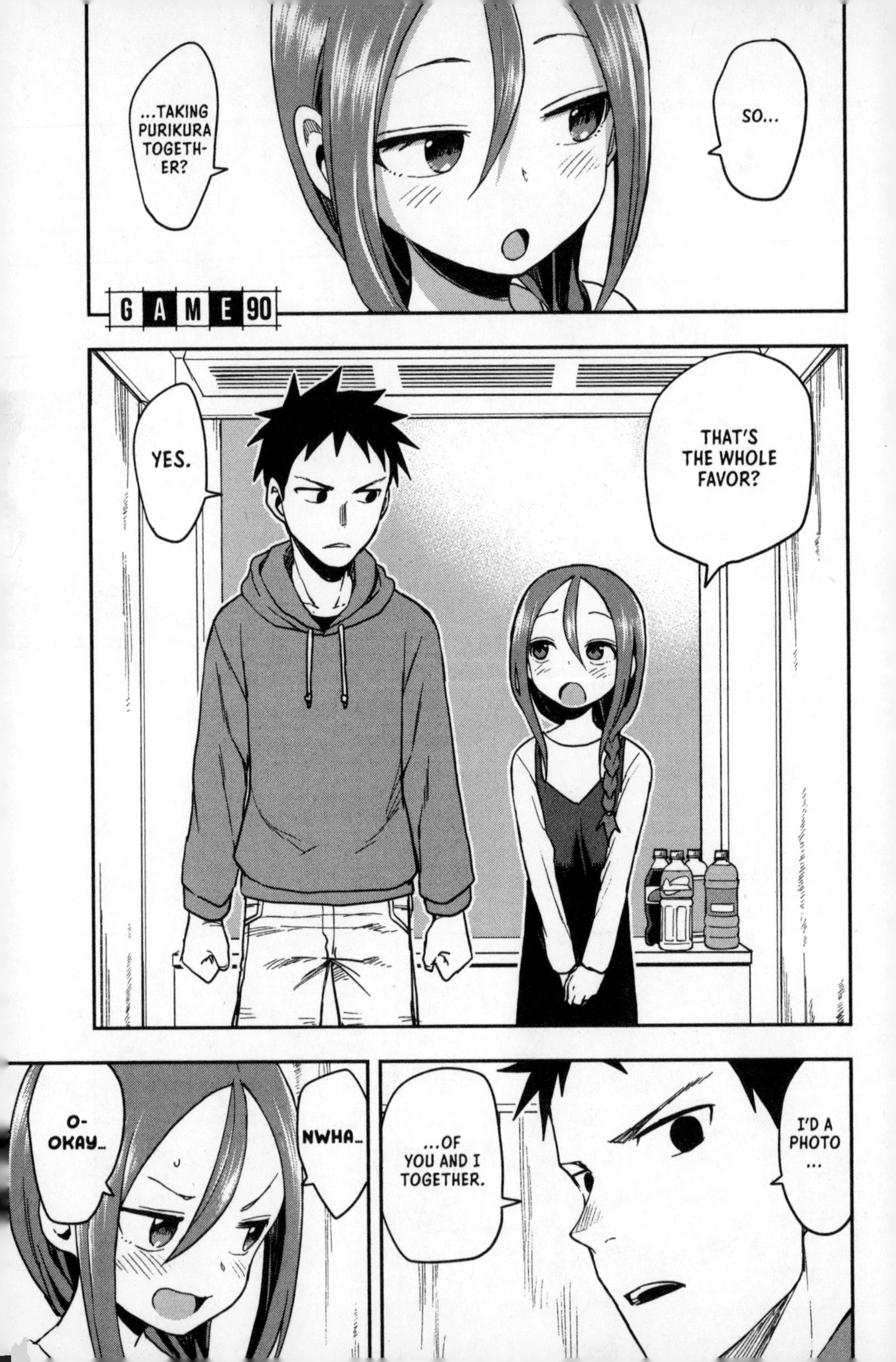
SO...
...TAKING PURIKURA TOGETH-ER?
GAME 90
THAT'S THE WHOLE FAVOR?
YES.
I'D A PHOTO ...
...OF YOU AND I TOGETHER.
NWHA...
O-OKAY...

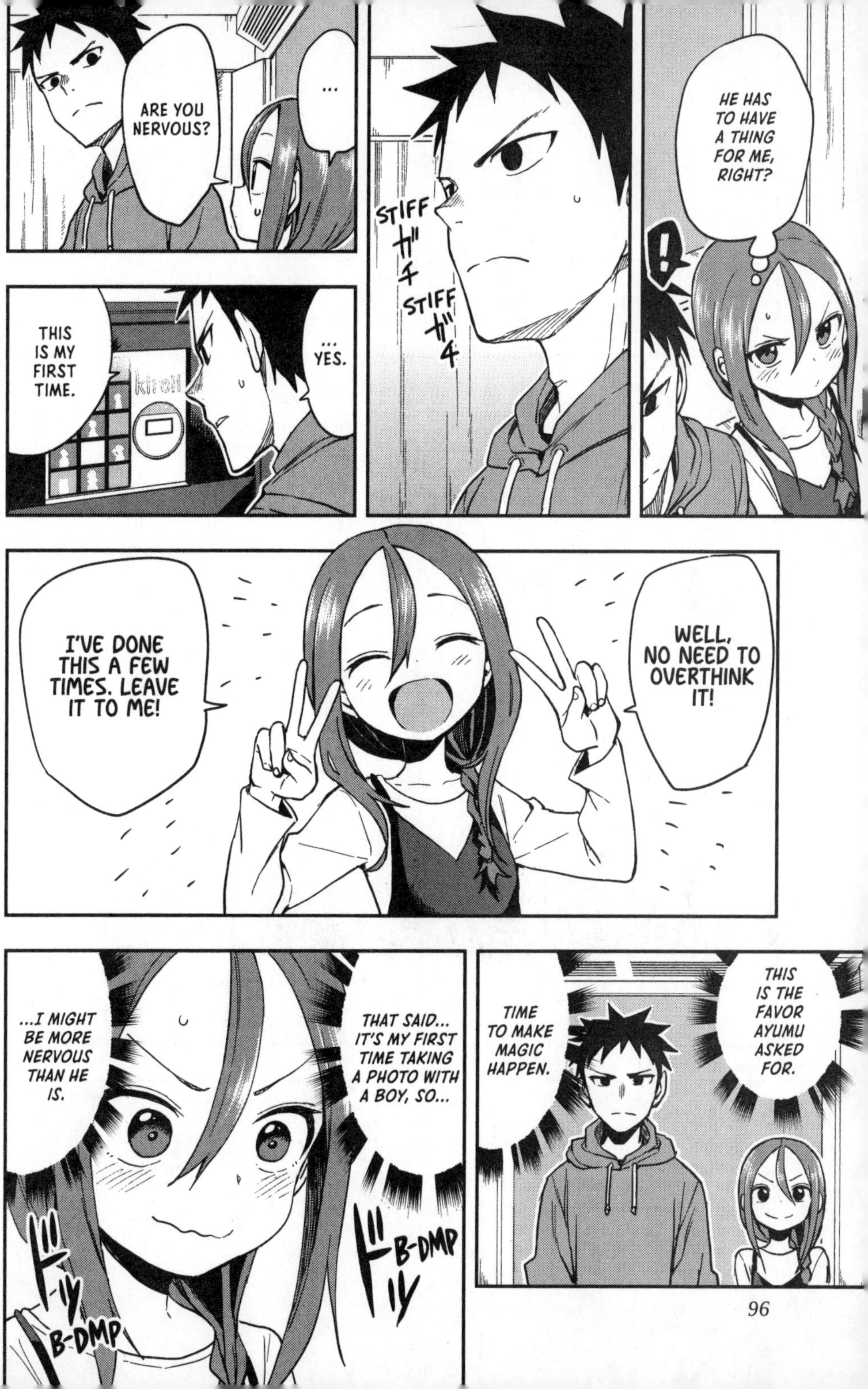

HE HAS TO HAVE A THING FOR ME, RIGHT?
!
STIFF
ガチ
STIFF
ガチ
...
ARE YOU NERVOUS?
... YES.
THIS IS MY FIRST TIME.
kireii
WELL, NO NEED TO OVERTHINK IT!
I'VE DONE THIS A FEW TIMES. LEAVE IT TO ME!
THIS IS THE FAVOR AYUMU ASKED FOR.
TIME TO MAKE MAGIC HAPPEN.
THAT SAID... IT'S MY FIRST TIME TAKING A PHOTO WITH A BOY, SO...
...I MIGHT BE MORE NERVOUS THAN HE IS.
ドリ
B-DMP
ドリ
B-DMP

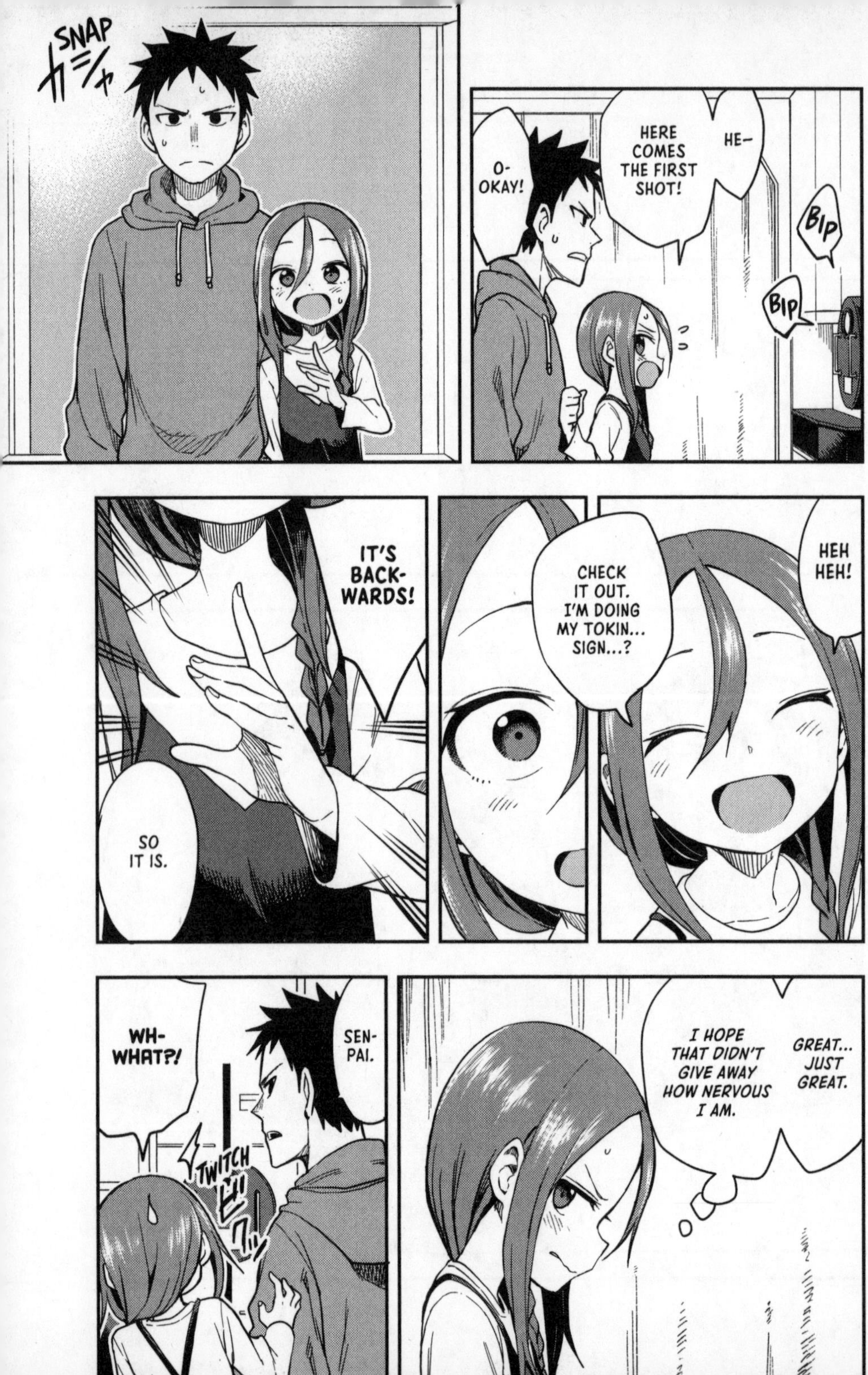
HE—
HERE COMES THE FIRST SHOT!
O-OKAY!
BIP
BIP
SNAP
カシャ
HEH HEH!
CHECK IT OUT. I'M DOING MY TOKIN... SIGN...?
IT'S BACKWARDS!
SO IT IS.
GREAT... JUST GREAT.
I HOPE THAT DIDN'T GIVE AWAY HOW NERVOUS I AM.
SEN-PAI.
WH-WHAT?!
TWITCH
ビクッ

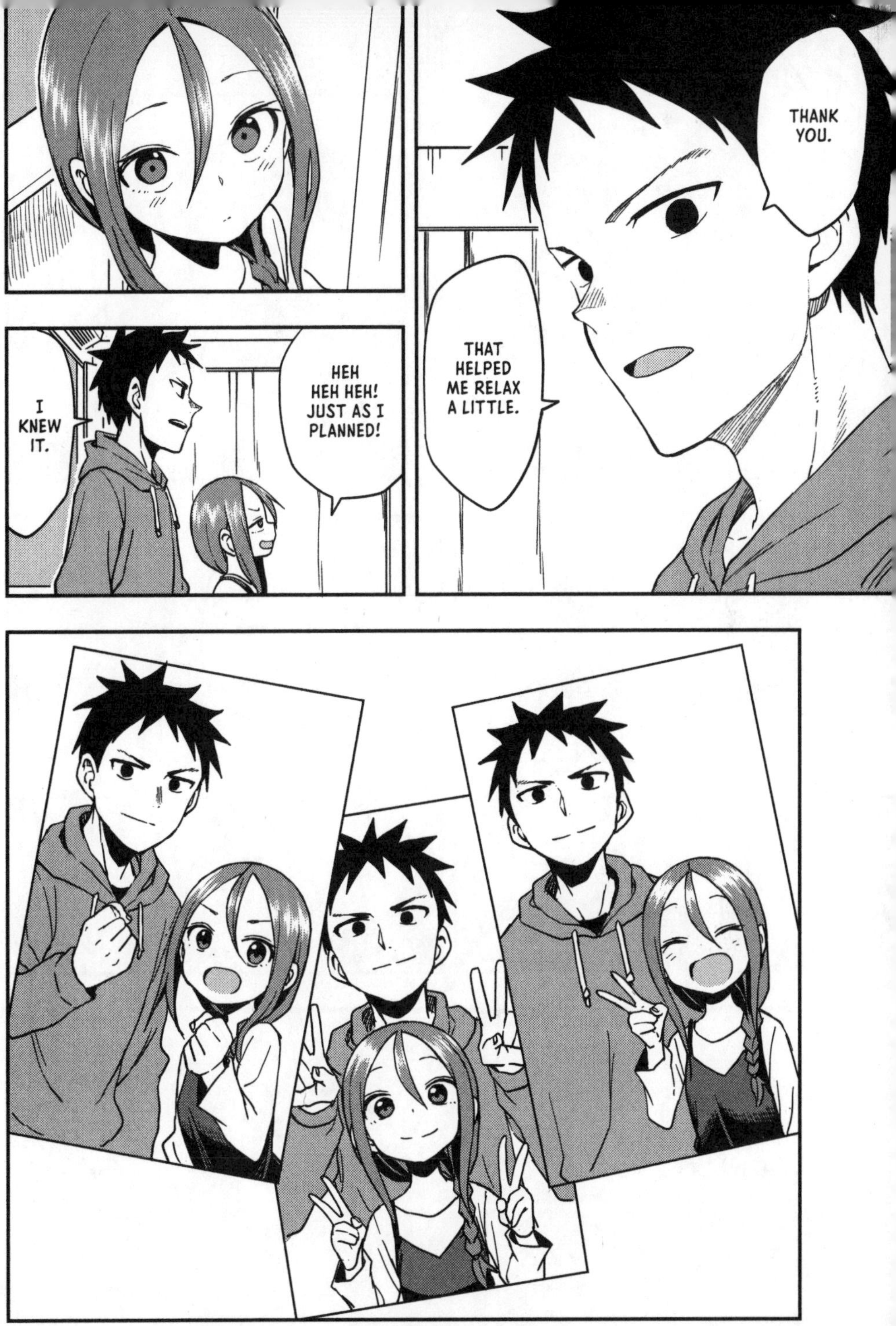
THANK YOU.
THAT HELPED ME RELAX A LITTLE.
HEH HEH HEH! JUST AS I PLANNED!
I KNEW IT.

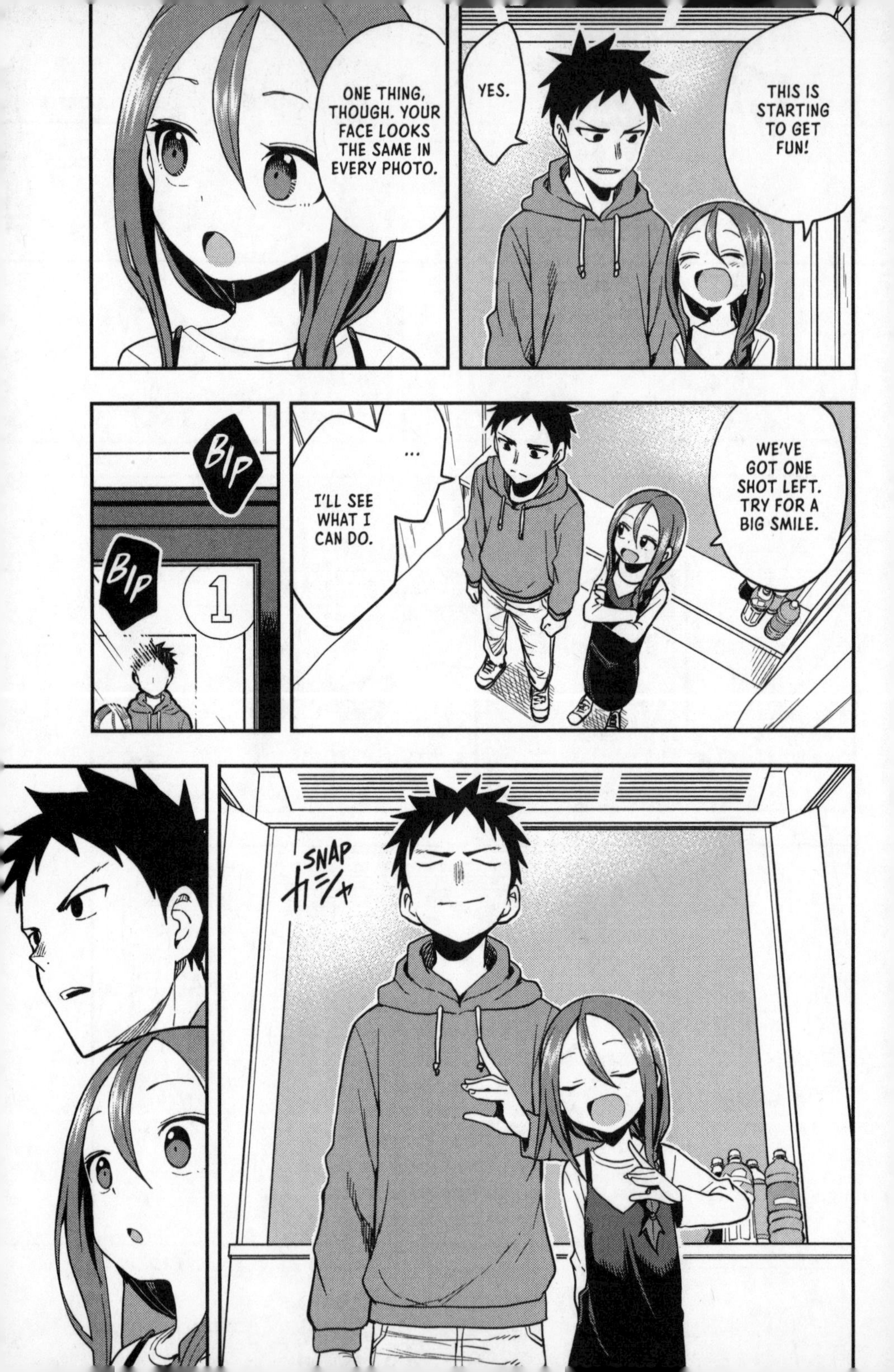
THIS IS STARTING TO GET FUN!
YES.
ONE THING, THOUGH. YOUR FACE LOOKS THE SAME IN EVERY PHOTO.
WE'VE GOT ONE SHOT LEFT. TRY FOR A BIG SMILE.
...
I'LL SEE WHAT I CAN DO.
BIP
BIP
1
SNAP
カシャ

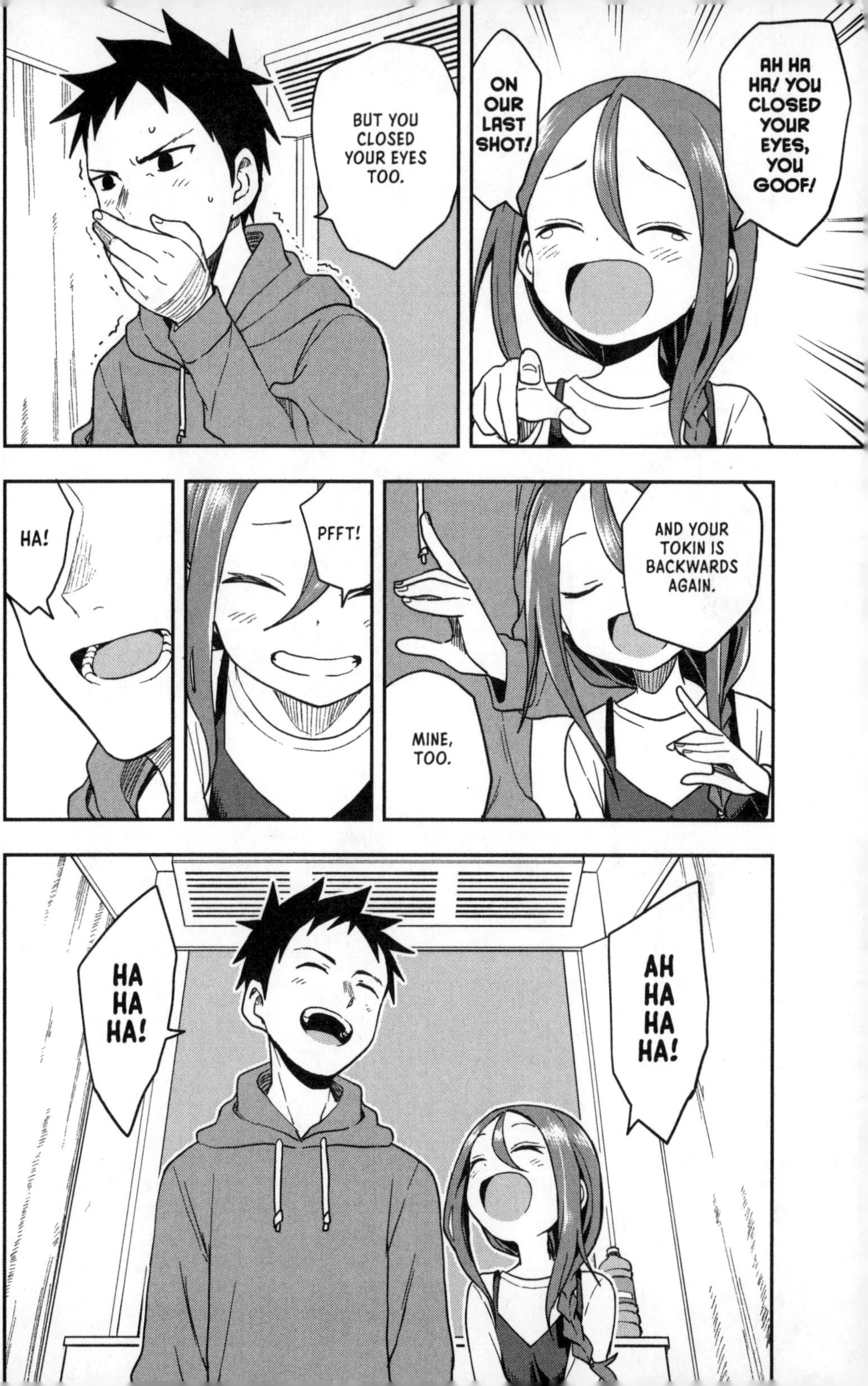
AH HA HA! YOU CLOSED YOUR EYES, YOU GOOF!
ON OUR LAST SHOT!
BUT YOU CLOSED YOUR EYES TOO.
AND YOUR TOKIN IS BACKWARDS AGAIN.
MINE, TOO.
PFFT!
HA!
AH HA HA HA!
HA HA HA!

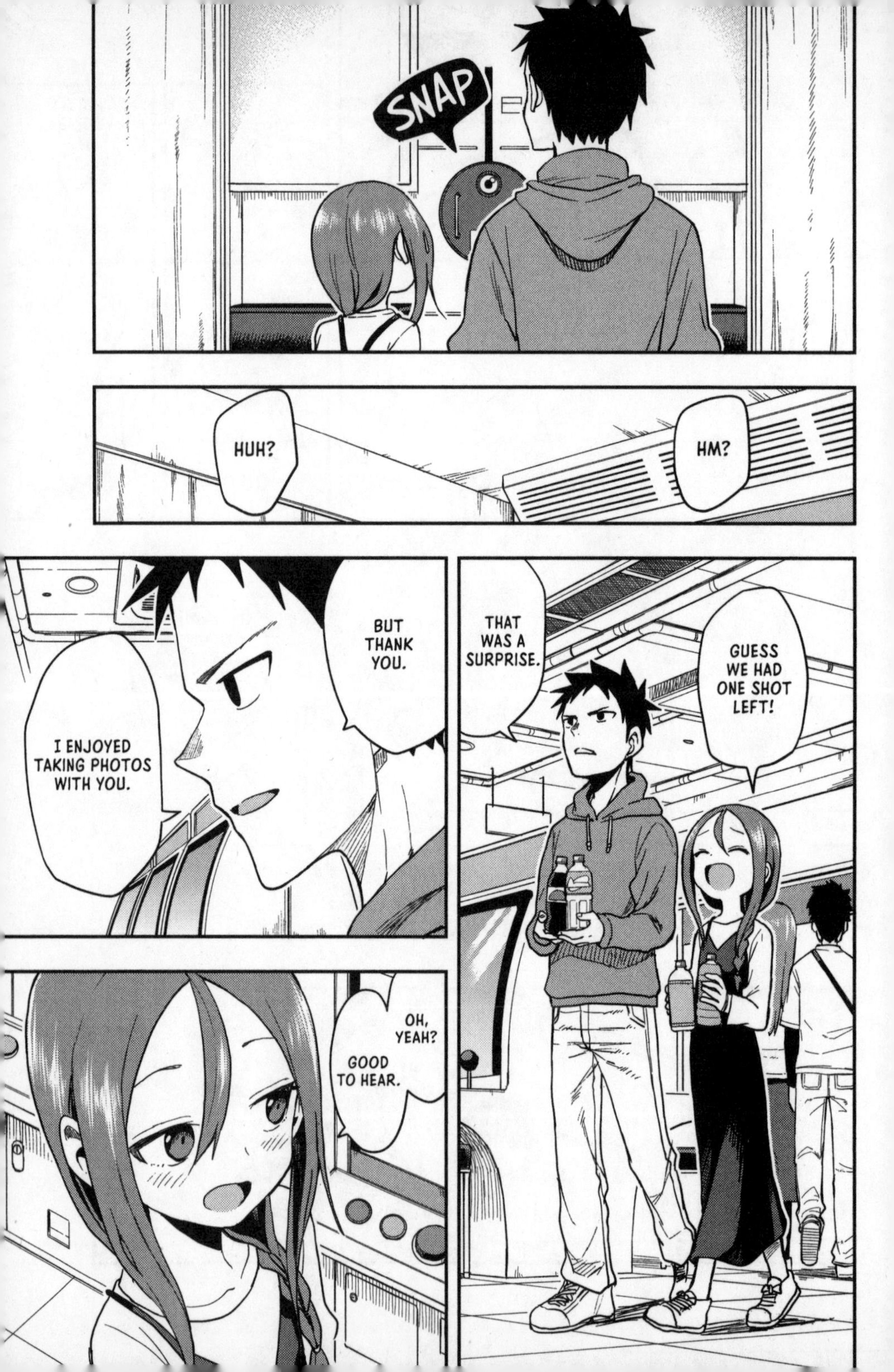
SNAP
HM?
HUH?
GUESS WE HAD ONE SHOT LEFT!
THAT WAS A SURPRISE.
BUT THANK YOU.
I ENJOYED TAKING PHOTOS WITH YOU.
OH, YEAH?
GOOD TO HEAR.

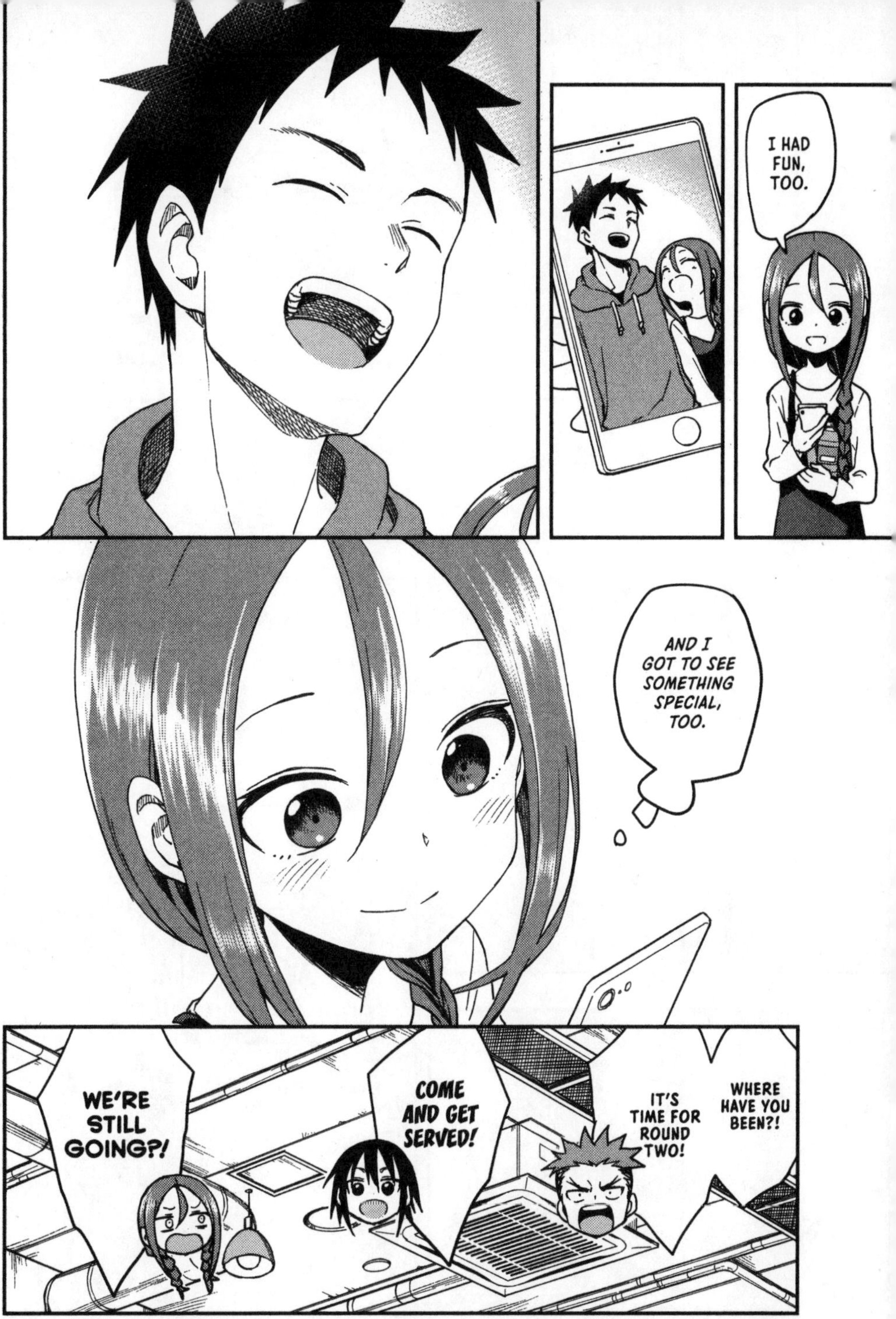
I HAD FUN, TOO.
AND I GOT TO SEE SOMETHING SPECIAL, TOO.
WHERE HAVE YOU BEEN?!
IT'S TIME FOR ROUND TWO!
COME AND GET SERVED!
WE'RE STILL GOING?!

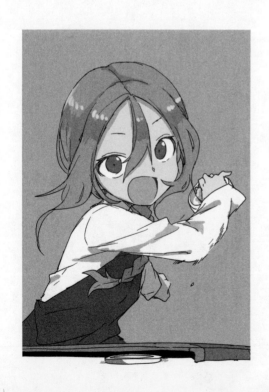

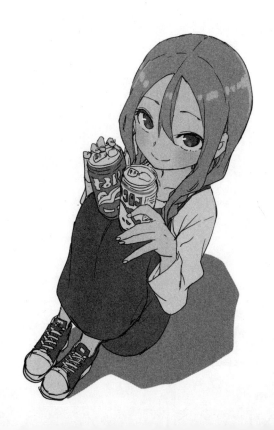

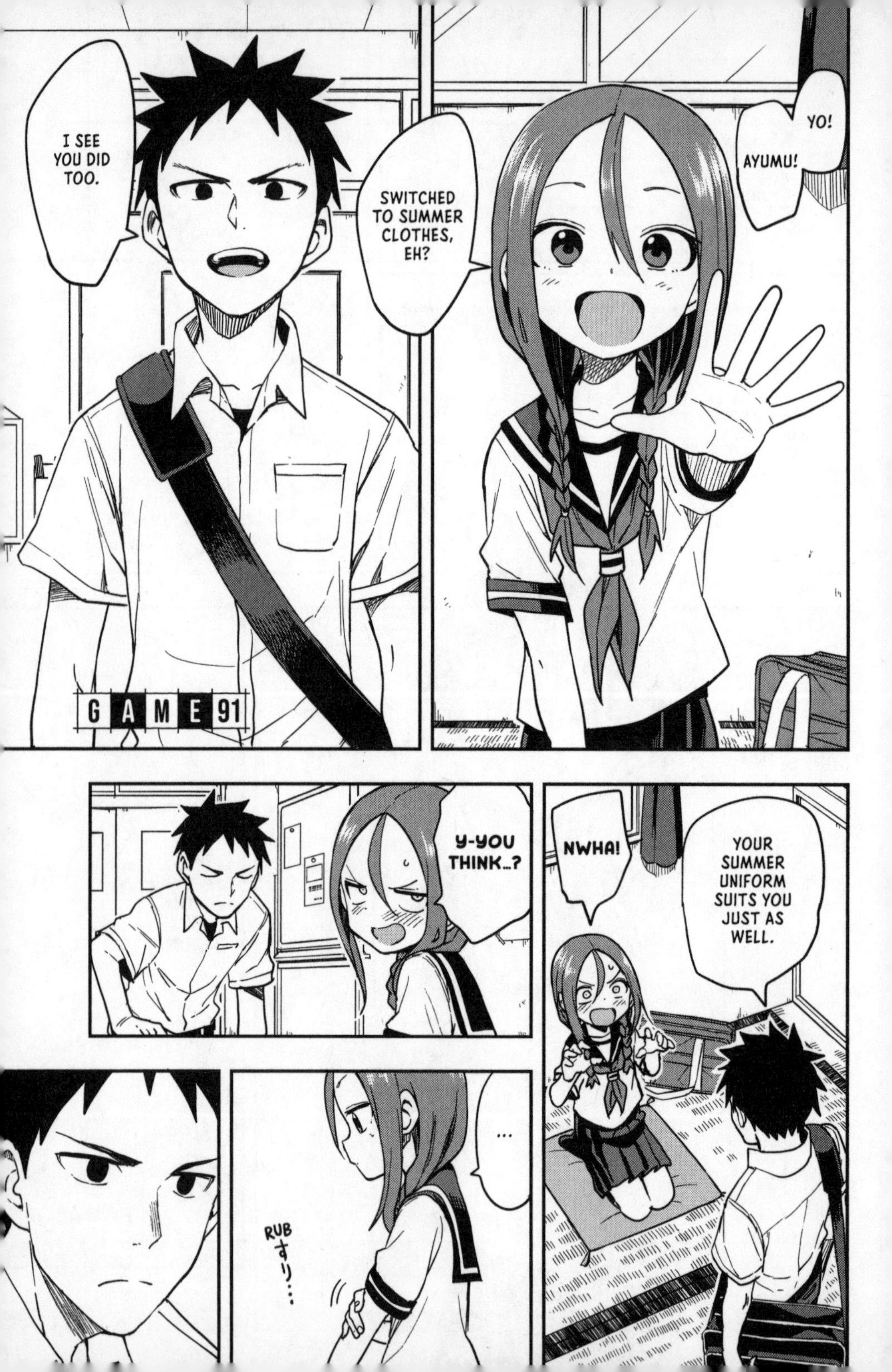
YO! AYUMU!
SWITCHED TO SUMMER CLOTHES, EH?
I SEE YOU DID TOO.
GAME 91
YOUR SUMMER UNIFORM SUITS YOU JUST AS WELL.
NWHA!
Y-YOU THINK..?
...
RUB すり…

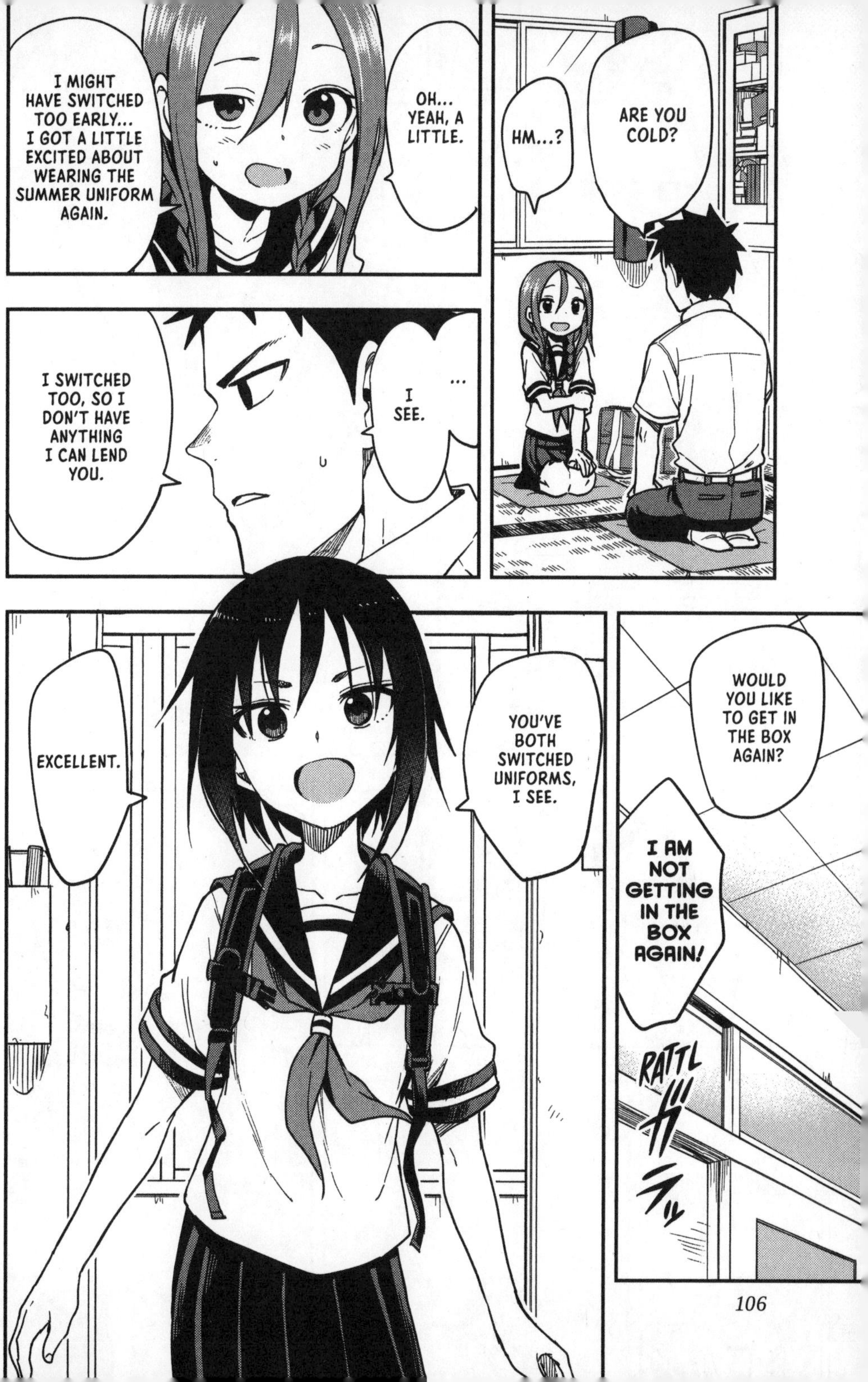
ARE YOU COLD?
HM...?
OH... YEAH, A LITTLE.
I MIGHT HAVE SWITCHED TOO EARLY... I GOT A LITTLE EXCITED ABOUT WEARING THE SUMMER UNIFORM AGAIN.
... I SEE.
I SWITCHED TOO, SO I DON'T HAVE ANYTHING I CAN LEND YOU.
WOULD YOU LIKE TO GET IN THE BOX AGAIN?
I AM NOT GETTING IN THE BOX AGAIN!
RATTL
YOU'VE BOTH SWITCHED UNIFORMS, I SEE.
EXCELLENT.

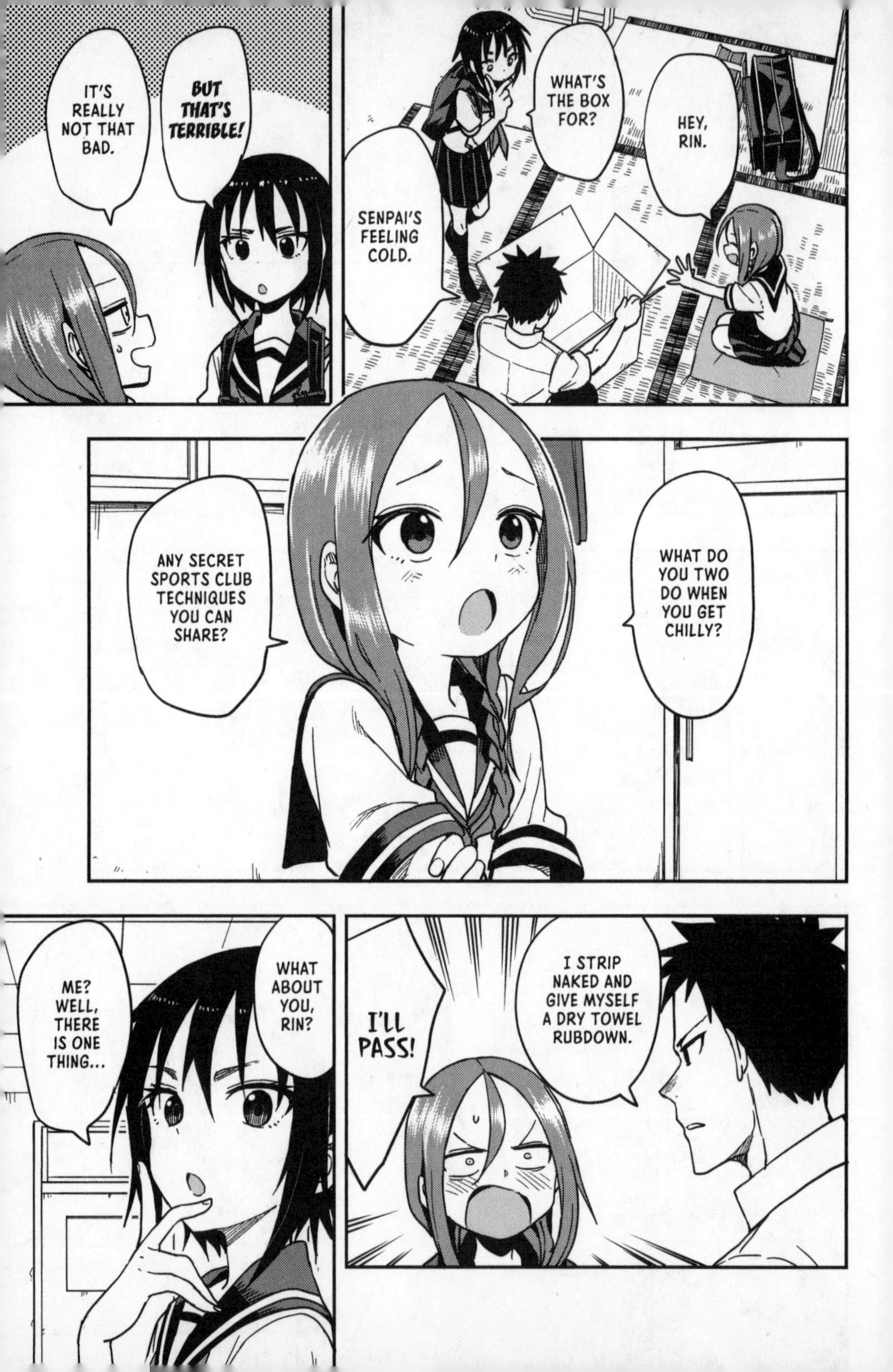
HEY, RIN.
WHAT'S THE BOX FOR?
SENPAI'S FEELING COLD.
BUT THAT'S TERRIBLE!
IT'S REALLY NOT THAT BAD.
WHAT DO YOU TWO DO WHEN YOU GET CHILLY?
ANY SECRET SPORTS CLUB TECHNIQUES YOU CAN SHARE?
I STRIP NAKED AND GIVE MYSELF A DRY TOWEL RUBDOWN.
I'LL PASS!
WHAT ABOUT YOU, RIN?
ME? WELL, THERE IS ONE THING...

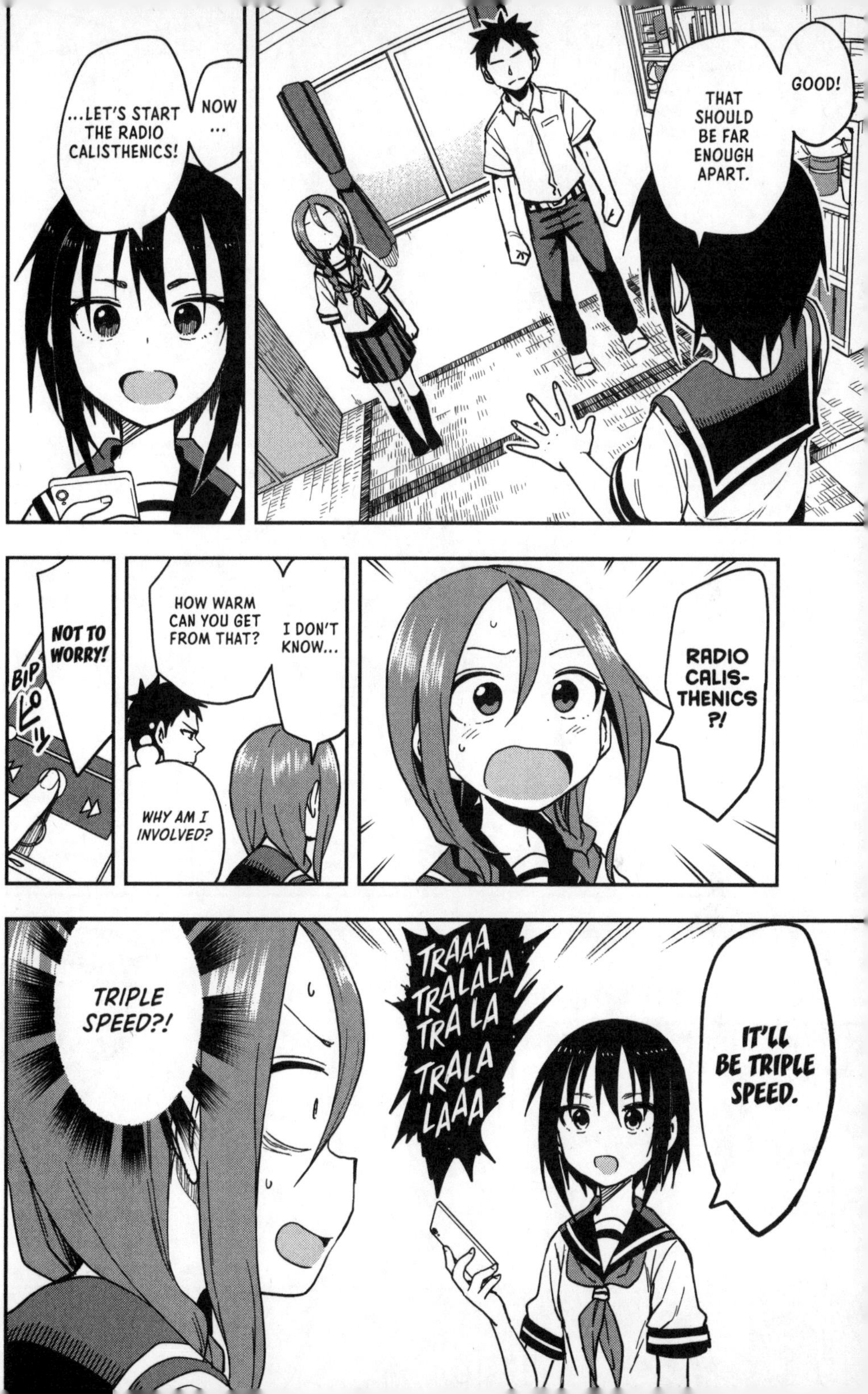
GOOD!
THAT SHOULD BE FAR ENOUGH APART.
NOW...
...LET'S START THE RADIO CALISTHENICS!
RADIO CALIS-THENICS?!
I DON'T KNOW...
HOW WARM CAN YOU GET FROM THAT?
WHY AM I INVOLVED?
NOT TO WORRY!
BIP
IT'LL BE TRIPLE SPEED.
TRAAA TRALALA TRA LA TRALA LAAA
TRIPLE SPEED?!

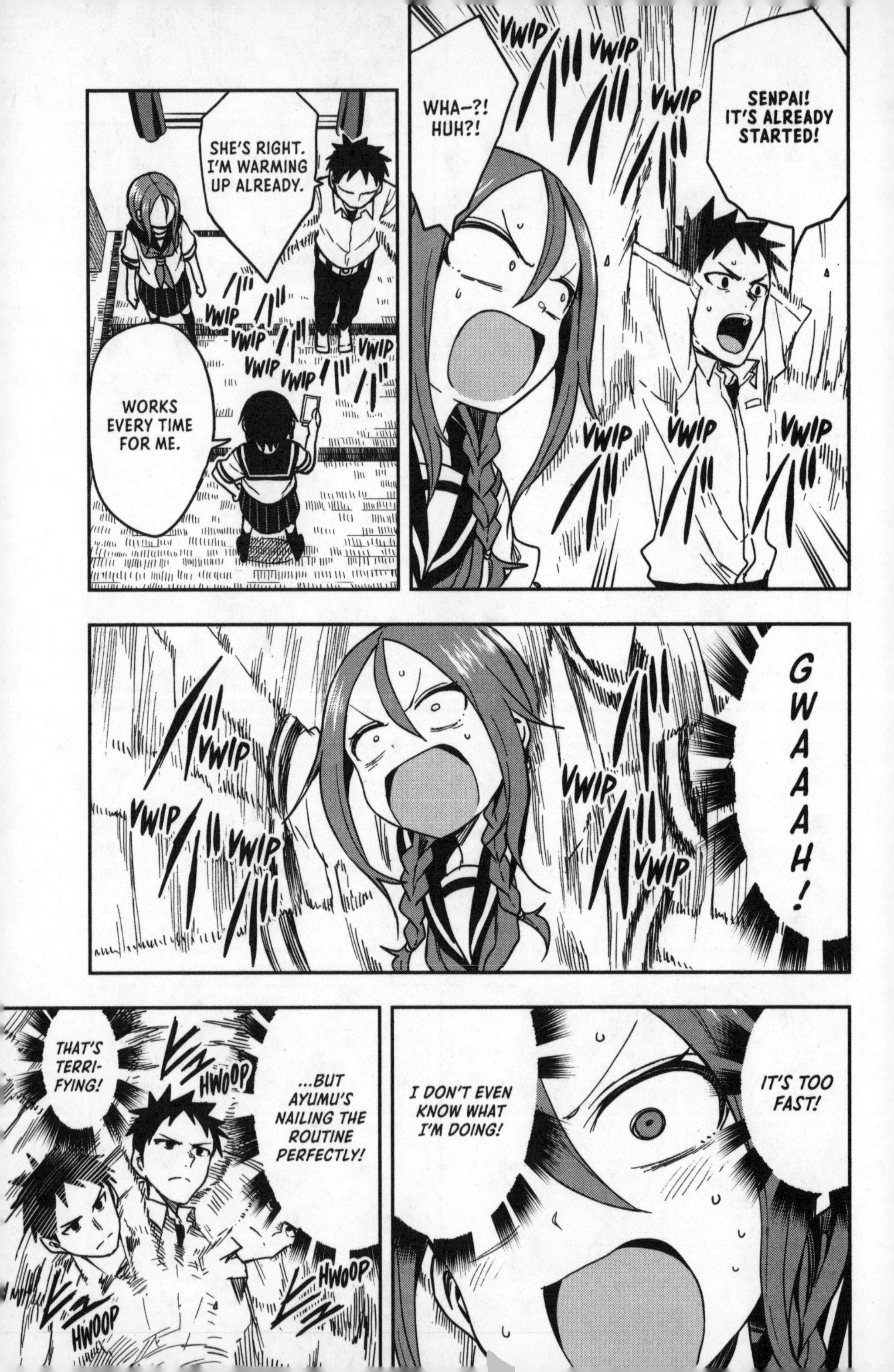
SENPAI! IT'S ALREADY STARTED!
VWIP
VWIP
VWIP
WHA–?! HUH?!
VWIP
VWIP
VWIP
SHE'S RIGHT. I'M WARMING UP ALREADY.
VWIP
VWIP
VWIP
VWIP
VWIP
WORKS EVERY TIME FOR ME.
GWAAAAH!
VWIP
VWIP
VWIP
VWIP
VWIP
IT'S TOO FAST!
I DON'T EVEN KNOW WHAT I'M DOING!
...BUT AYUMU'S NAILING THE ROUTINE PERFECTLY!
HWOOP
THAT'S TERRI-FYING!
HWOOP
HWOOP

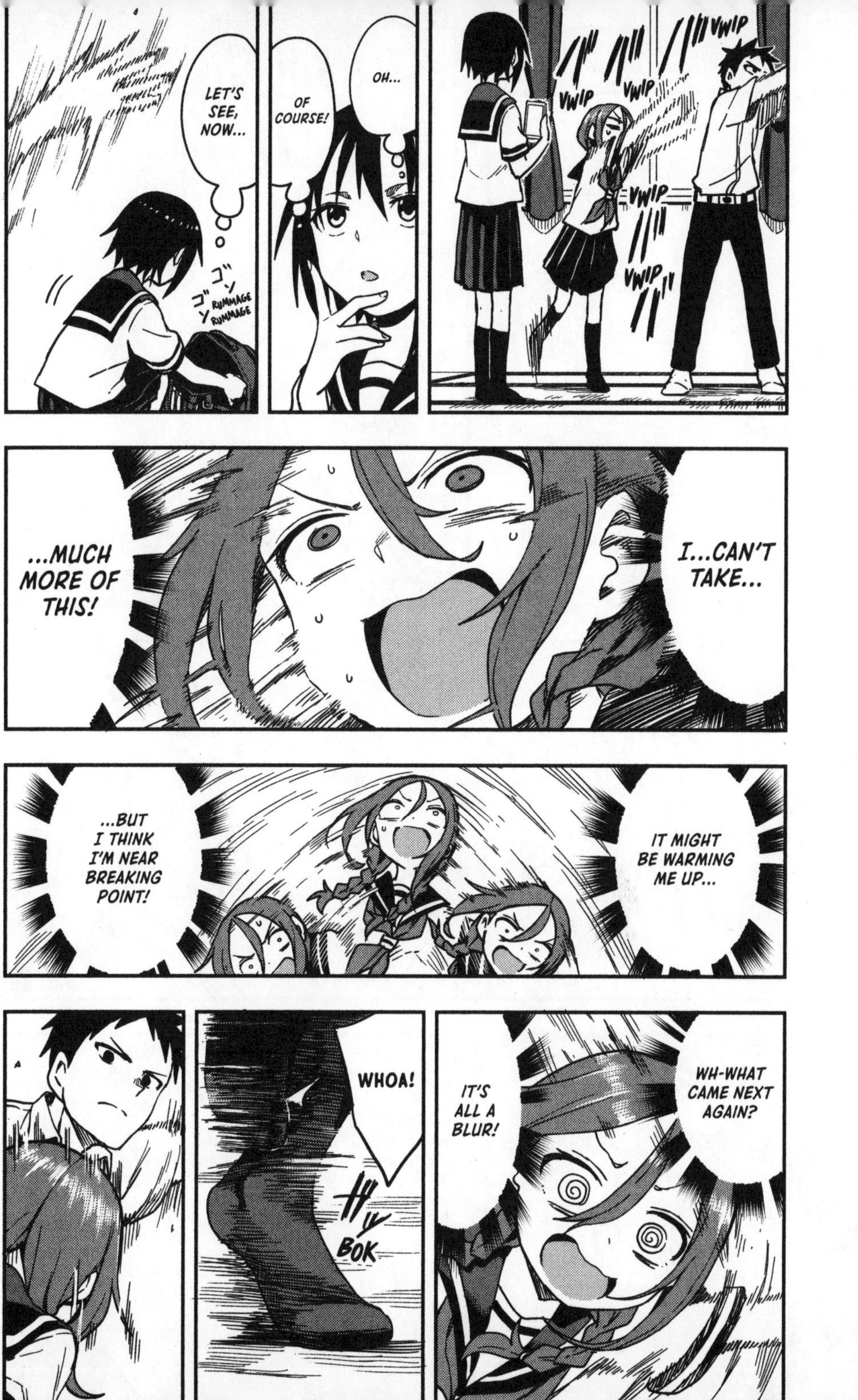
VWIP
VWIP
VWIP
VWIP
VWIP
OH...
OF COURSE!
LET'S SEE, NOW...
ゴソゴソ
RUMMAGE RUMMAGE
I...CAN'T TAKE...
...MUCH MORE OF THIS!
IT MIGHT BE WARMING ME UP...
...BUT I THINK I'M NEAR BREAKING POINT!
WH-WHAT CAME NEXT AGAIN?
IT'S ALL A BLUR!
WHOA!
BOK

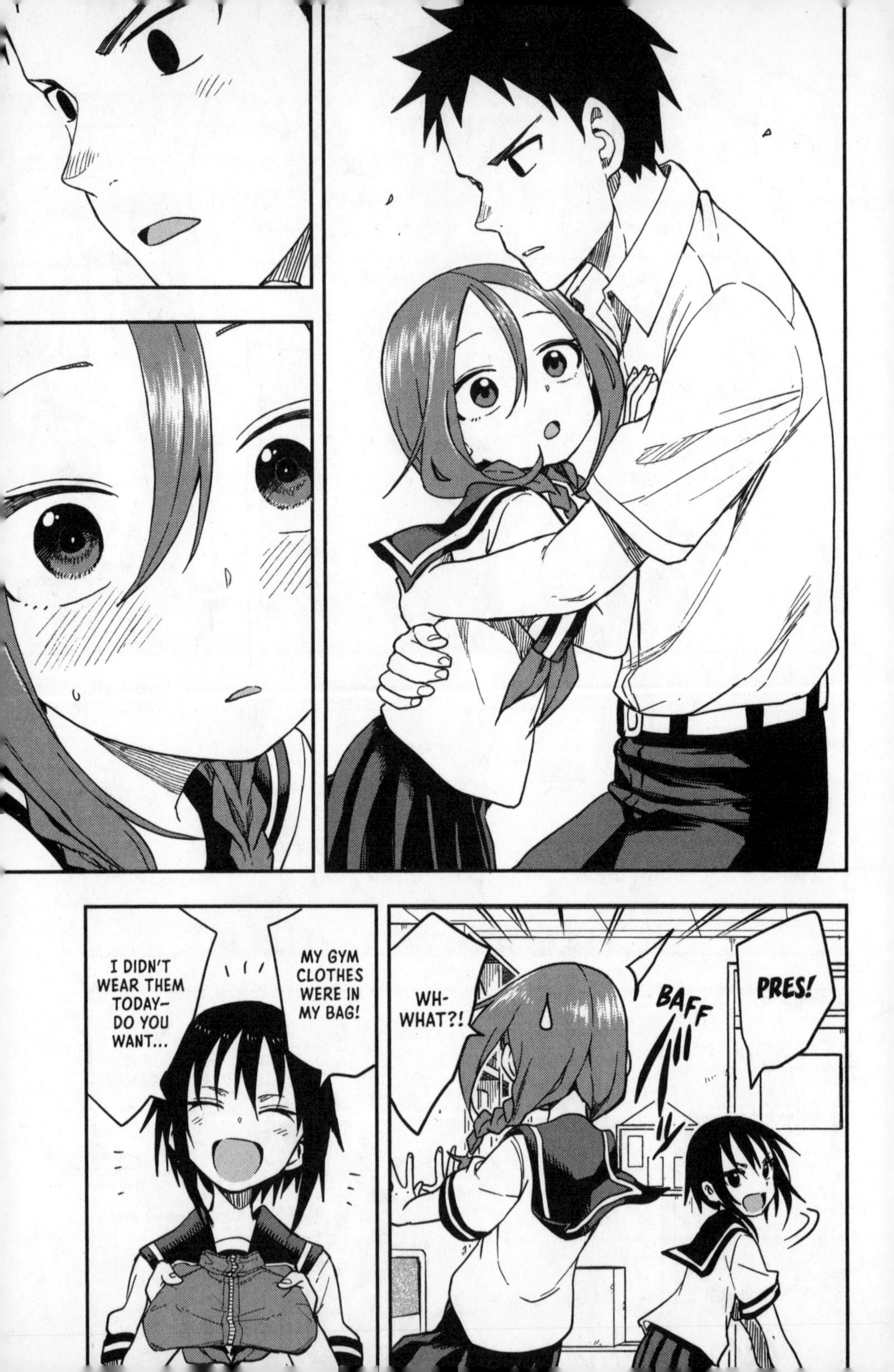
PRES!
BAFF
WH- WHAT?!
MY GYM CLOTHES WERE IN MY BAG!
I DIDN'T WEAR THEM TODAY— DO YOU WANT...

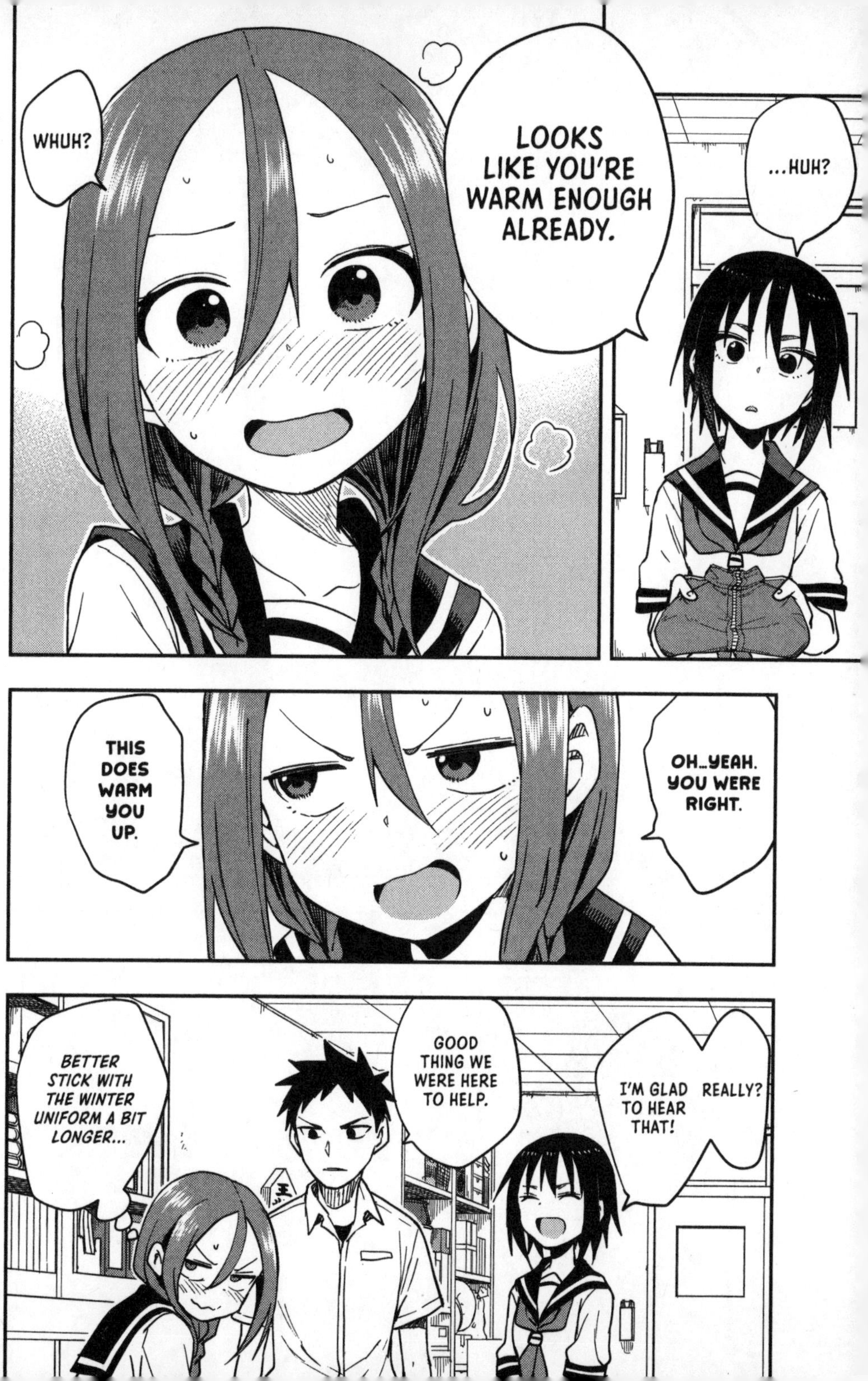
...HUH?
LOOKS LIKE YOU'RE WARM ENOUGH ALREADY.
WHUH?
OH...YEAH. YOU WERE RIGHT.
THIS DOES WARM YOU UP.
REALLY? I'M GLAD TO HEAR THAT!
GOOD THING WE WERE HERE TO HELP.
BETTER STICK WITH THE WINTER UNIFORM A BIT LONGER...

Brr...

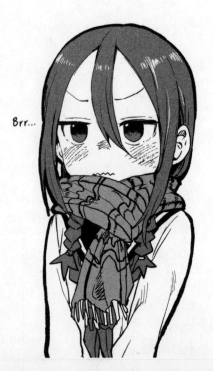

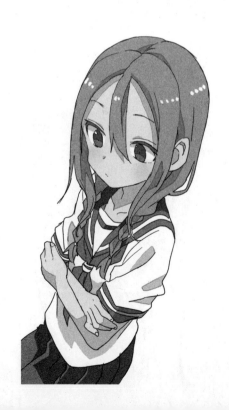

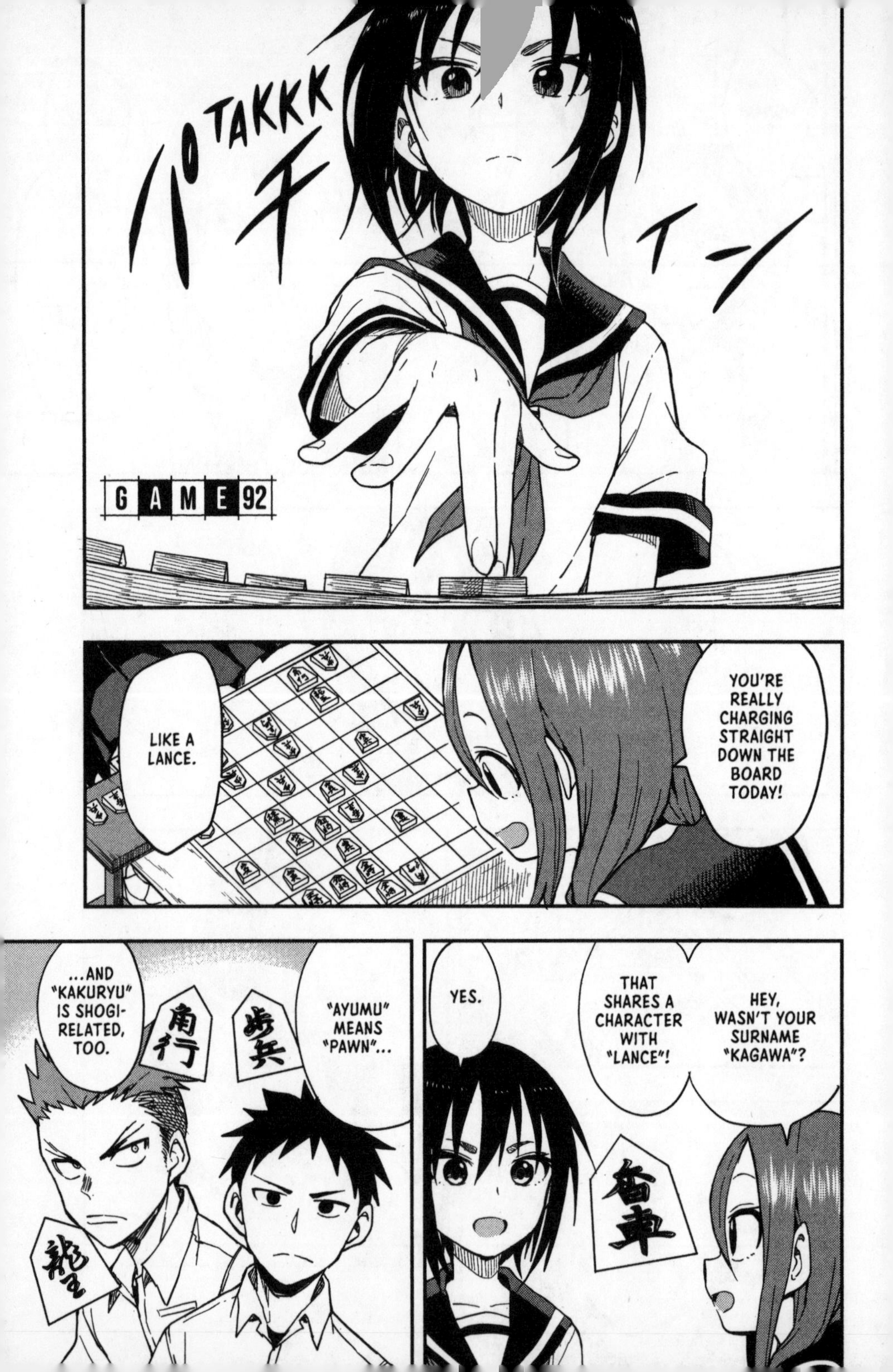
TAKKK
GAME 92
YOU'RE REALLY CHARGING STRAIGHT DOWN THE BOARD TODAY!
LIKE A LANCE.
HEY, WASN'T YOUR SURNAME "KAGAWA"?
THAT SHARES A CHARACTER WITH "LANCE"!
香車
YES.
"AYUMU" MEANS "PAWN"...
歩兵
...AND "KAKURYU" IS SHOGI-RELATED, TOO.
角行

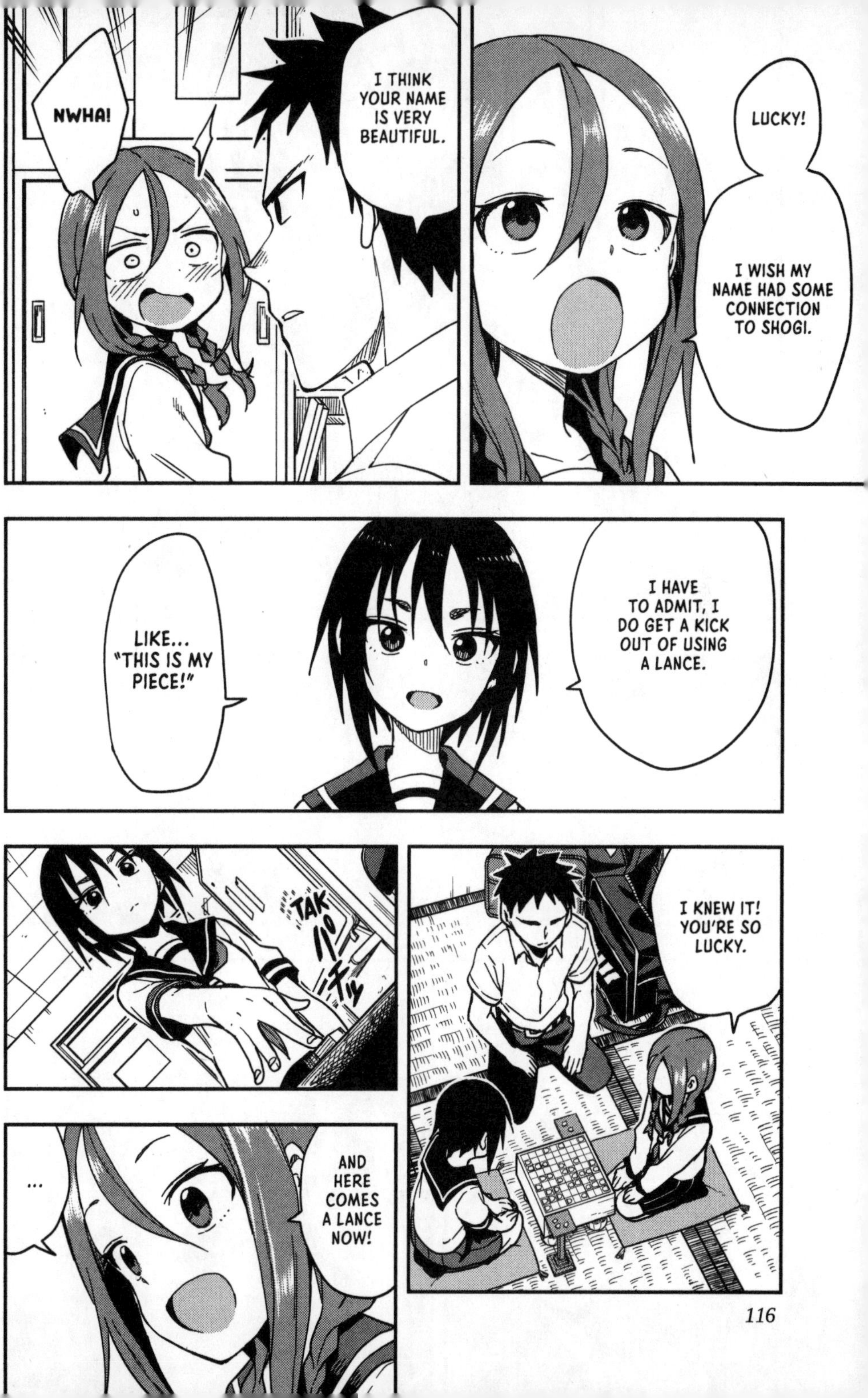
LUCKY!
I WISH MY NAME HAD SOME CONNECTION TO SHOGI.
I THINK YOUR NAME IS VERY BEAUTIFUL.
NWHA!
I HAVE TO ADMIT, I DO GET A KICK OUT OF USING A LANCE.
LIKE... "THIS IS MY PIECE!"
I KNEW IT! YOU'RE SO LUCKY.
TAK
パチッ
AND HERE COMES A LANCE NOW!
...

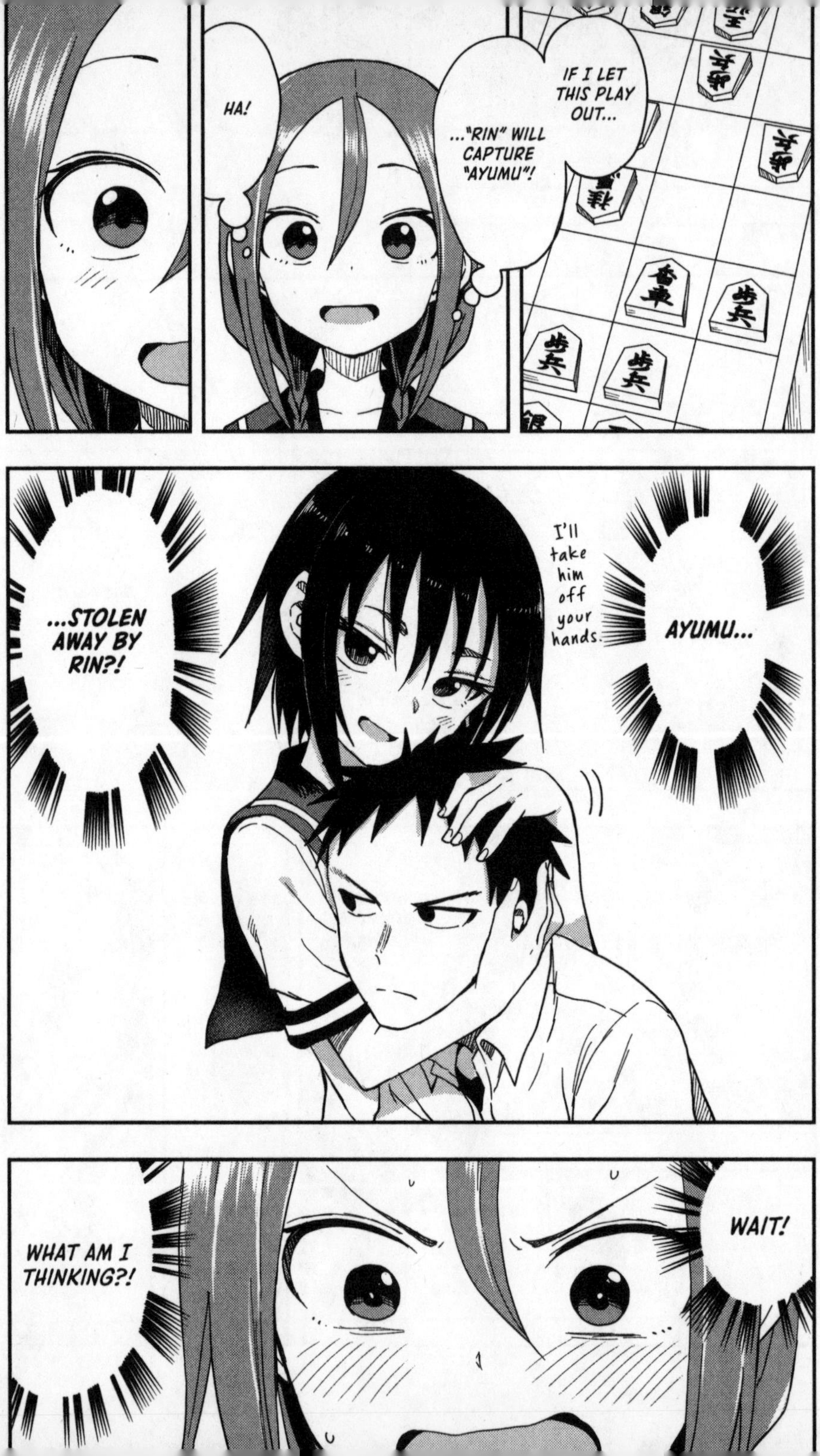
IF I LET THIS PLAY OUT...
..."RIN" WILL CAPTURE "AYUMU"!
HA!
AYUMU...
I'll take him off your hands.
...STOLEN AWAY BY RIN?!
WAIT!
WHAT AM I THINKING?!

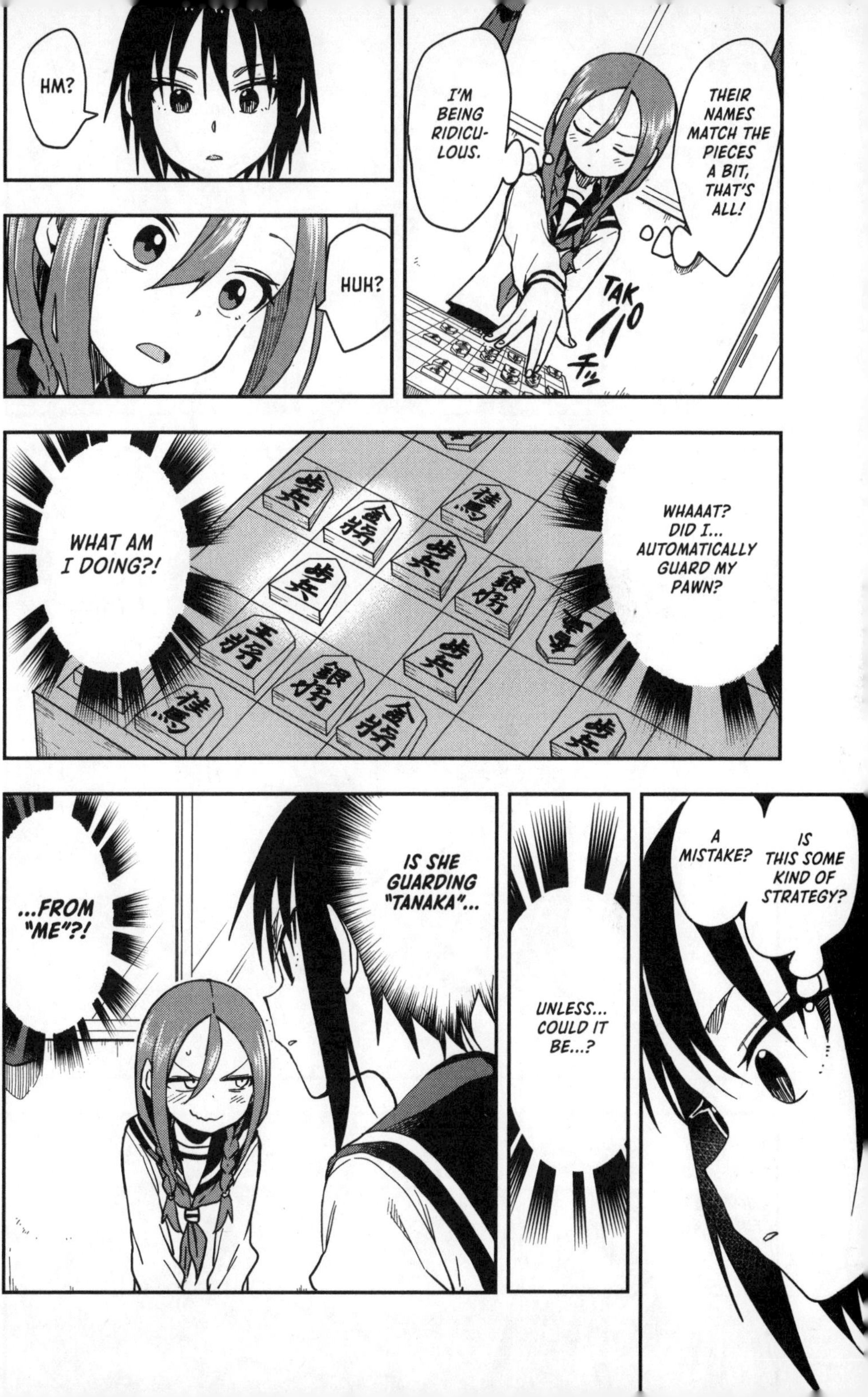
THEIR NAMES MATCH THE PIECES A BIT, THAT'S ALL!
I'M BEING RIDICULOUS.
TAK
チッ
HM?
HUH?
WHAAAT? DID I... AUTOMATICALLY GUARD MY PAWN?
WHAT AM I DOING?!
IS THIS SOME KIND OF STRATEGY?
A MISTAKE?
UNLESS... COULD IT BE...?
IS SHE GUARDING "TANAKA"...
...FROM "ME"?!

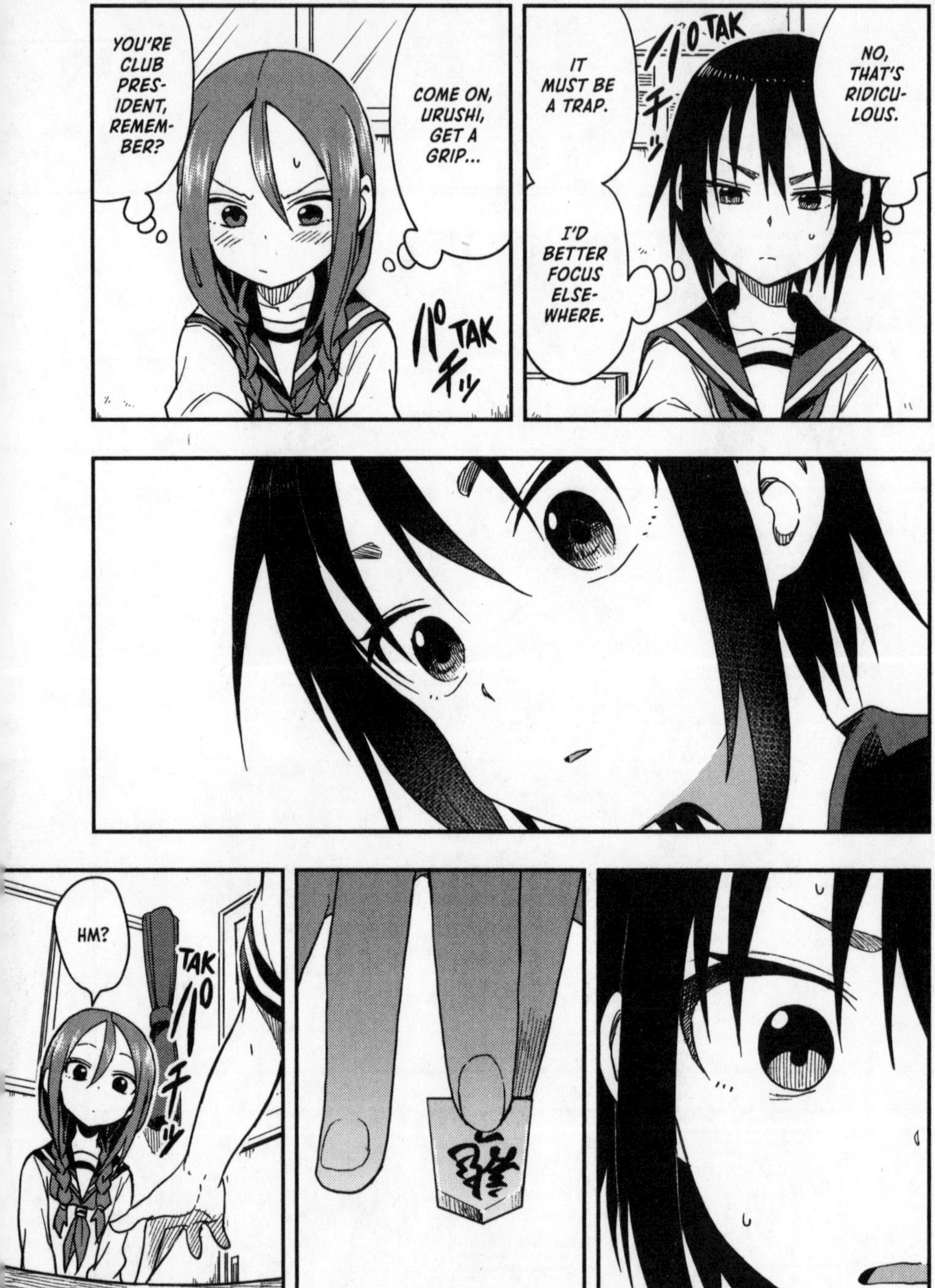
NO, THAT'S RIDICULOUS.
IT MUST BE A TRAP.
パチッ TAK
I'D BETTER FOCUS ELSEWHERE.
COME ON, URUSHI, GET A GRIP...
YOU'RE CLUB PRESIDENT, REMEMBER?
パチッ TAK
HM?
TAK パチッ

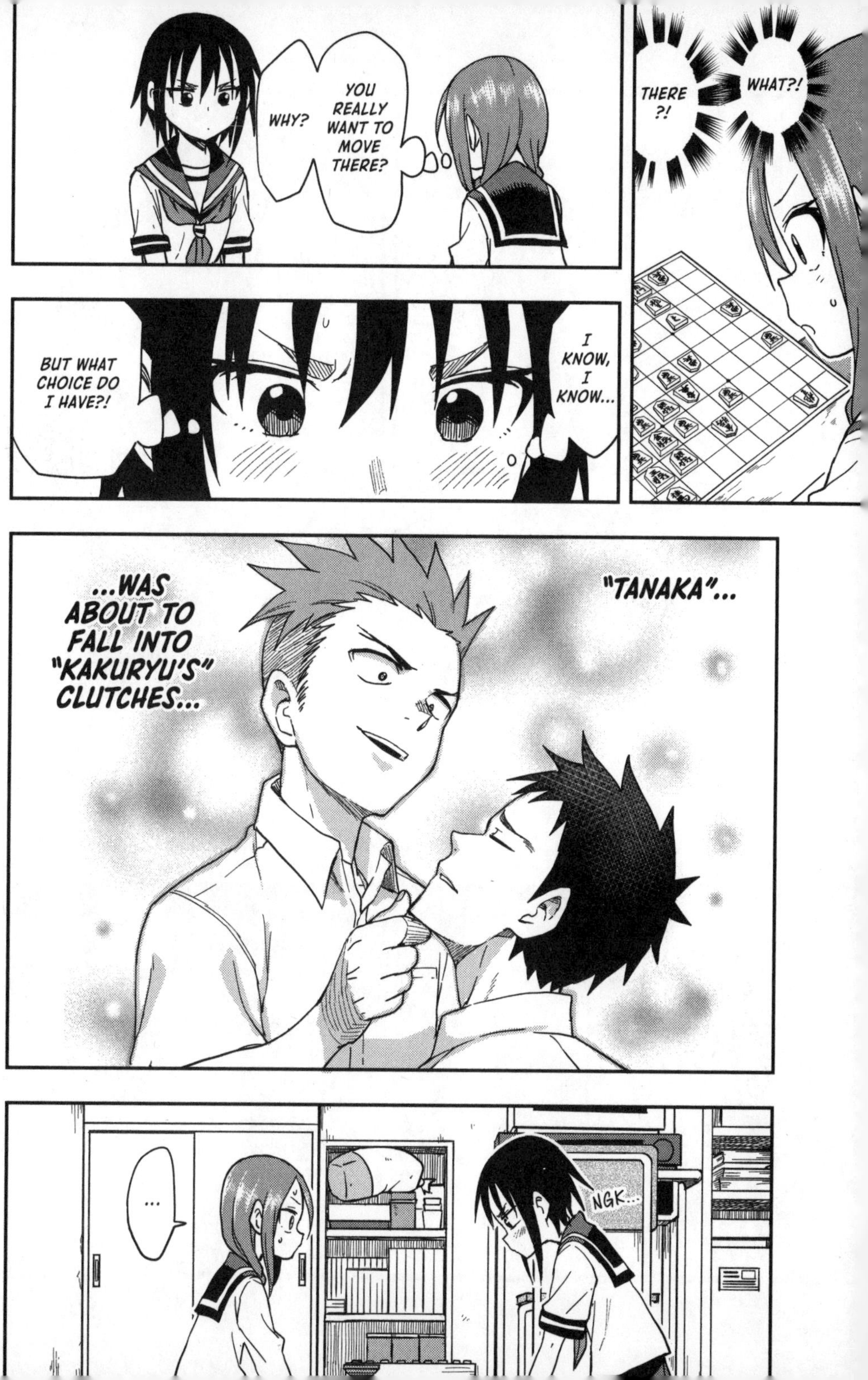
WHAT?!
THERE ?!
WHY? YOU REALLY WANT TO MOVE THERE?
I KNOW, I KNOW...
BUT WHAT CHOICE DO I HAVE?!
"TANAKA"...
...WAS ABOUT TO FALL INTO "KAKURYU'S" CLUTCHES...
NGK...
...

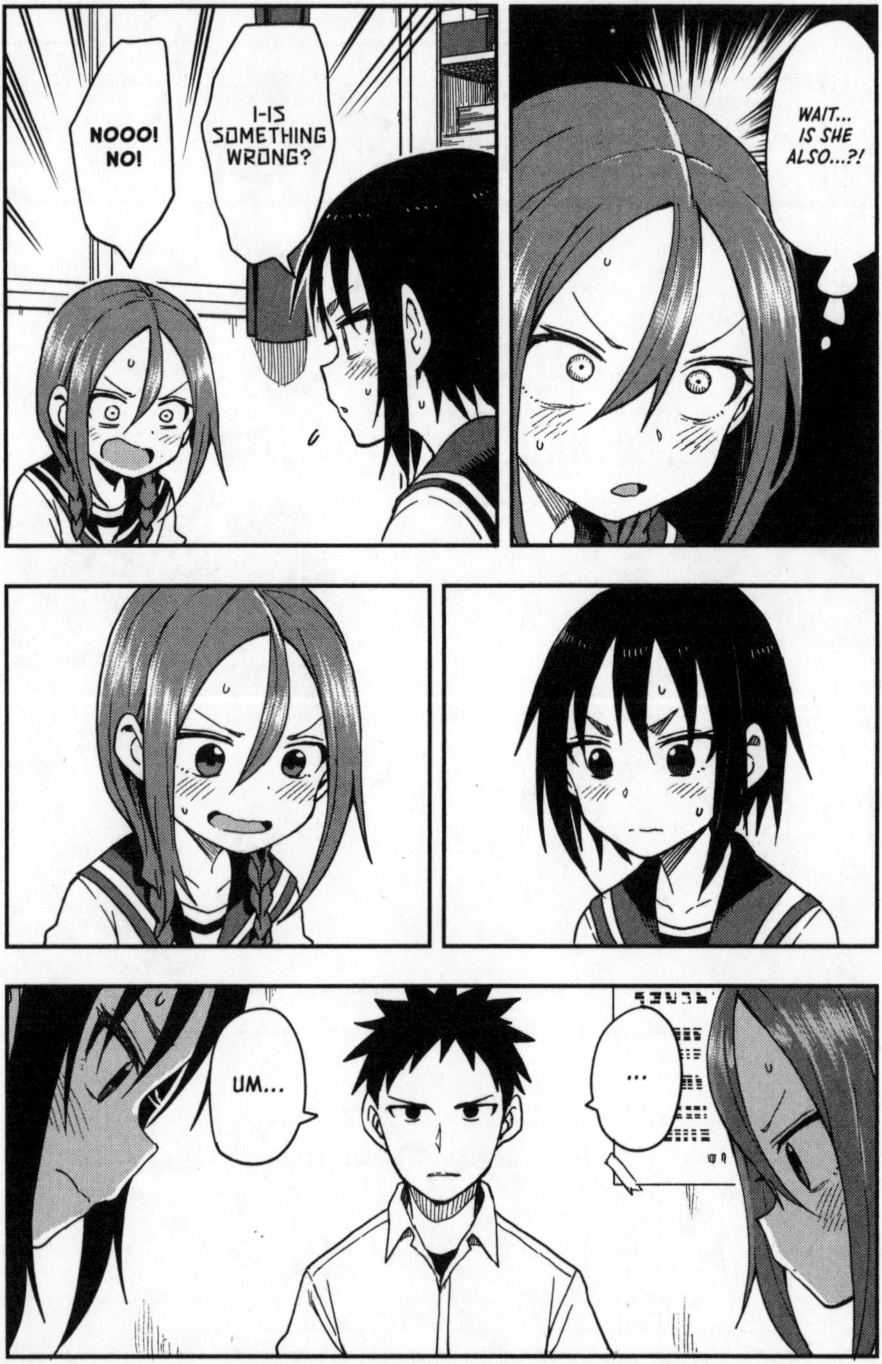
WAIT... IS SHE ALSO...?!
I-IS SOMETHING WRONG?
NOOO! NO!
...
UM...

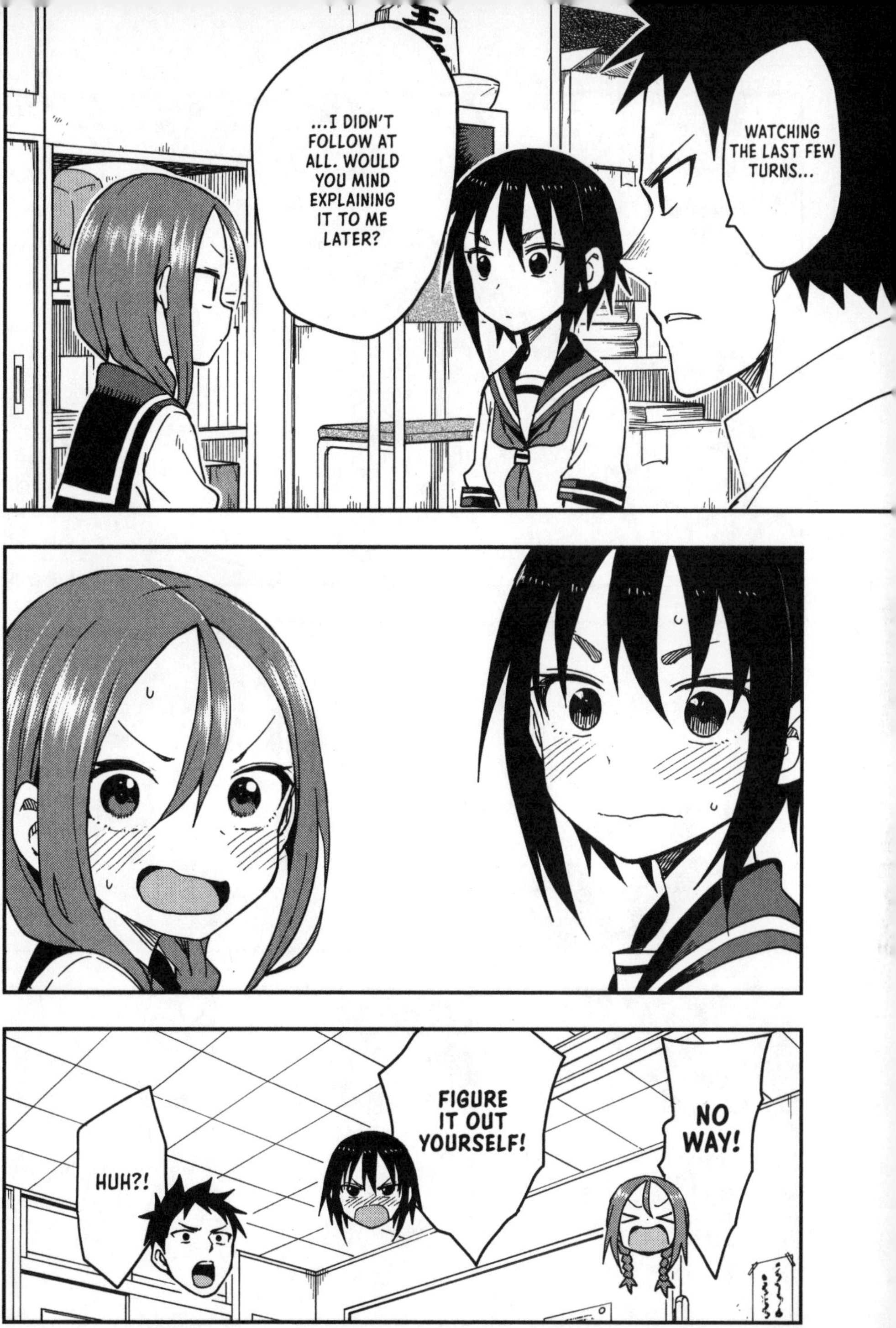
WATCHING THE LAST FEW TURNS...
...I DIDN'T FOLLOW AT ALL. WOULD YOU MIND EXPLAINING IT TO ME LATER?
NO WAY!
FIGURE IT OUT YOURSELF!
HUH?!

GAME 92 RECORD

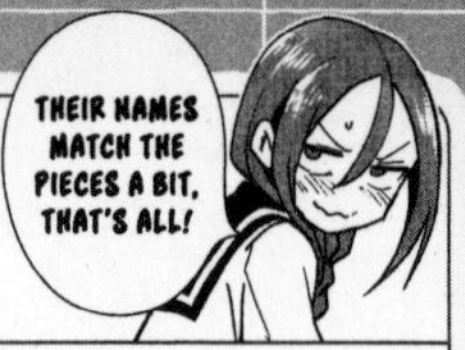

THEIR NAMES MATCH THE PIECES A BIT, THAT'S ALL!

▲ BLACK (SENTE): RIN KAGAWA △ WHITE (GOTE): YAOTOME URUSHI

(DIAGRAM SHOWS BOARD AFTER MOVE 98, △ +B×3I)

◁URUSHI: G, P×3

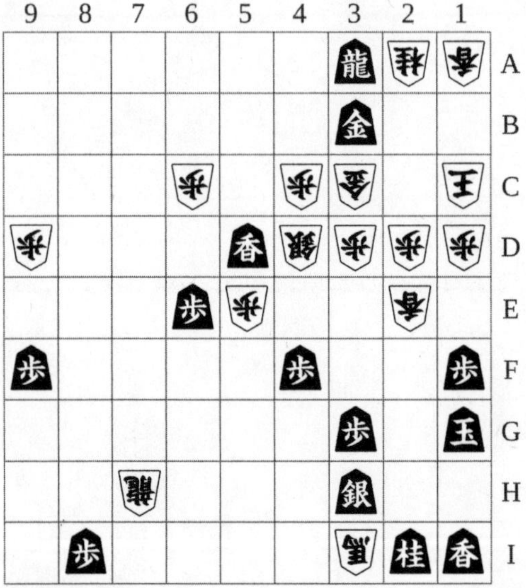

9
8
7
6
5
4
3
2
1
A
B
C
D
E
F
G
H
I

▲RIN: B, G, S×2, N×2, P×2

▲ R-7H	△ P-8D	▲ B-6H	△ B-4B	▲ B×5A	△ P-7G+
▲ P-7F	△ P-8E	▲ R-8H	△ P-7E	▲ L×2F	△ G×2D
▲ B-7G	△ P-3D	▲ P×7E	△ B×7E	▲ B×4B+	△ G×4B
▲ P-6F	△ S-6B	▲ R-7H	△ P×7D	▲ G×5B	△ G-3C
▲ K-4H	△ K-4B	▲ G-6G	△ P-8F	▲ +R-8A	△ +P-6H
▲ K-3H	△ K-3B	▲ P×8F	△ B×8F	▲ G-4H	△ +P-5I
▲ K-2H	△ G6A-5B	▲ R×7D	△ B×6H+	▲ L×2D	△ P×2D
▲ S-3H	△ P-5D	▲ G×6H	△ R×8I+	▲ G-4B	△ +P×4I
▲ P-1F	△ P-1D	▲ R-7A+	△ +R×9I	▲ G×4I	△ B×5G+
▲ S-6H	△ P-7D	▲ +R×8A	△ N×3E	▲ +R-3A	△ K-1C
▲ S-6G	△ B-3C	▲ S-5H	△ L×4G	▲ G×3B	△ N×2G+
▲ G6I-5H	△ S-5C	▲ P×8I	△ L×4I+	▲ K×2G	△ S×2F
▲ S-5F	△ S-4D	▲ S5H×4I	△ +R-9H	▲ K×2F	△ L×2E
▲ P-4F	△ P-5E	▲ P×7H	△ B×7I	▲ K-1G	△ B×3I
▲ S5F-4G	△ K-2B	▲ G-5H	△ +R×7H	▲ G×3I	△ +B×3I
▲ P-6E	△ P-9D	▲ +R×9A	△ P×7F		
▲ P-9F	△ S-3B	▲ L×5D	△ G5B-4B		

(RIN WINS AT MOVE 98)

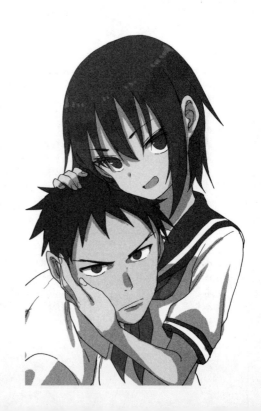

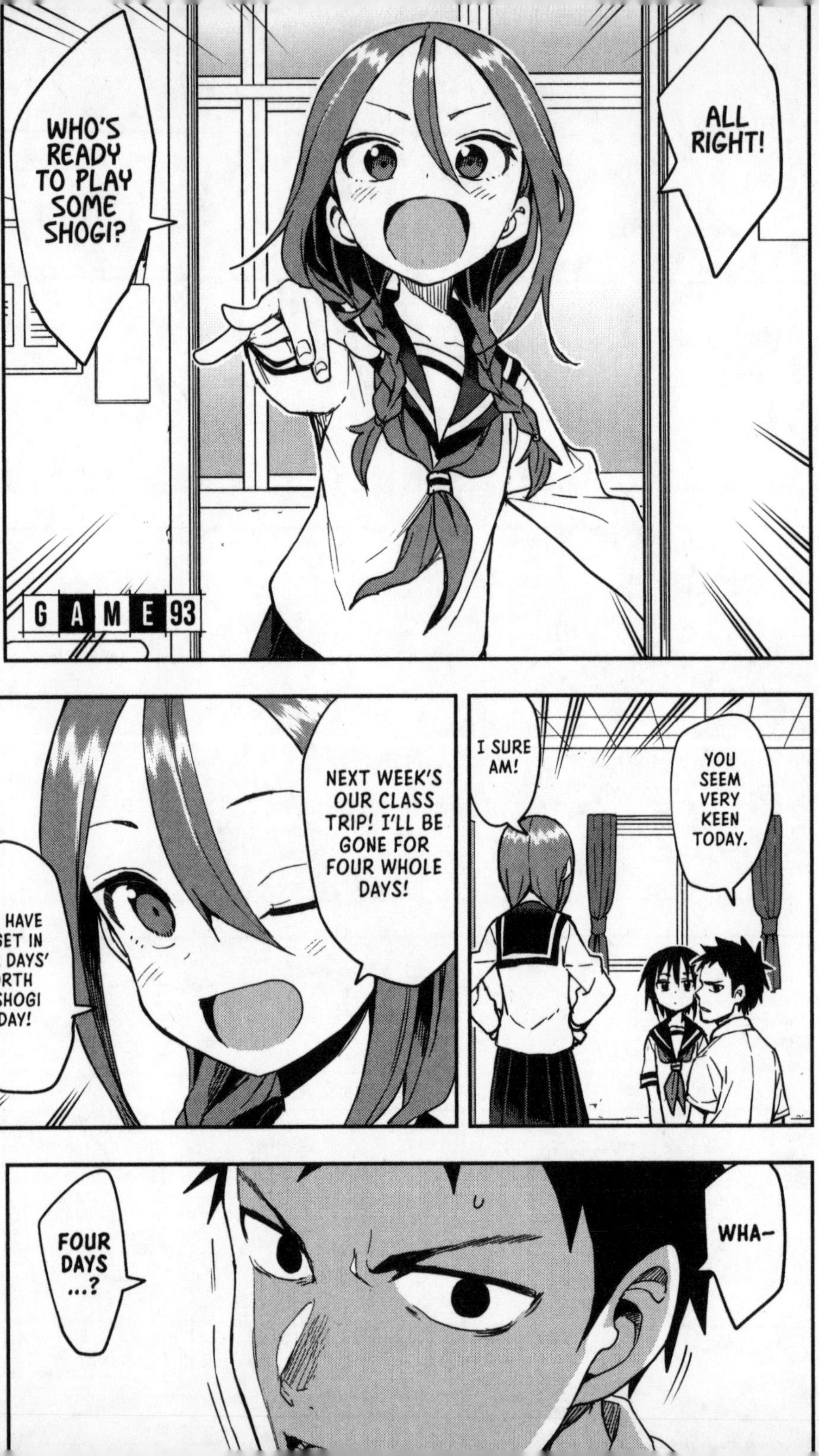
ALL RIGHT!
WHO'S READY TO PLAY SOME SHOGI?
GAME 93
YOU SEEM VERY KEEN TODAY.
I SURE AM!
NEXT WEEK'S OUR CLASS TRIP! I'LL BE GONE FOR FOUR WHOLE DAYS!
SO I HAVE TO GET IN FOUR DAYS' WORTH OF SHOGI TODAY!
WHA-
FOUR DAYS ...?

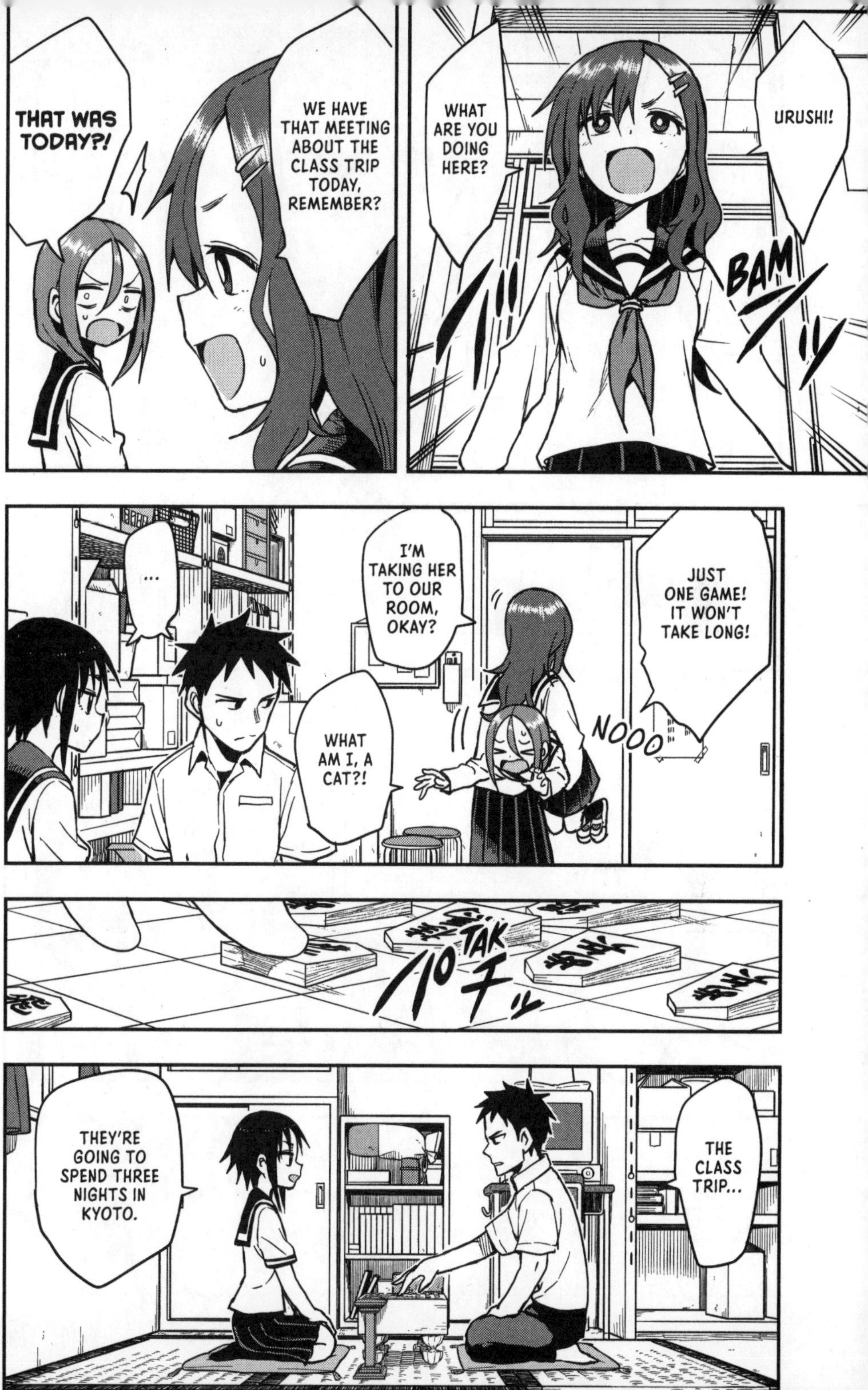
URUSHI!
BAM
WHAT ARE YOU DOING HERE?
WE HAVE THAT MEETING ABOUT THE CLASS TRIP TODAY, REMEMBER?
THAT WAS TODAY?!
JUST ONE GAME! IT WON'T TAKE LONG!
NOOO
I'M TAKING HER TO OUR ROOM, OKAY?
...
WHAT AM I, A CAT?!
TAK
THE CLASS TRIP...
THEY'RE GOING TO SPEND THREE NIGHTS IN KYOTO.

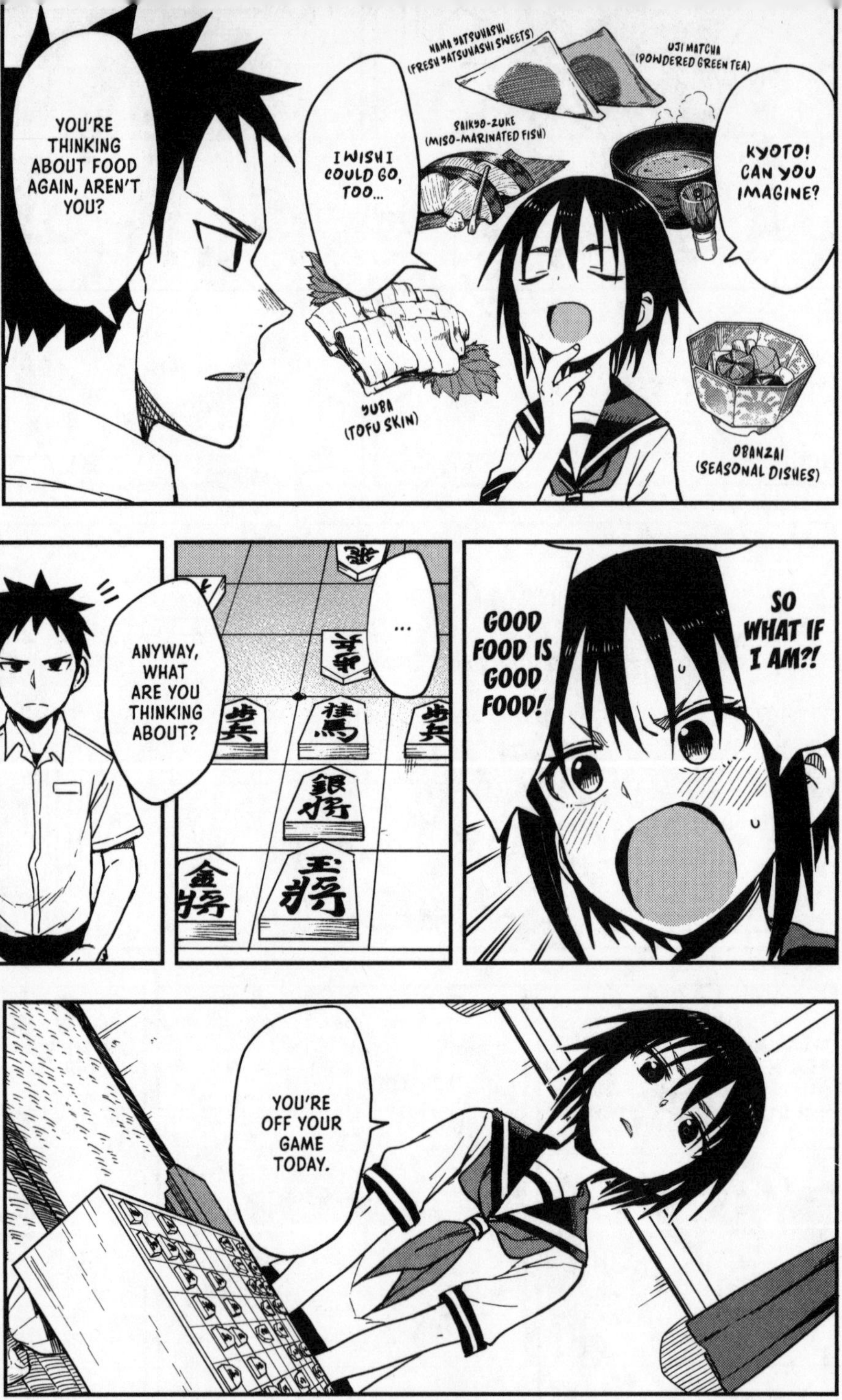
UJI MATCHA (POWDERED GREEN TEA)
NAMA YATSUHASHI (FRESH YATSUHASHI SWEETS)
KYOTO! CAN YOU IMAGINE?
SAIKYO-ZUKE (MISO-MARINATED FISH)
I WISH I COULD GO, TOO...
YOU'RE THINKING ABOUT FOOD AGAIN, AREN'T YOU?
OBANZAI (SEASONAL DISHES)
YUBA (TOFU SKIN)
SO WHAT IF I AM?!
GOOD FOOD IS GOOD FOOD!
...
ANYWAY, WHAT ARE YOU THINKING ABOUT?
YOU'RE OFF YOUR GAME TODAY.

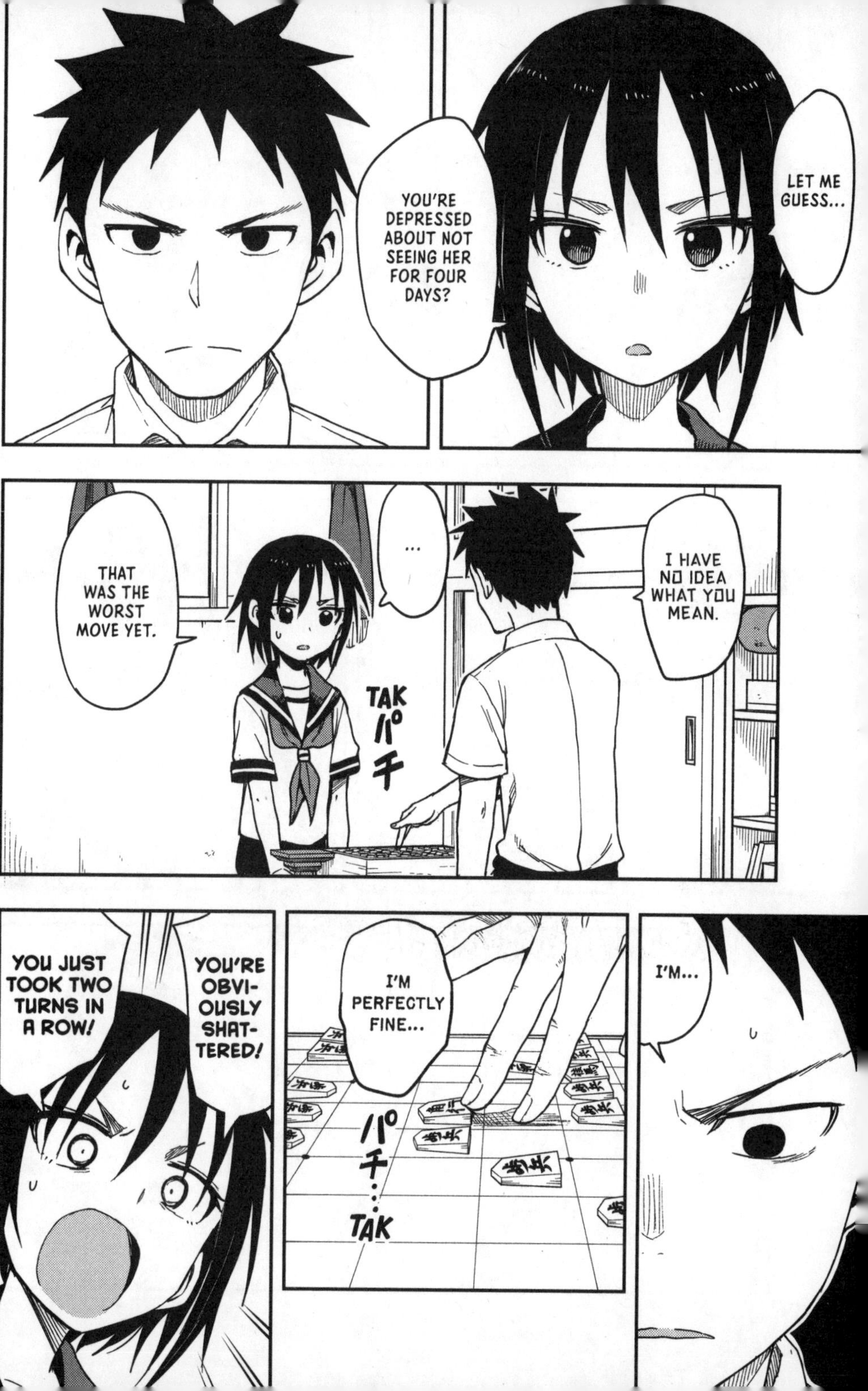
LET ME GUESS...
YOU'RE DEPRESSED ABOUT NOT SEEING HER FOR FOUR DAYS?
I HAVE NO IDEA WHAT YOU MEAN.
...
THAT WAS THE WORST MOVE YET.
TAK パチ
I'M...
I'M PERFECTLY FINE...
パチ... TAK
YOU'RE OBVI-OUSLY SHAT-TERED!
YOU JUST TOOK TWO TURNS IN A ROW!

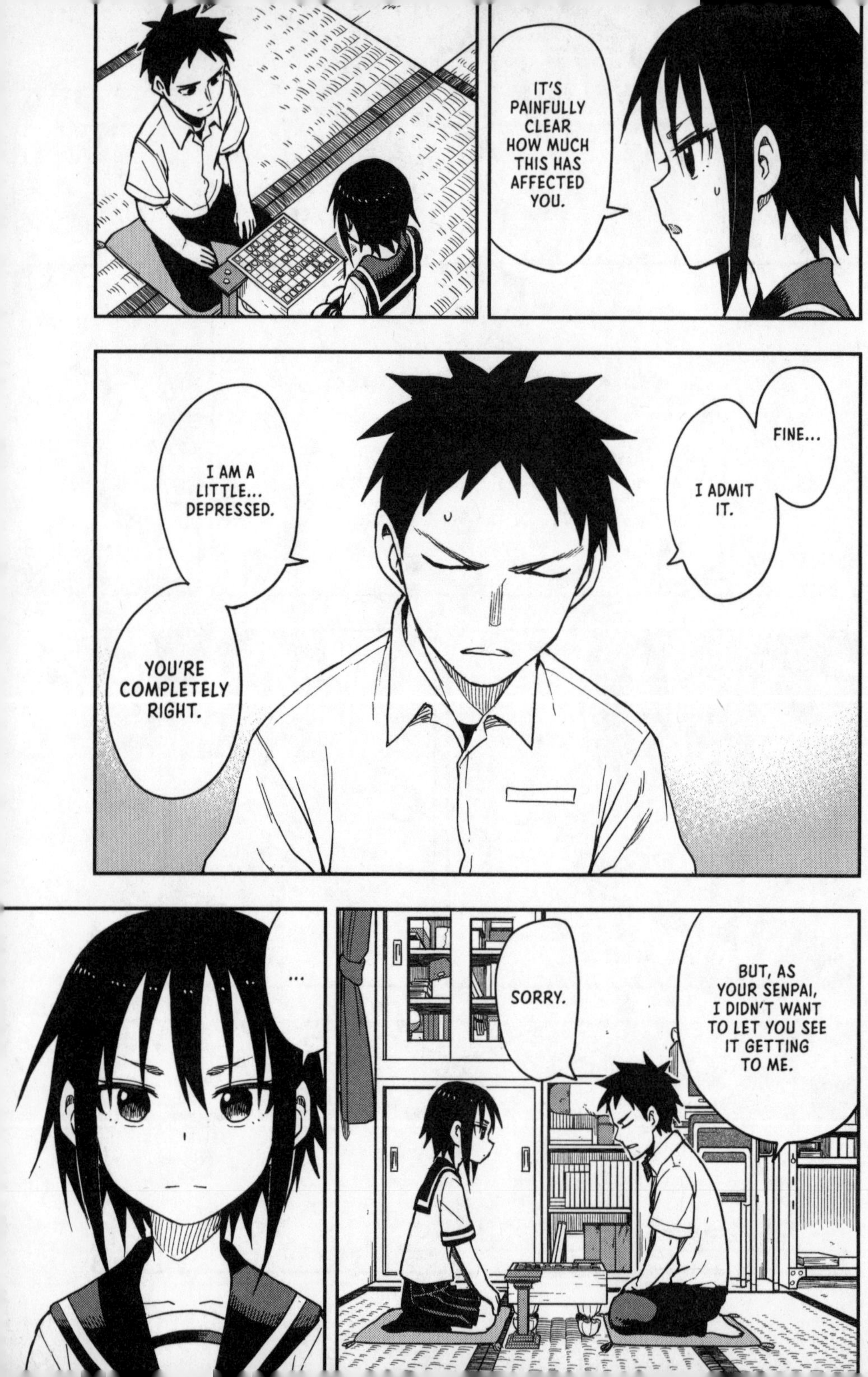
IT'S PAINFULLY CLEAR HOW MUCH THIS HAS AFFECTED YOU.
FINE...
I ADMIT IT.
I AM A LITTLE... DEPRESSED.
YOU'RE COMPLETELY RIGHT.
BUT, AS YOUR SENPAI, I DIDN'T WANT TO LET YOU SEE IT GETTING TO ME.
SORRY.
...

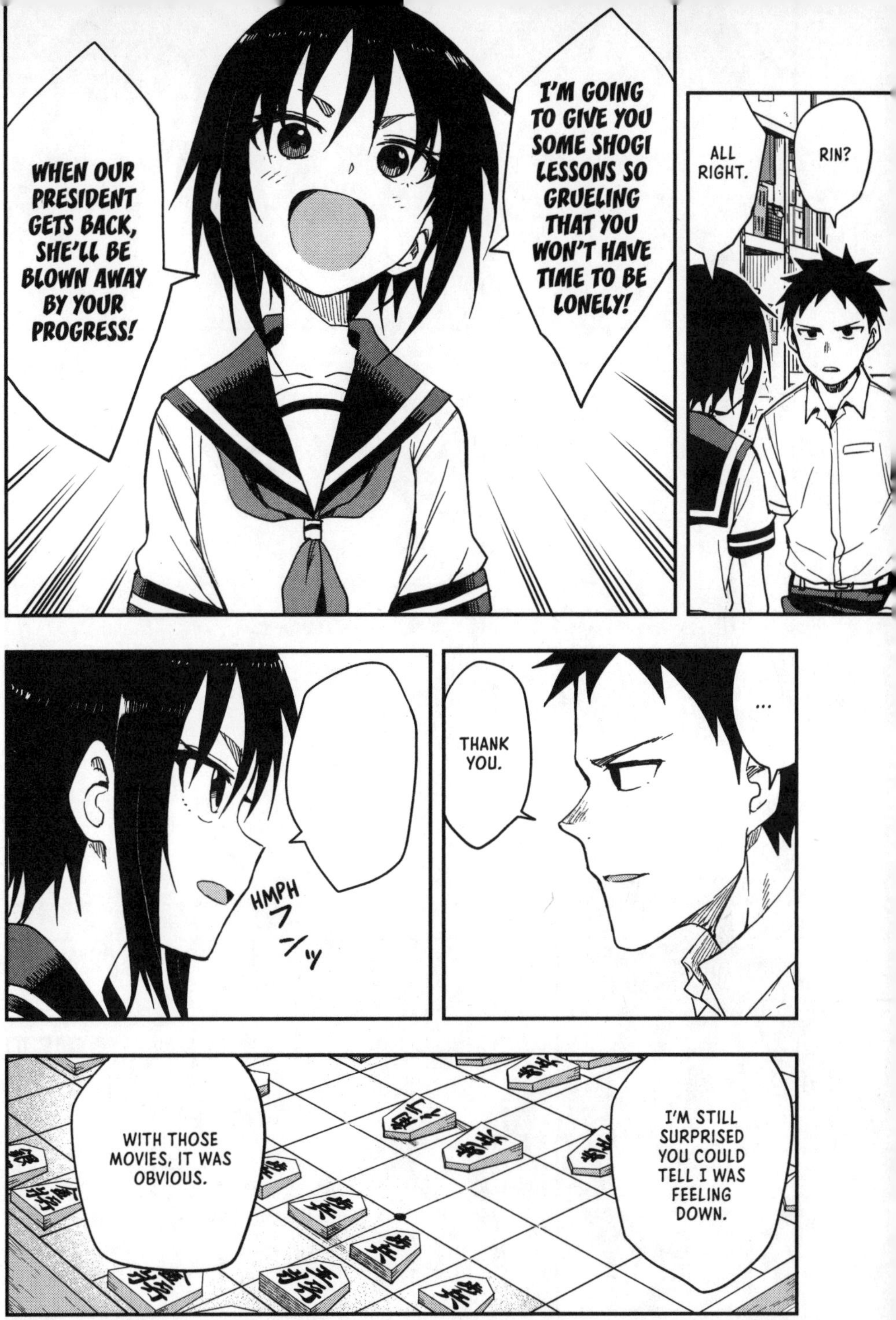
RIN?
ALL RIGHT.
I'M GOING TO GIVE YOU SOME SHOGI LESSONS SO GRUELING THAT YOU WON'T HAVE TIME TO BE LONELY!
WHEN OUR PRESIDENT GETS BACK, SHE'LL BE BLOWN AWAY BY YOUR PROGRESS!
...
THANK YOU.
HMPH
フンッ
I'M STILL SURPRISED YOU COULD TELL I WAS FEELING DOWN.
WITH THOSE MOVIES, IT WAS OBVIOUS.

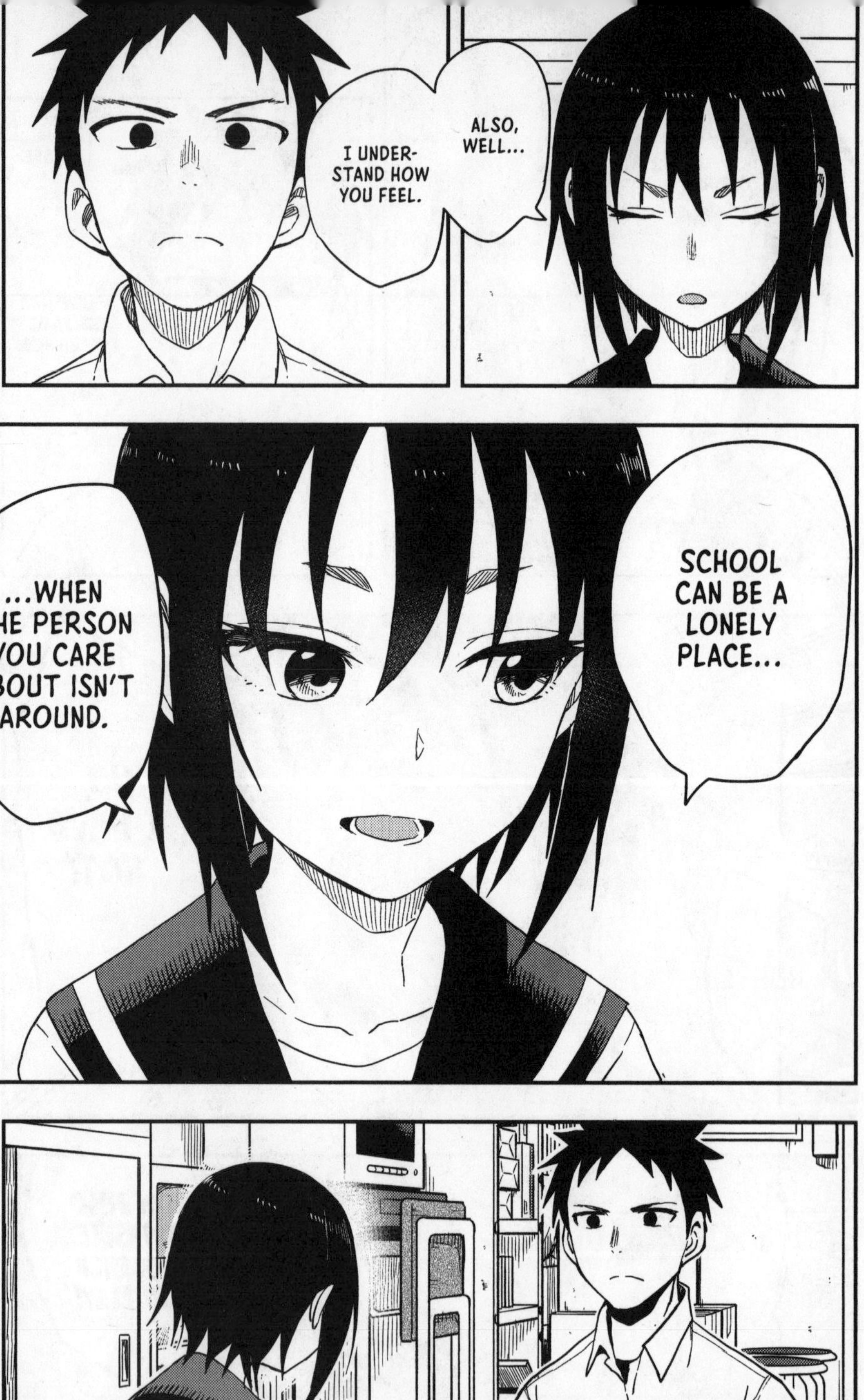
ALSO, WELL...
I UNDER-STAND HOW YOU FEEL.
SCHOOL CAN BE A LONELY PLACE...
...WHEN THE PERSON YOU CARE ABOUT ISN'T AROUND.

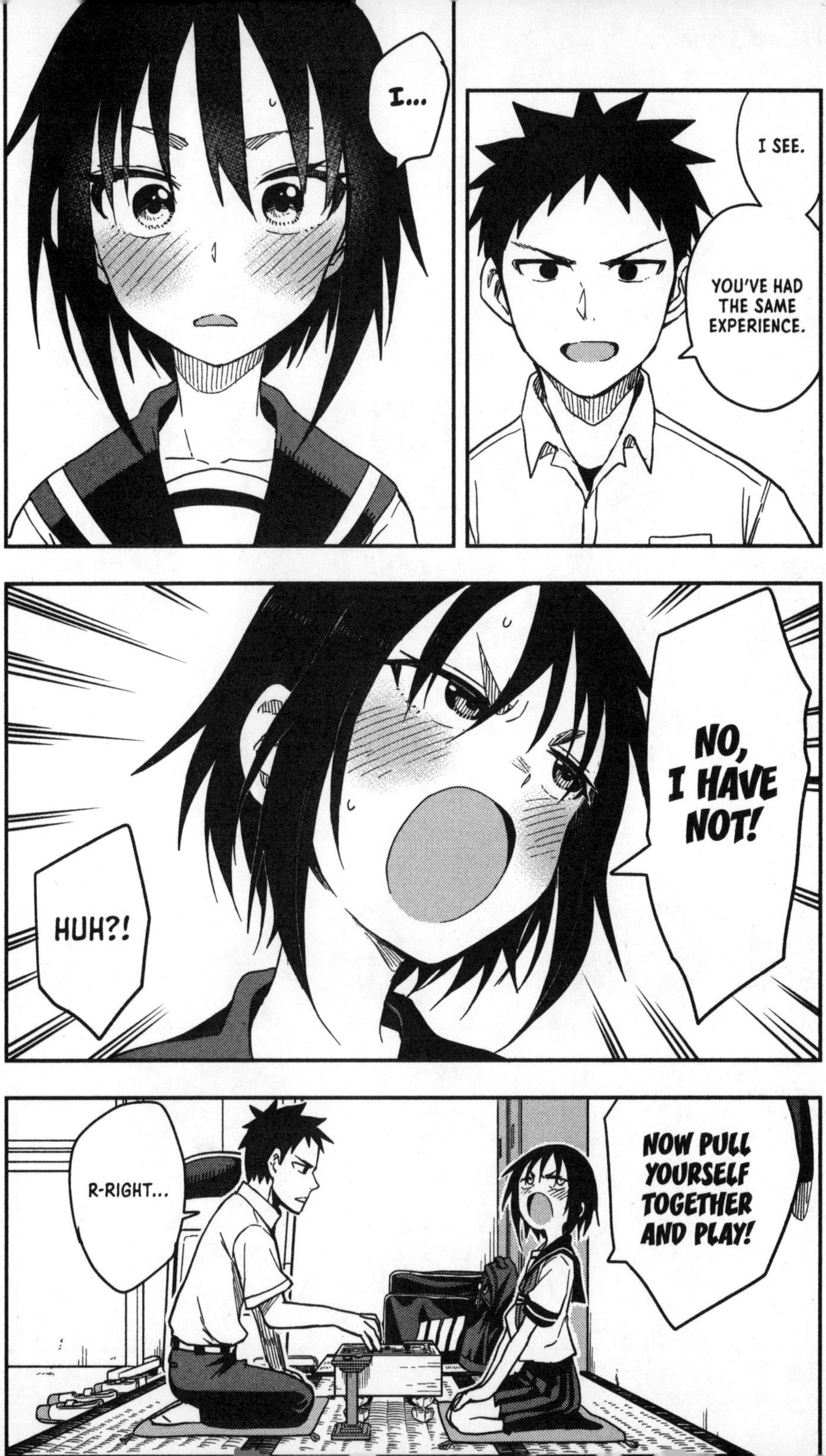
I SEE.
YOU'VE HAD THE SAME EXPERIENCE.
I...
NO, I HAVE NOT!
HUH?!
NOW PULL YOURSELF TOGETHER AND PLAY!
R-RIGHT...

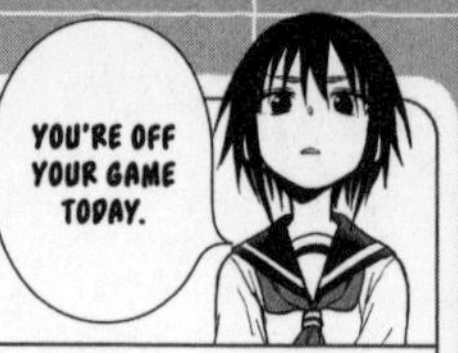

▲ BLACK (SENTE): AYUMU TANAKA △ WHITE (GOTE): RIN KAGAWA

(DIAGRAM SHOWS BOARD AFTER MOVE 22, △ B-5E)

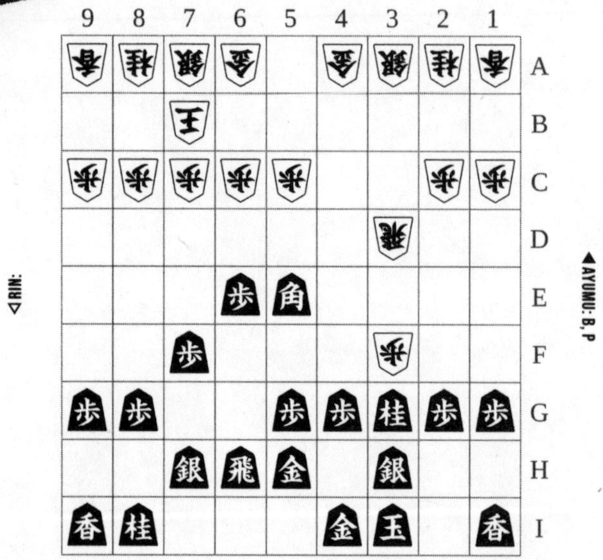

YOU'RE OFF YOUR GAME TODAY.

◁ RIN:

▲ AYUMU: B, P

	9	8	7	6	5	4	3	2	1	
A	香	桂	銀	金		金	銀	桂	香	A
B			王							B
C	歩		歩		歩		歩		歩	C
D							角			D
E				歩	角					E
F			歩				歩			F
G	歩	歩			歩	歩	桂	歩	歩	G
H			銀	飛	金		銀			H
I	香	桂				金	玉		香	I

▲ P-7F	△ P-3D	▲ N-3G	△ R×3F
▲ P-6F	△ P-3E	▲ S-3H	△ R-3D
▲ R-6H	△ R-3B	▲ K-3I	△ P×3F
▲ K-4H	△ K-6B	▲ P-6E	▲ B-5E
▲ G6I-5H	△ K-7B		
▲ S-7H	△ P-3F		
▲ P×3F	△ B-5E		

(RIN WINS AT MOVE 22 DUE TO AYUMU ILLEGALLY PLAYING TWO MOVES IN A ROW)

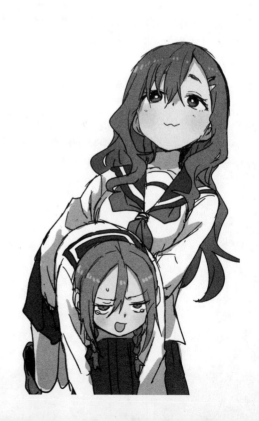

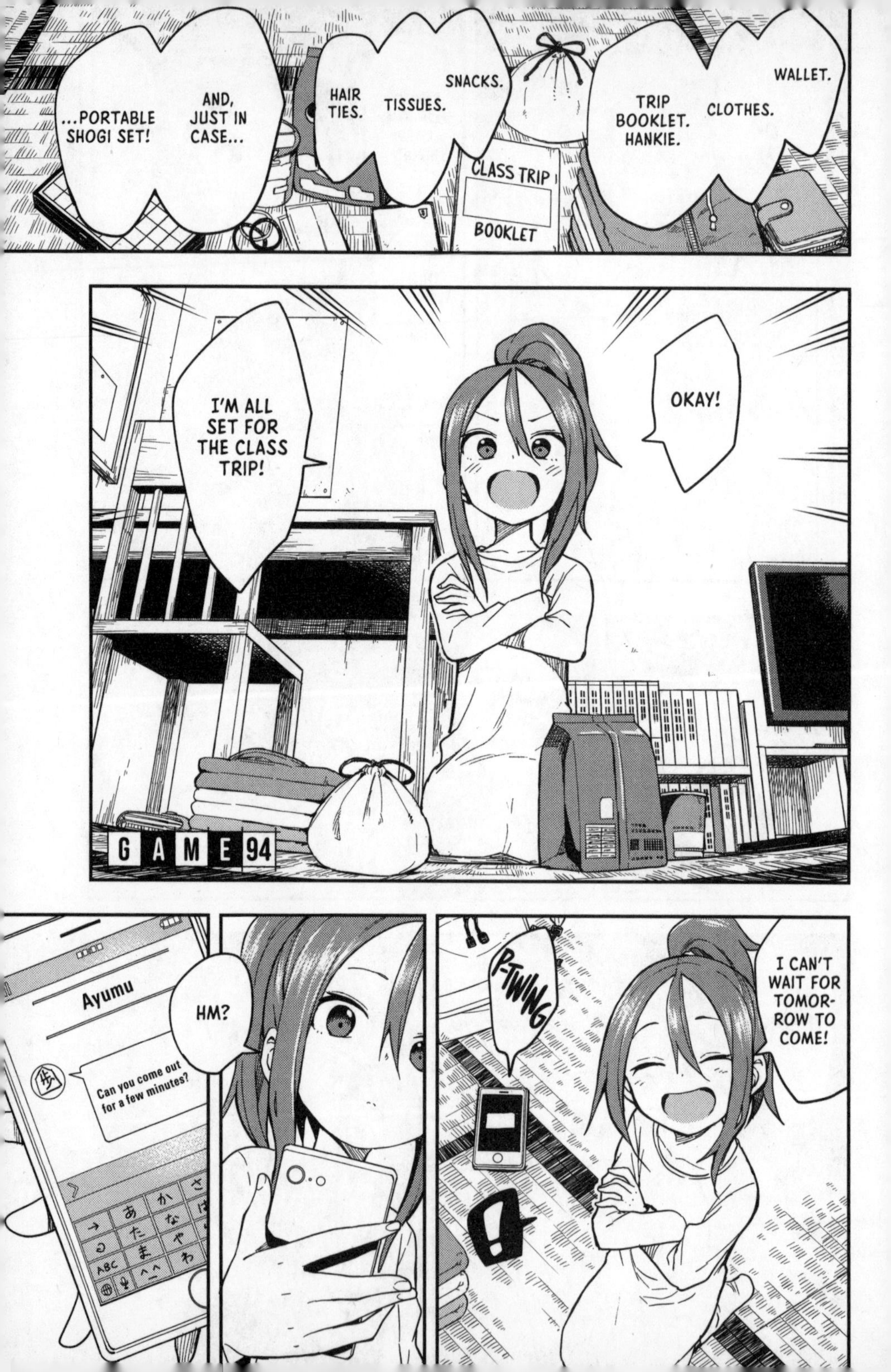
WALLET.
CLOTHES.
TRIP BOOKLET. HANKIE.
SNACKS.
TISSUES.
HAIR TIES.
AND, JUST IN CASE...
...PORTABLE SHOGI SET!
CLASS TRIP BOOKLET
OKAY!
I'M ALL SET FOR THE CLASS TRIP!
GAME 94
I CAN'T WAIT FOR TOMORROW TO COME!
P-TWING
!
HM?
Ayumu
Can you come out for a few minutes?

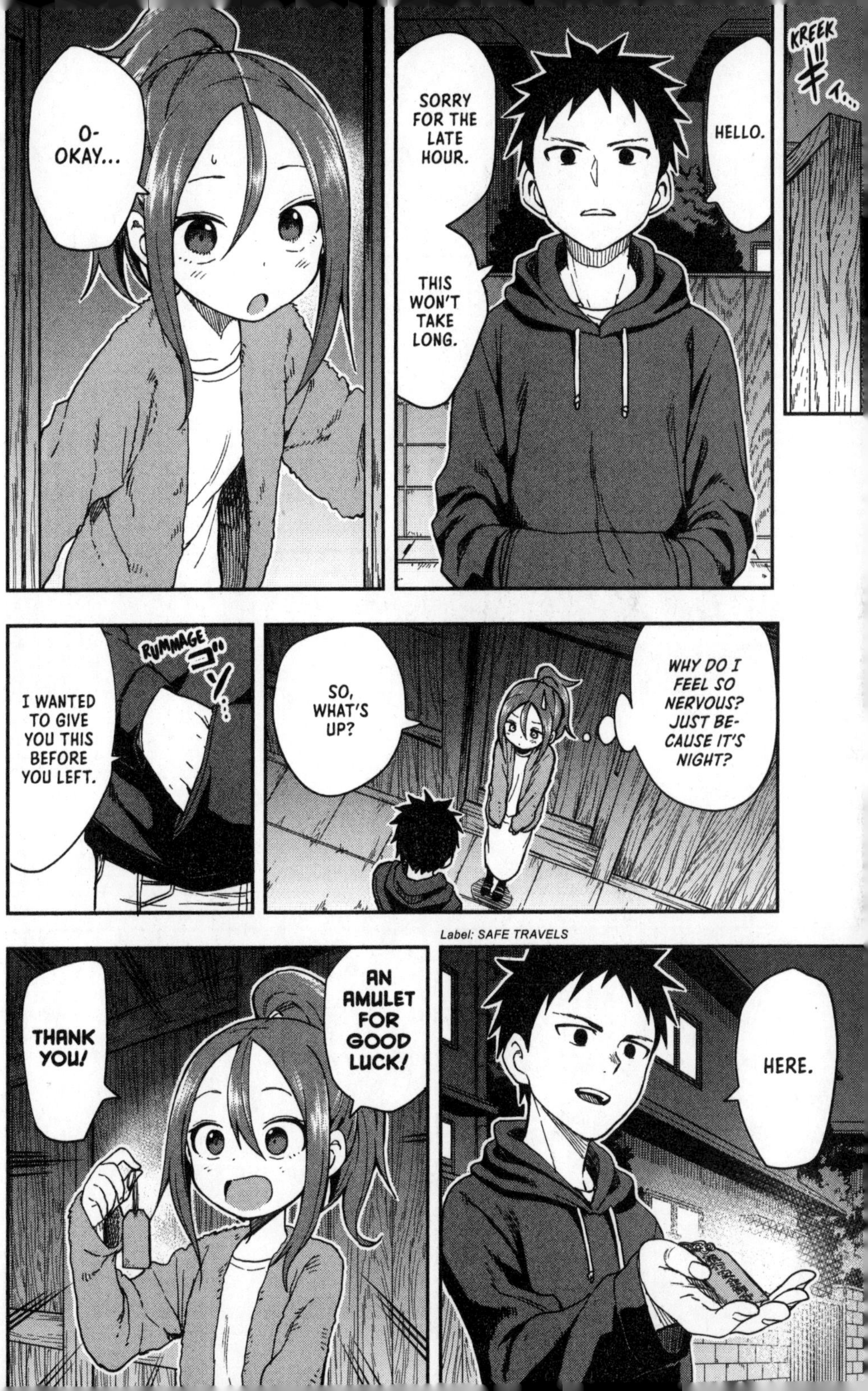
KREEK
HELLO.
SORRY FOR THE LATE HOUR.
THIS WON'T TAKE LONG.
O-OKAY...
WHY DO I FEEL SO NERVOUS? JUST BE-CAUSE IT'S NIGHT?
SO, WHAT'S UP?
RUMMAGE
I WANTED TO GIVE YOU THIS BEFORE YOU LEFT.
Label: SAFE TRAVELS
HERE.
AN AMULET FOR GOOD LUCK!
THANK YOU!

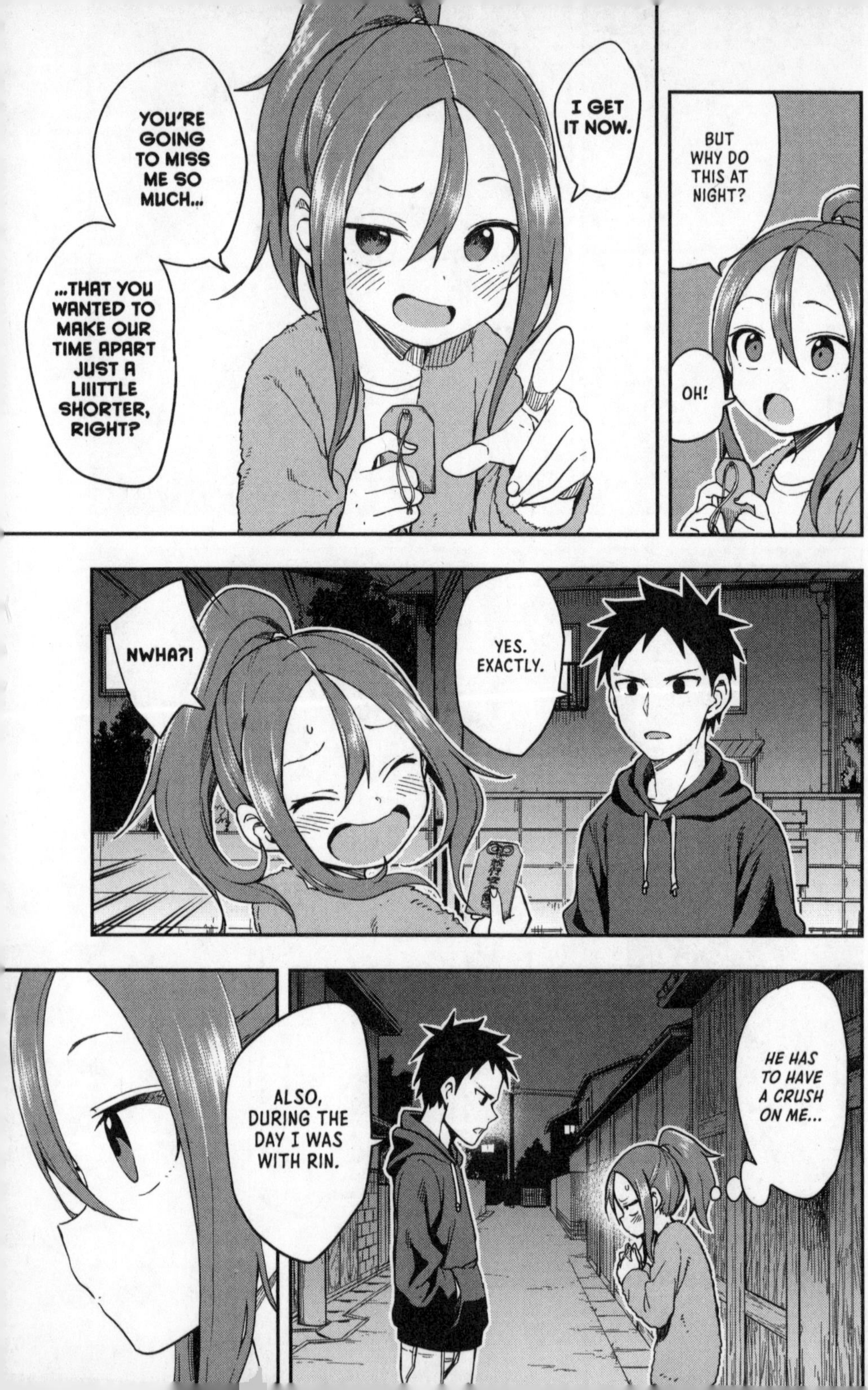
BUT WHY DO THIS AT NIGHT?
OH!
I GET IT NOW.
YOU'RE GOING TO MISS ME SO MUCH...
...THAT YOU WANTED TO MAKE OUR TIME APART JUST A LIIITTLE SHORTER, RIGHT?
YES. EXACTLY.
NWHA?!
HE HAS TO HAVE A CRUSH ON ME...
ALSO, DURING THE DAY I WAS WITH RIN.

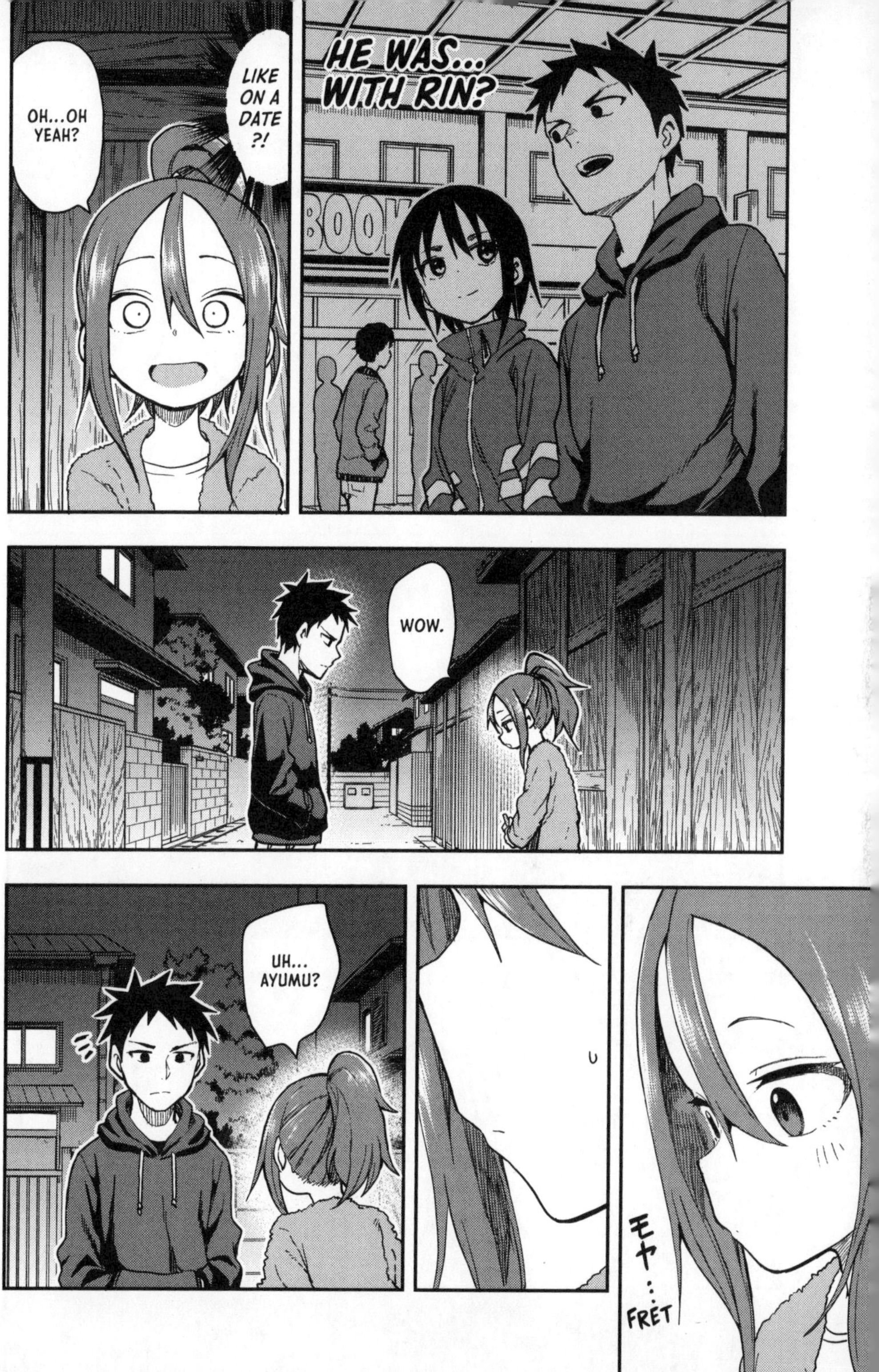
HE WAS... WITH RIN?
LIKE ON A DATE ?!
OH...OH YEAH?
WOW.
モヤ... FRET
UH... AYUMU?

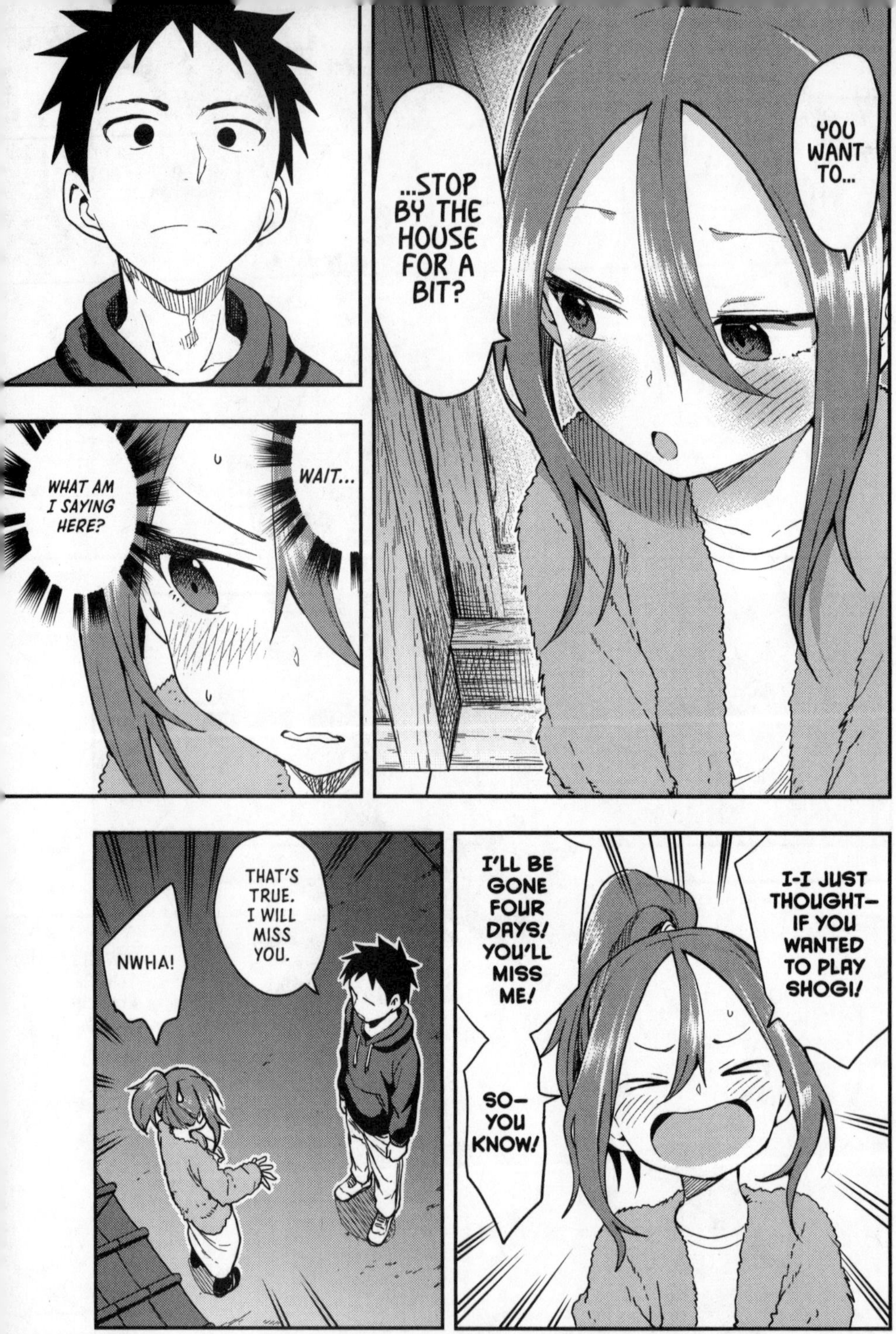
YOU WANT TO...
...STOP BY THE HOUSE FOR A BIT?
WAIT...
WHAT AM I SAYING HERE?
I-I JUST THOUGHT— IF YOU WANTED TO PLAY SHOGI!
I'LL BE GONE FOUR DAYS! YOU'LL MISS ME!
SO— YOU KNOW!
THAT'S TRUE. I WILL MISS YOU.
NWHA!

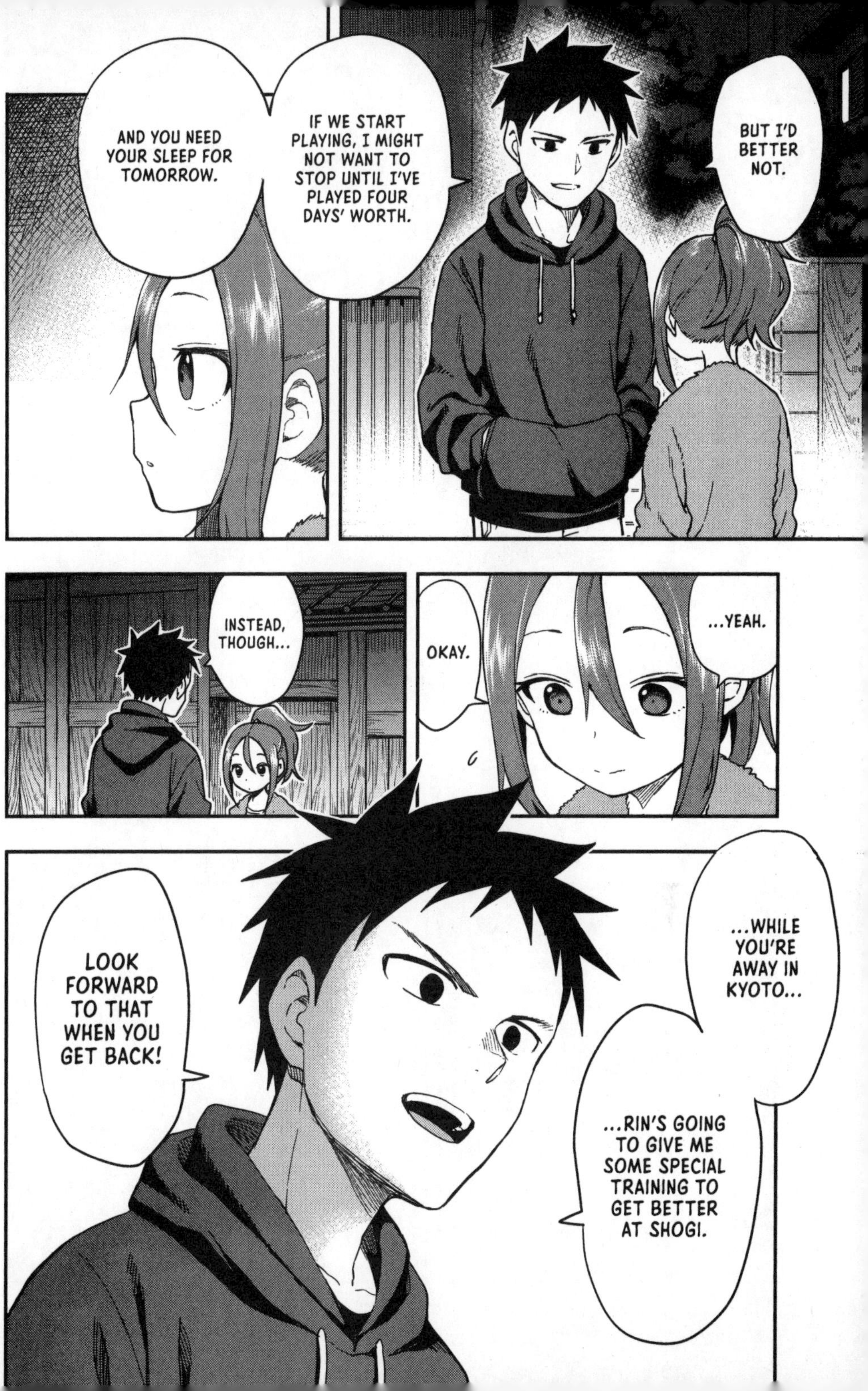
BUT I'D BETTER NOT.
IF WE START PLAYING, I MIGHT NOT WANT TO STOP UNTIL I'VE PLAYED FOUR DAYS' WORTH.
AND YOU NEED YOUR SLEEP FOR TOMORROW.
...YEAH.
OKAY.
INSTEAD, THOUGH...
...WHILE YOU'RE AWAY IN KYOTO...
...RIN'S GOING TO GIVE ME SOME SPECIAL TRAINING TO GET BETTER AT SHOGI.
LOOK FORWARD TO THAT WHEN YOU GET BACK!

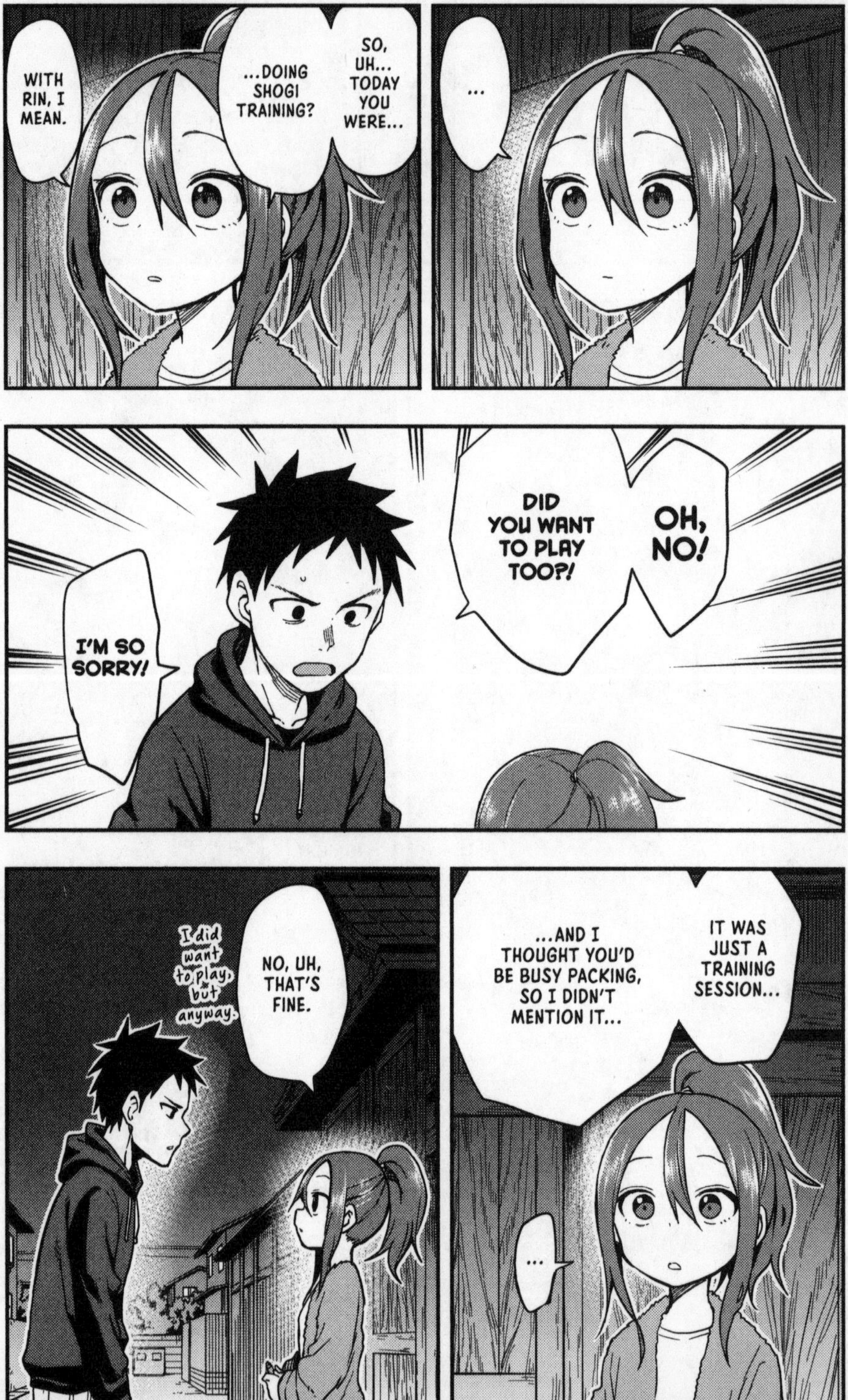
...
SO, UH... TODAY YOU WERE...
...DOING SHOGI TRAINING?
WITH RIN, I MEAN.
OH, NO!
DID YOU WANT TO PLAY TOO?!
I'M SO SORRY!
IT WAS JUST A TRAINING SESSION...
...AND I THOUGHT YOU'D BE BUSY PACKING, SO I DIDN'T MENTION IT...
...
NO, UH, THAT'S FINE.
I did want to play, but anyway.

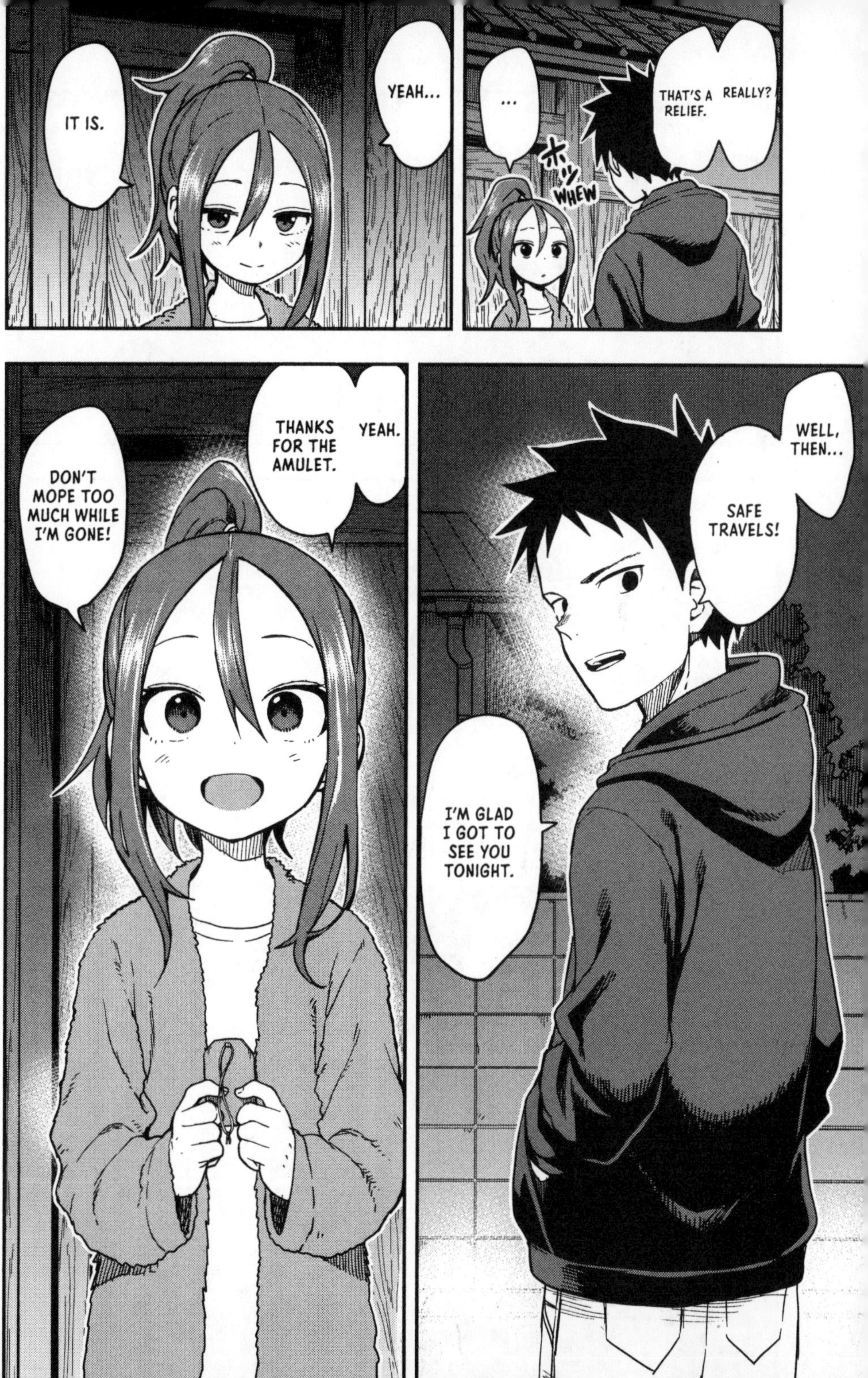
REALLY?
THAT'S A RELIEF.
...
ホッ
WHEW
YEAH...
IT IS.
WELL, THEN...
SAFE TRAVELS!
I'M GLAD I GOT TO SEE YOU TONIGHT.
YEAH.
THANKS FOR THE AMULET.
DON'T MOPE TOO MUCH WHILE I'M GONE!

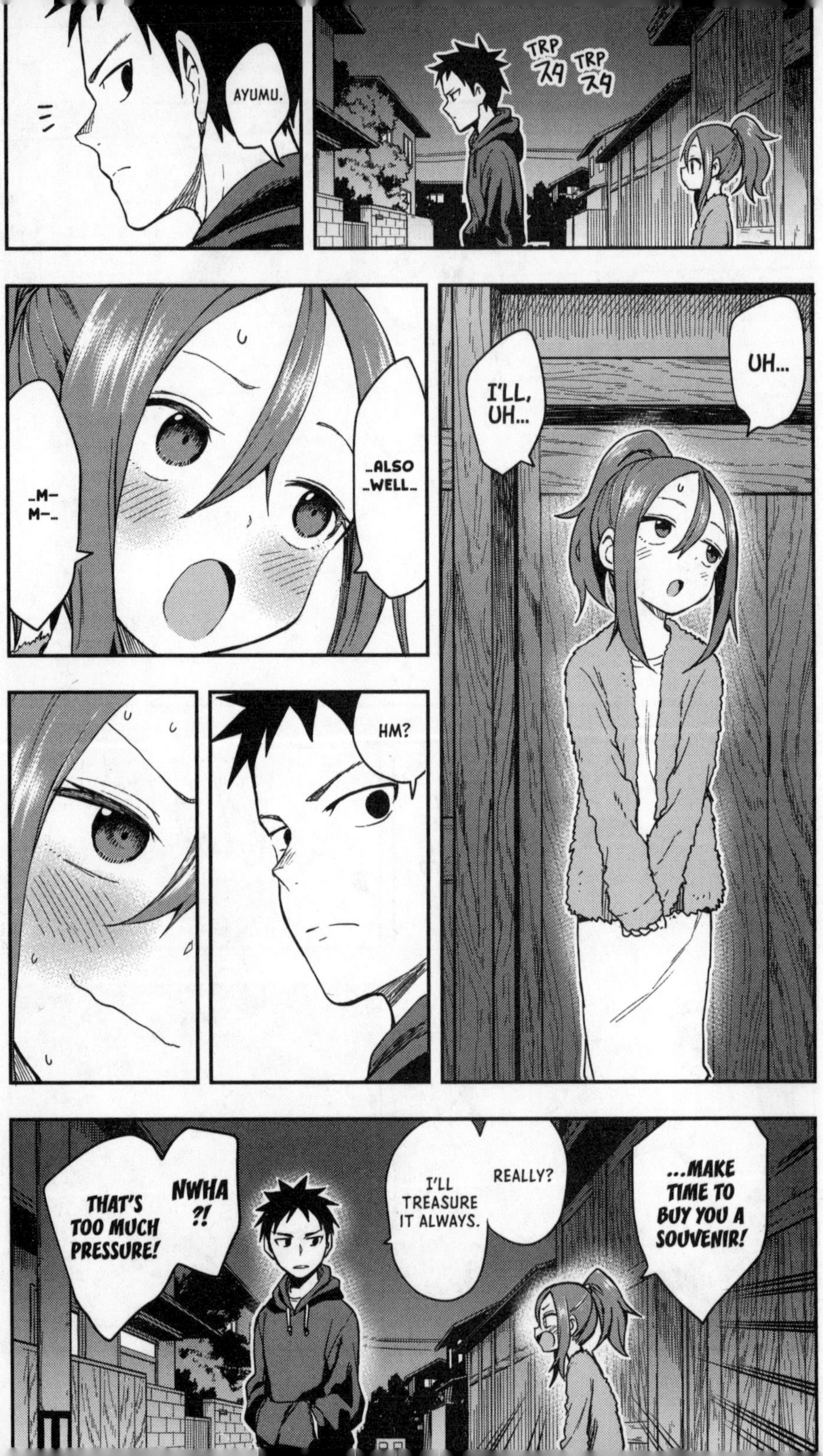
TRP
スタ
TRP
スタ
AYUMU.
UH...
I'LL, UH...
...ALSO ...WELL...
...M– M–...
HM?
...MAKE TIME TO BUY YOU A SOUVENIR!
REALLY?
I'LL TREASURE IT ALWAYS.
NWHA ?!
THAT'S TOO MUCH PRESSURE!

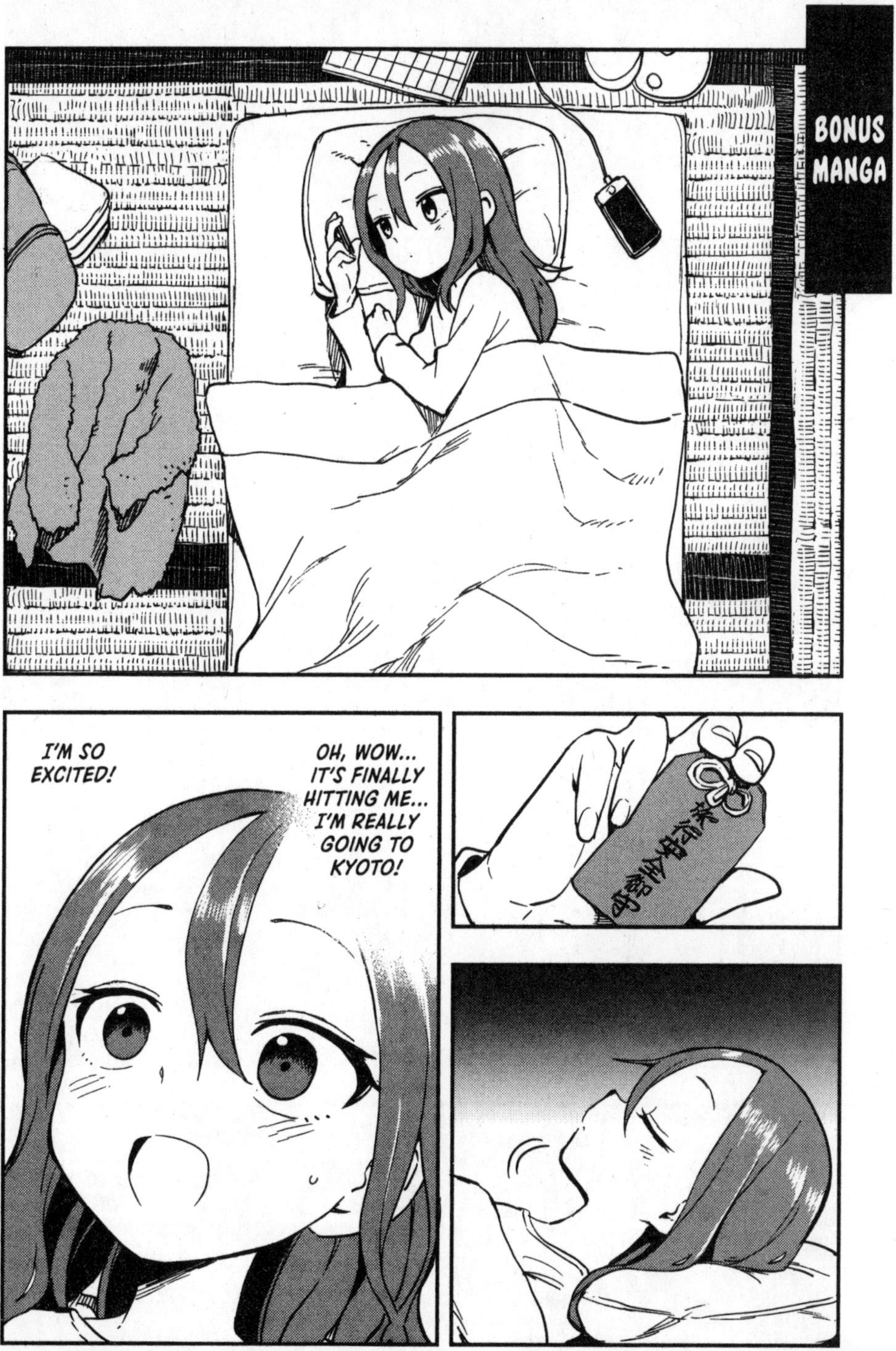
BONUS MANGA
OH, WOW... IT'S FINALLY HITTING ME... I'M REALLY GOING TO KYOTO!
I'M SO EXCITED!

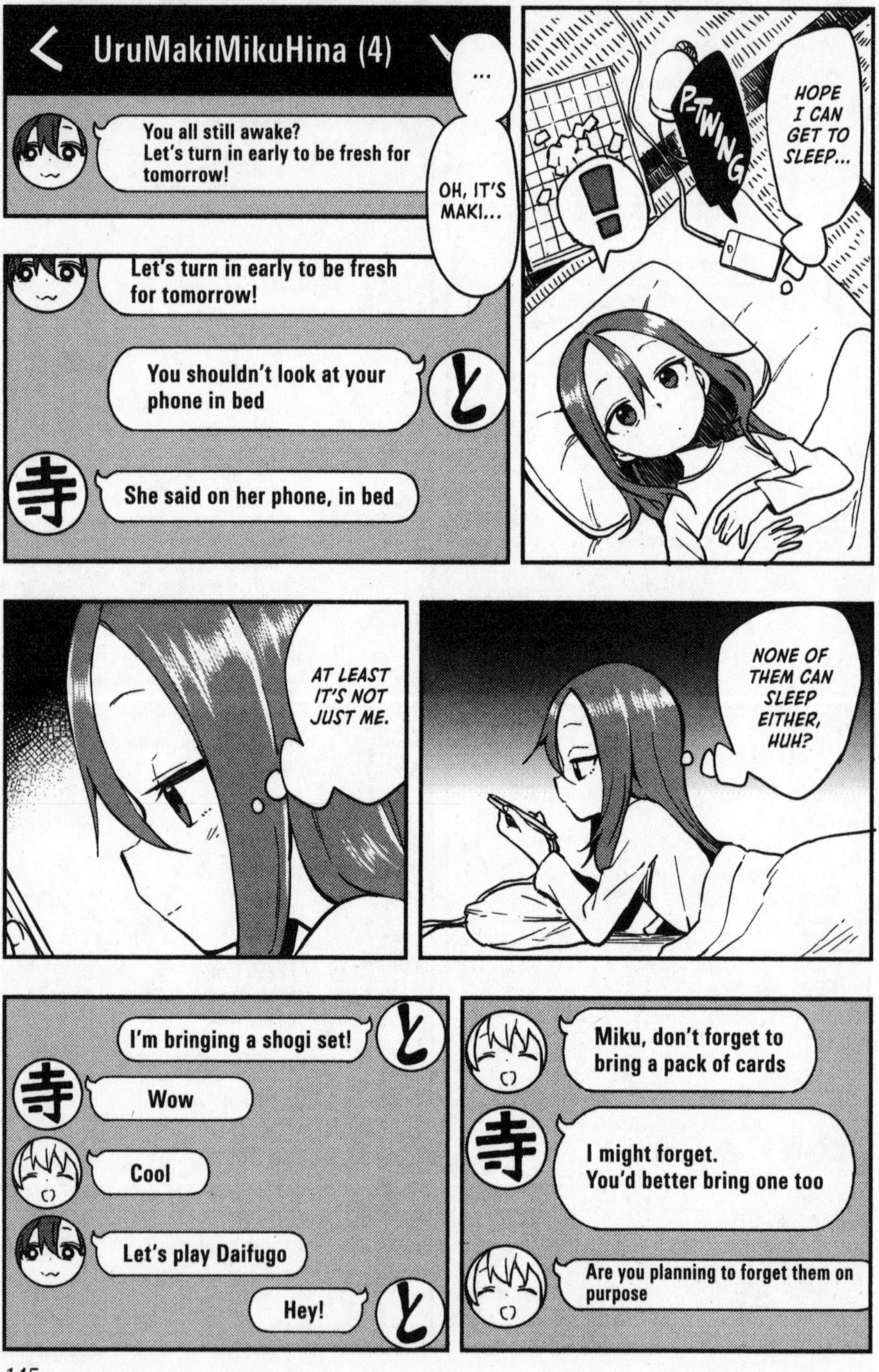

HOPE I CAN GET TO SLEEP...
P-TWING
!
...
OH, IT'S MAKI...
UruMakiMikuHina (4)
You all still awake? Let's turn in early to be fresh for tomorrow!
Let's turn in early to be fresh for tomorrow!
You shouldn't look at your phone in bed
She said on her phone, in bed
NONE OF THEM CAN SLEEP EITHER, HUH?
AT LEAST IT'S NOT JUST ME.
Miku, don't forget to bring a pack of cards
I might forget. You'd better bring one too
Are you planning to forget them on purpose
I'm bringing a shogi set!
Wow
Cool
Let's play Daifugo
Hey!

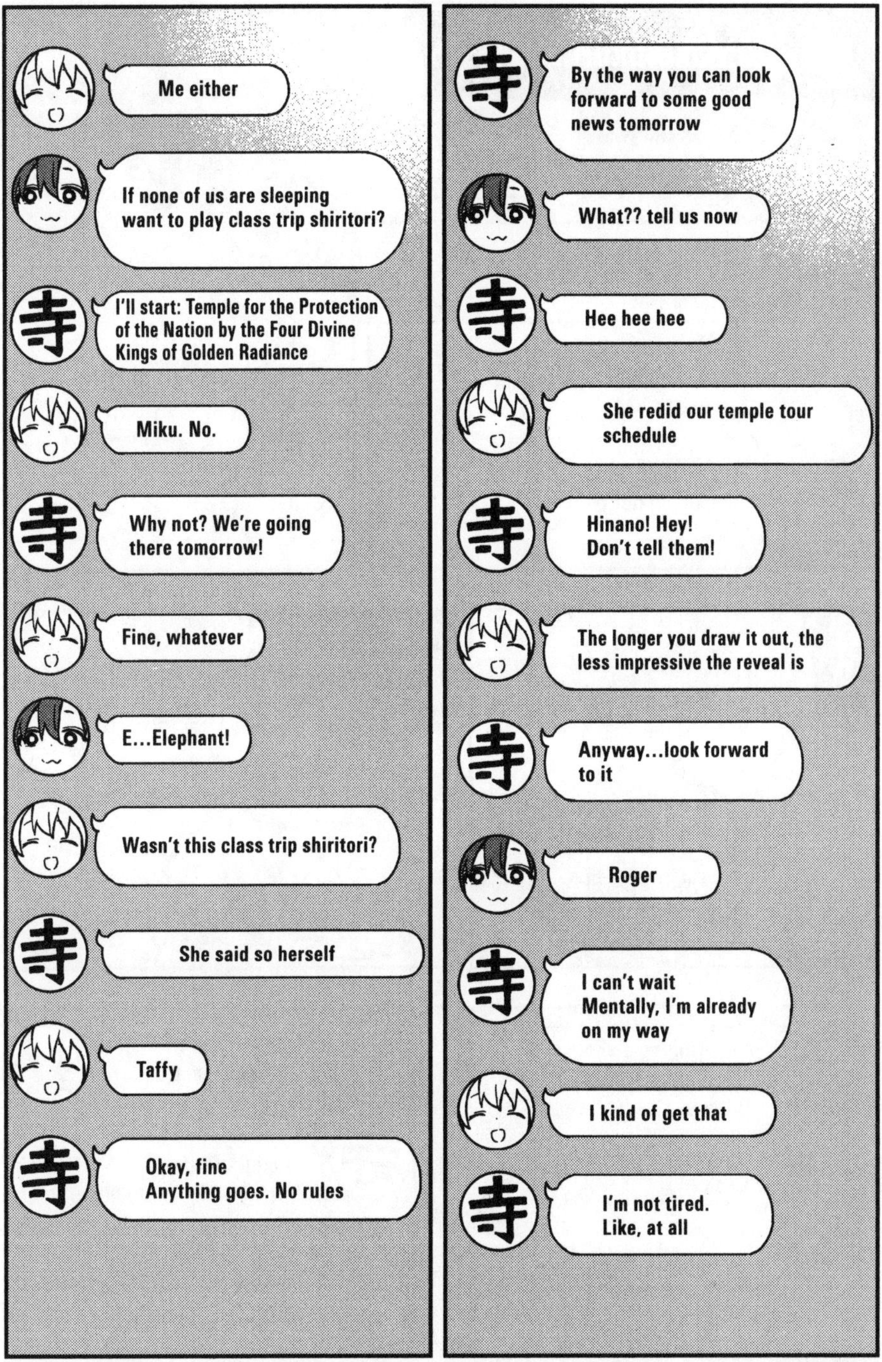
By the way you can look forward to some good news tomorrow
What?? tell us now
Hee hee hee
She redid our temple tour schedule
Hinano! Hey! Don't tell them!
The longer you draw it out, the less impressive the reveal is
Anyway...look forward to it
Roger
I can't wait
Mentally, I'm already on my way
I kind of get that
I'm not tired.
Like, at all
Me either
If none of us are sleeping want to play class trip shiritori?
I'll start: Temple for the Protection of the Nation by the Four Divine Kings of Golden Radiance
Miku. No.
Why not? We're going there tomorrow!
Fine, whatever
E...Elephant!
Wasn't this class trip shiritori?
She said so herself
Taffy
Okay, fine
Anything goes. No rules

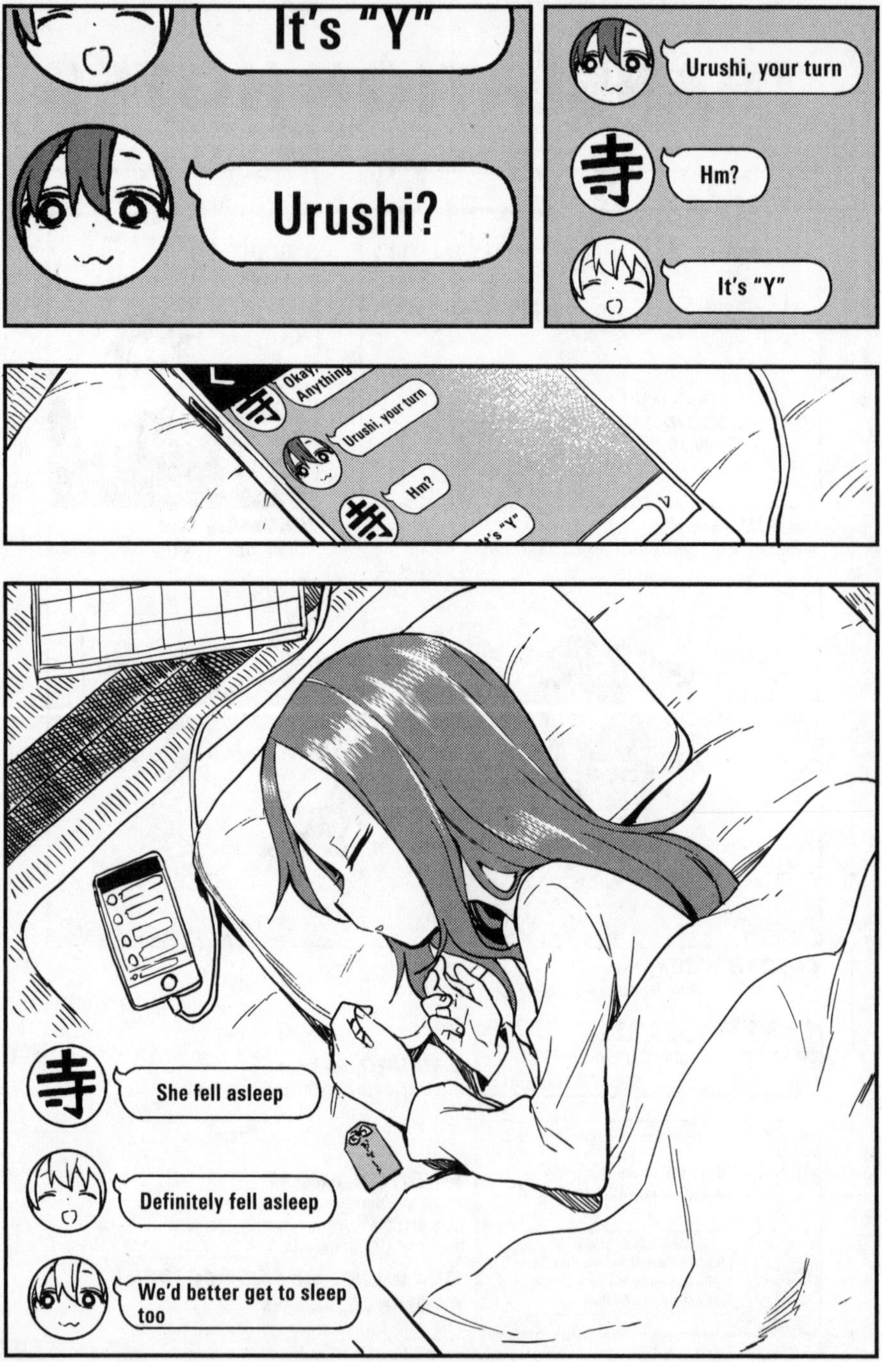
Urushi, your turn
Hm?
It's "Y"
It's "Y"
Urushi?
Okay, Anything
Urushi, your turn
Hm?
She fell asleep
Definitely fell asleep
We'd better get to sleep too

THE END

TRANSLATION NOTES

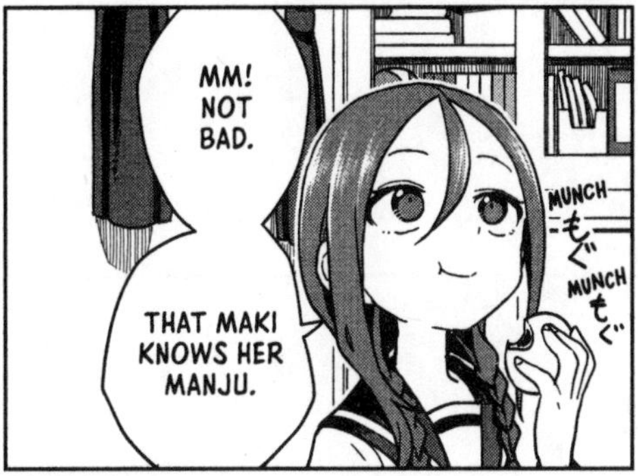
MM! NOT BAD.
MUNCH
もぐ
MUNCH
もぐ
THAT MAKI KNOWS HER MANJU.

***MANJU*, PAGE 7**
Steamed buns with sweet red bean paste filling.

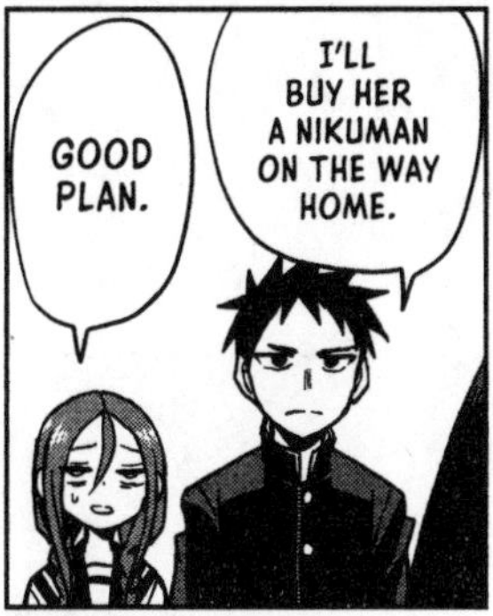
I'LL BUY HER A NIKUMAN ON THE WAY HOME.
GOOD PLAN.

***NIKUMAN*, PAGE 16**
Steamed bun with meat filling.

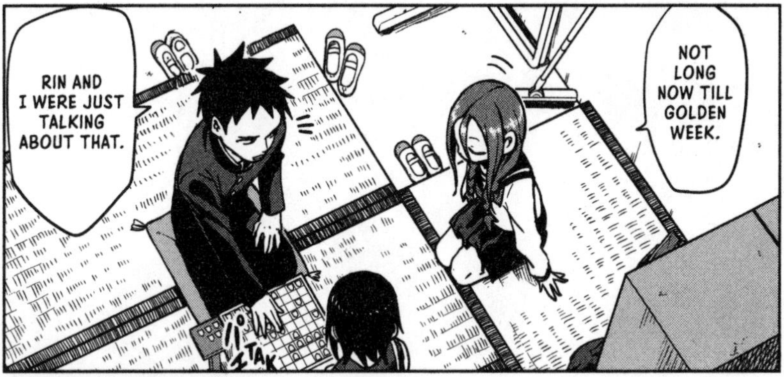
NOT LONG NOW TILL GOLDEN WEEK.
RIN AND I WERE JUST TALKING ABOUT THAT.
TAK

***GOLDEN WEEK*, PAGE 75**
A cluster of public holidays in late April/early May.

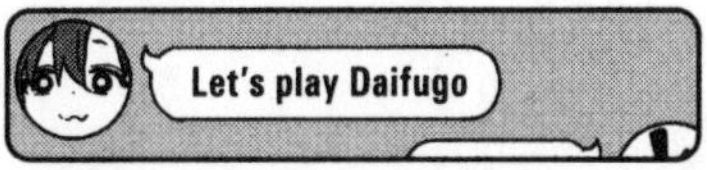
Let's play Daifugo

***DAIFUGO*, PAGE 145**
A card game similar to President.

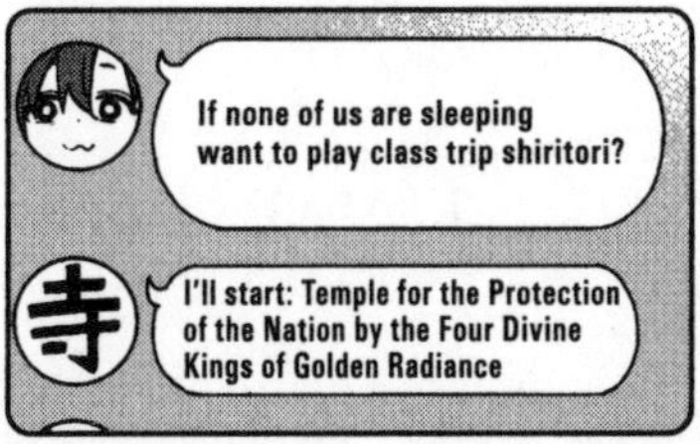
If none of us are sleeping want to play class trip shiritori?
寺
I'll start: Temple for the Protection of the Nation by the Four Divine Kings of Golden Radiance

***SHIRITOR*, PAGE 146**
A word game where the first letter of each word must match the last letter of the previous one.

***OUR DIVINE KINGS OF GOLDEN RADIANCE*, PAGE 146**
The full, formal name of Todaiji temple

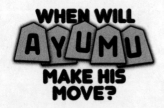
WHEN WILL AYUMU MAKE HIS MOVE?

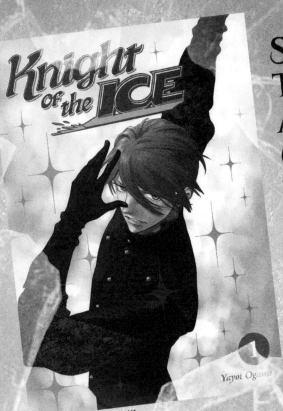

Knight of the Ice ©Yayoi Ogawa/Kodansha Ltd.

SKATING THRILLS AND ICY CHILLS WITH THIS NEW TINGLY ROMANCE SERIES!

A rom-com on ice, perfect for fans of *Princess Jellyfish* and *Wotakoi*. Kokoro is the talk of the figure-skating world, winning trophies and hearts. But little do they know... he's actually a huge nerd! From the beloved creator of *You're My Pet* (*Tramps Like Us*).

Chitose is a serious young woman, working for the health magazine *SASSO*. Or at least, she would be, if she wasn't constantly getting distracted by her childhood friend, international figure skating star Kokoro Kijinami! In the public eye and on the ice, Kokoro is a gallant, flawless knight, but behind his glittery costumes and breathtaking spins lies a secret: He's actually a hopelessly romantic otaku, who can only land his quad jumps when Chitose is on hand to recite a spell from his favorite magical girl anime!

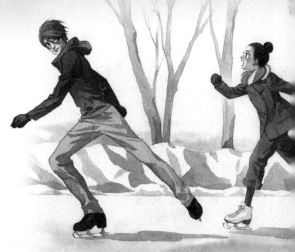

KODANSHA COMICS

Young characters and steampunk setting, like *Howl's Moving Castle* and *Battle Angel Alita*

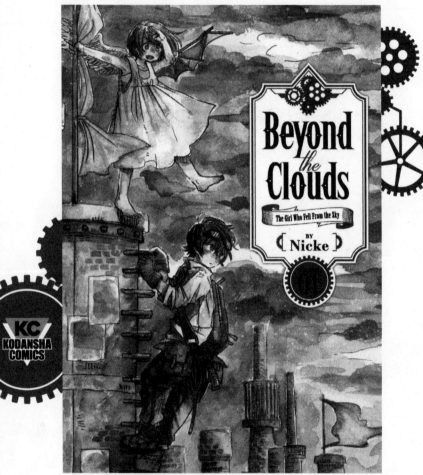

Beyond the Clouds © 2018 Nicke / Ki-oon

A boy with a talent for machines and a mysterious girl whose wings he's fixed will take you beyond the clouds! In the tradition of the high-flying, resonant adventure stories of Studio Ghibli comes a gorgeous tale about the longing of young hearts for adventure and friendship!

PERFECT WORLD

Rie Aruga

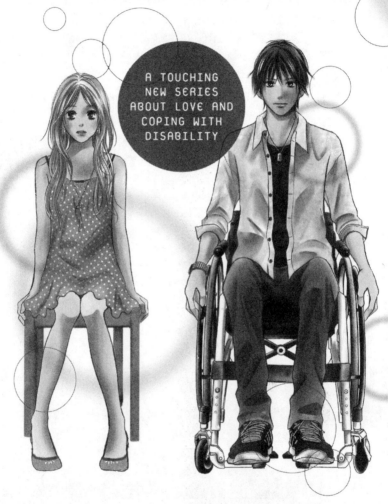

A TOUCHING NEW SERIES ABOUT LOVE AND COPING WITH DISABILITY

An office party reunites Tsugumi with her high school crush Itsuki. He's realized his dream of becoming an architect, but along the way, he experienced a spinal injury that put him in a wheelchair. Now Tsugumi's rekindled feelings will butt up against prejudices she never considered — and Itsuki will have to decide if he's ready to let someone into his heart...

KC KODANSHA COMICS

A SMART, NEW ROMANTIC COMEDY FOR FANS OF *SHORTCAKE CAKE* AND *TERRACE HOUSE*!

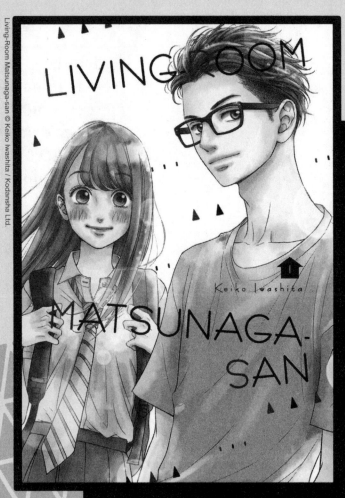

A romance manga starring high school girl Meeko, who learns to live on her own in a boarding house whose living room is home to the odd (but handsome) Matsunaga-san. She begins to adjust to her new life away from her parents, but Meeko soon learns that no matter how far away from home she is, she's still a young girl at heart — especially when she finds herself falling for Matsunaga-san.

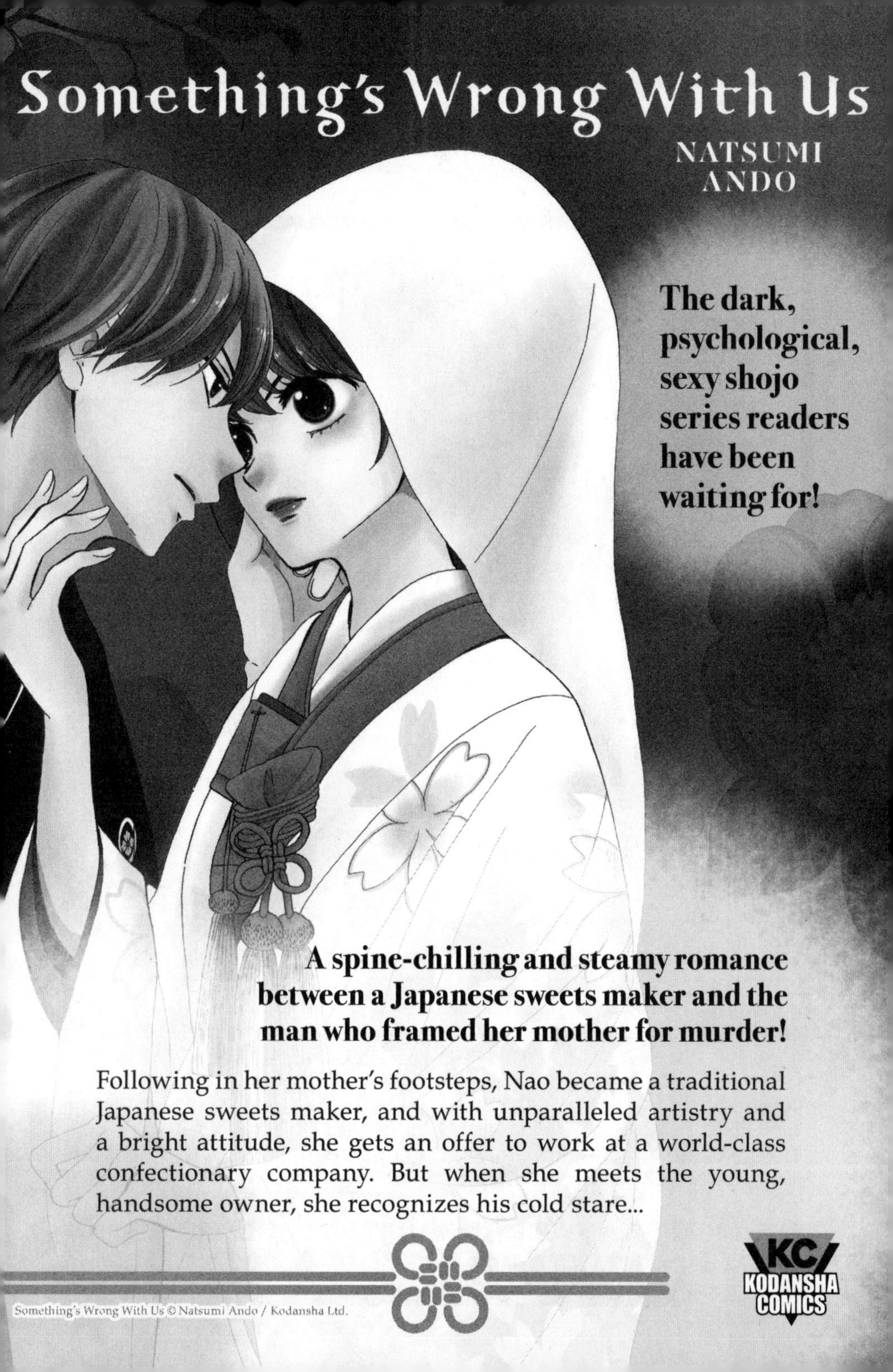

Something's Wrong With Us

NATSUMI ANDO

The dark, psychological, sexy shojo series readers have been waiting for!

A spine-chilling and steamy romance between a Japanese sweets maker and the man who framed her mother for murder!

Following in her mother's footsteps, Nao became a traditional Japanese sweets maker, and with unparalleled artistry and a bright attitude, she gets an offer to work at a world-class confectionary company. But when she meets the young, handsome owner, she recognizes his cold stare...

KC/
KODANSHA
COMICS

The boys are back, in 400-page hardcovers that are as pretty and badass as they are!

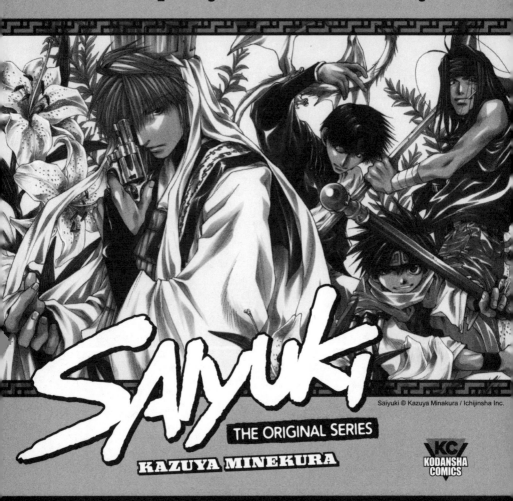

Saiyuki © Kazuya Minakura / Ichijinsha Inc.

SAIYUKI
THE ORIGINAL SERIES
KAZUYA MINEKURA

"AN EDGY COMIC LOOK AT AN ANCIENT CHINESE TALE." —YALSA

Genjo Sanzo is a Buddhist priest in the city of Togenkyo, which is being ravaged by yokai spirits that have fallen out of balance with the natural order. His superiors send him on a journey far to the west to discover why this is happening and how to stop it. His companions are three yokai with human souls. But this is no day trip — the four will encounter many discoveries and horrors on the way.

FEATURES NEW TRANSLATION, COLOR PAGES, AND BEAUTIFUL WRAPAROUND COVER ART!

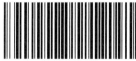

A Kodansha Trade Paperback Original

When Will Ayumu Make His Move? 7 copyright ©
2021 Soichiro Yamamoto
English translation copyright © 2022 Soichiro Yamamoto

Published in the United States by
Kodansha USA Publishing, LLC, New York.

Publication rights for this English edition arranged through
Kodansha Ltd., Tokyo.

First published in Japan in 2021 by Kodansha Ltd., Tokyo
as *Sore demo Ayumu ha yosetekuru*, volume 7.

ISBN 978-1-64651-531-8

Printed in the United States of America.

1st Printing

Translation: Max Greenway
Lettering: Phil Christie
Editing: Nathaniel Gallant
Kodansha USA Publishing edition cover design by Adam Del Re

Publisher: Kiichiro Sugawara

Director of Publishing Services: Ben Applegate
Director of Publishing Operations: Dave Barrett
Associate Director, Publishing Operations: Stephen Pakula
Publishing Services Managing Editors: Madison Salters, Alanna Ruse
Production Managers: Emi Lotto, Angela Zurlo

KODANSHA.US

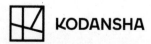